D1001964

# THE NESBIT TRADITION

# The Nesbit Tradition

## THE CHILDREN'S NOVEL
## IN ENGLAND
## 1945-1970

MARCUS CROUCH

'I have often thought that if people who wrote books
for children knew a little more it would be better'

OSWALD BASTABLE

LONDON
ERNEST BENN LIMITED

*First published 1972 by Ernest Benn Limited*
*25 New Street Square, Fleet Street, London EC4A 3JA*

*Distributed in Canada by*
*The General Publishing Company Limited, Toronto*

© *Marcus Crouch 1972*

*Printed in Great Britain*

ISBN 0 510-31351-5

FOR
EILEEN COLWELL

# Foreword

NEVER IN HISTORY have so many critical words been spilt over children's literature. Where *The Junior Bookshelf* laboured alone for almost twenty years there are now nine journals—if I have counted aright—devoted to their critical assessment, while even the dailies and weeklies give them a more than seasonal look and allocate the task to someone other than the 'brisk uncle' of A. A. Milne's day. Hardly a day goes by but some group of professionally eminent people meet to debate them.

This immense activity notwithstanding, I come more and more to the view that there *are* no children's books. They are a concept invented for commercial reasons and kept alive by the human instinct for classification and categorizing. There are books for children, certainly, picture-books and little stories which train the child's observation and feed his imagination and sense of wonder. When a child has mastered the technique of reading, however, the world opens for him, and not one artificially isolated segment of it. The honest writer—and I am not concerned with the others—does not sit down to write a children's book. He writes what is inside him and must out. Sometimes what he writes will chime with the instincts and interests of young people, sometimes it will not. But both sorts are just books, not books for children and books for adults. If you must have a classification, it is into books good and bad.

What possible excuse is there for yet another book about children's literature, especially from one who has already declared his dislike of the current escalation of adult interest in children and what they read? It is not merely a decision to jump upon a bandwaggon which I cannot hope to stop. It is

7

perhaps—and it is notoriously difficult for anyone to identify his own motives—that in the deluge of words which pour over us what tends to get washed away is, first, the absolute quality of the books under debate, and second, the fact that books are for pleasure. I have tried to convey in the following pages my personal appreciation of the many books which I have shared with children over the past twenty-five years and my delight in the delights which they so generously offer.

One of the hazards of looking at children's books in isolation is that one will apply to them different and probably lower standards of criticism. In fact the reverse is essential to a proper assessment. One examines books which children will read with the aid of all the criteria applied to books read by adults and with one additional consideration—accessibility. However sincere, imaginative and accurate a book may be, it will fail if young readers cannot penetrate its defences.

In looking at some of the books which children have read since the war I have sought the qualities which make the true novel: vivid, sustained and developed narrative, honestly observed and consistent characterization, a critical examination of society, and identifiable objectives, the whole presented in a style which is adapted to its purpose yet still expresses the personality of the writer. So rich is the present age that I have had no difficulty in finding these exacting standards met in a great many books, so many indeed that I have necessarily been selective, reluctantly omitting reference to many novels which have given me real pleasure. To the writers of these neglected books my sincere apologies.

It is a truism to say that today's children are lucky. So far as books are concerned they always have been, for each generation inherits the best of the past and adds its own contribution. Ours is often called the Golden Age of children's literature. I am not sure that it is, qualitatively, better than the age of Nesbit and Beatrix Potter, or that of Ransome and the early Ardizzone. Children today, however, can enjoy the best of these ages and at the same time share in the exciting experiments of those enterprising new writers who are leading the young boldly into the Seventies.

# Contents

# List of Illustrations & Artists

# Acknowledgements

The publishers make grateful acknowledgement to copyright owners for permission to reproduce the following:

To G. Bell & Sons Ltd., for the illustration from *The Namesake*, author and illustrator, Walter Hodges.

To The Bodley Head Ltd., for the illustration by Edward Ardizzone in *The Otterbury Incident* by C. Day Lewis.

To Brockhampton Press Limited, for the illustration by Charles Keeping from *The Dream-Time* by Henry Treece, and also that by Pearl Falconer from *The Winter Princess* by Mary Treadgold.

To J. M. Dent & Sons Ltd., for the illustration by Michel Leszczynski from *Sea Change*, by Richard Armstrong.

To Faber & Faber Ltd., for the illustration by V. H. Drummond from *The Piemakers* by Helen Cresswell.

To William Heinemann Ltd., for the illustration by John Ward, A.R.A. from *The White Doe* by Richard Church.

To Longman Young Books Limited, for the illustration by Anthony Maitland from *Smith* by Leon Garfield.

To Oxford University Press Limited, for the illustration by Brian Wildsmith from *Tangara* by Nan Chauncy, also for that by Charles Keeping from *The Latchkey Children* by Eric Allen, and that by William Papas from *Beat of the City*, H. F. Brinsmead.

The author is indebted to Oswald Bastable for the chapter headings.

# CHAPTER ONE

# *Foundations*

'Oswald took care she had plenty of the right sort of books
to read'

THE NOVEL FOR CHILDREN was not an invention of post-
war Britain although, so completely have the traditional forms
been broken down and rebuilt, one readily assumes that it is as
much the creation of this age as that other transformed and
revitalized expression, the children's picture-book. The contemporary revival of Victorian children's books, including
some which had been forgotten and others whose titles—
*Froggy's Little Brother* and the like—used to evoke superior
derision, has shocked some readers of the Seventies with a realization that the children's book revolution of our time had been
anticipated a century earlier. The Victorians may have
lingered overlong beside deathbeds and permitted themselves
a self-indulgent excess of sententiousness; they were often
masters of narrative and of atmosphere, they showed considerable depth of insight into behaviour, and they were concerned
resolutely and—often—honestly with complex personal and
social problems. Their books were shorter than the three-
deckers of the 'adult' novelists; they were not less dedicated to
the psychological and sociological functions of the novel.

If, with a few exceptions, these novels have failed to find
readers among mid-twentieth-century children—for the re-
prints have been enjoyed mostly by adults—this is no criticism
of their integrity. Indeed, they have dated because they were
true to the spirit of their age. No book fades more quickly than
the social novel. One reads Dickens today not for his rage
against poverty and injustice but for the gaiety and truth of
his exploration of human oddities.

Similarly, E. Nesbit has survived despite, not because of, her Fabian conscience. The book in which she shows most sincerely and passionately her concern for the dignity of ordinary people is *Harding's Luck*; it is a good book, provocative in its ideas and illuminated with deep understanding, but it has died—or very nearly. The social content of the 'Bastable' stories is subordinated to the portraits of real, timelessly naughty children, and the stories have lost none of their vitality in seventy years. E. Nesbit stands squarely in the doorway between the nineteenth and the twentieth centuries. She owed much to the Victorians, even if she made affectionate fun of them. She transmuted their good solid base metal into pure gold. In her hands the Victorian conscience lost its self-consciousness; their insight became sharper and more richly aware of the incongruities which make for humour; above all, she threw away their strong, sober, essentially literary style and replaced it with the miraculously colloquial, flexible and revealing prose which was her unique contribution to the children's novel. After E. Nesbit children's literature might explore new worlds of ideas and themes; it would never return to the stuffily enclosed nurseries of the nineteenth century.

No writer for children today is free of debt to this remarkable woman. Although she had, I believe, no strong sense of purpose in most of her writing and certainly no exaggerated opinion of her importance, being content in the main to make good stories out of the resources of her experience and her imagination, she managed to create the prototypes of many of the basic patterns in modern children's fiction. The three books about the Treasure Seekers are the firm foundations of all our family comedies. In her 'Five Children' stories she initiated the comedy of magic applied to the commonplaces of daily life, and in *The Enchanted Castle* she showed how poetic and comic fantasy might be blended. Her 'Arden' books are, with Kipling's, the pioneers of the 'time' theme in historical reconstruction; and even *The Railway Children*, which is perhaps the most conventional and obviously dated of her novels and the one which looks backwards, not forwards, has retained the affections of several generations of children and fostered a host of other tales of family fortunes and misfortunes.

The true heirs to the Nesbit heritage did not appear until the Thirties. War and the aftermath of war inhibited experiment, and much of the work done in the second and third decades of the century was derivative and sterile. Perhaps significantly, the best books for children were almost all fantasies. Writers who had forsworn the realism, harsh or sentimental by turns, of the Victorians found little inspiration in the grimness and false gaiety of post-war England. The hacks—and this was the great age of the 'Reward'—wrote 'formula' stories of adventure in exotic places or in schools no less remote from common experience. Writers of sensibility, like Walter de la Mare, Eleanor Farjeon and John Masefield, turned to worlds of the imagination or to remote times. Such writers were not hiding from reality; they preferred to interpret timeless themes, like the necessity of courage and the truth of love, without relating them directly to the ills of contemporary society. Such books as *The Three Mulla-Mulgars* (1910) and *The Midnight Folk* (1927) were 'minority' books of their day and have remained so, but they have survived and show a sturdy resistance to decay, while other, more obviously relevant, books died with the circumstances which prompted them.

Looking from the privileged viewpoint of the Seventies, one sees the Thirties as one of the most important decades in the history of the children's book. Even at the time one was aware of change and experiment. Writers, illustrators and publishers were bringing to the genre new attitudes and ideas, with enthusiasm and humour but without the self-conscious dedication which knocks the high spirits out of some areas of the children's book today. Writers for children in the new dawn of the Thirties did not commonly think of themselves as a force in education or in sociology. More commonly, they approached their task in Ransome's spirit. In 1937 Arthur Ransome wrote, quoting Stevenson: 'You just indulge the pleasure of your heart. You write not for children but for yourself, and if, by good fortune, children enjoy what you enjoy, why then you are a writer of children's books. No special credit to you, but simply thumping good luck.' The great man had his coat off at the time, at ease in his cabin, and he did not bother to polish his words. They might, nevertheless, be inscribed on the study walls of every writer who aspires to sail in the perilous waters of children's literature.

Arthur Ransome straddles the Thirties. He gave all his books the care and skill of an accomplished professional writer, trained in the tough school of international journalism, but he applied to them no aesthetic or sociological principles. He chose to write sincerely and modestly about things that mattered to him personally, and to associate them with children whom he knew and liked. The result was startlingly original. Here are stories about children passionately concerned with realities. We see them only at play, for they are always on holiday, but it is a serious play, applying hard-won skills to difficult and responsible tasks.

Ransome chose to look upon these books always as 'yarns' and never dignified them with a higher title. They have, nevertheless, some of the qualities of the novel. They offer detailed studies of society, a small-scale society but one in which the relationships between individual members and their responsibilities to the whole are examined closely. One might feel a theoretical regret that Ransome did not choose to show children and adults in partnership, and that, with the exception of Captain Flint and a few others, the adults are hostile and barbarous, like the Hullabaloos, or tyrannous like Great Aunt Maria. With Ransome, however, rather more than with most writers, one accepts gladly the writer's chosen limitations, recognizing that he knew precisely what he was about. He shows with beautiful clarity and conviction how children grow by contact with one another and with their environment, submitting to their own voluntary disciplines while retaining their personal integrity. Like a good novelist, too, he uses the setting of his stories as if it were an actor in them. He writes only about places for which he has a strong feeling, like the Lakes—their topography drastically reshaped but their spirit faithfully portrayed—and the Broads and the estuaries of Suffolk. To each of these settings his characters react according to their natures and according to the nature of the landscape.

For the first time in children's literature since *Bevis*—and this was an isolated phenomenon—Ransome showed not only *what* happened but *how* it happened. He and his characters are deeply concerned with the mechanics of living. They examine the detailed processes by which they sail a boat or light a fire until, in Eric Linklater's revealing sentence, Ransome 'makes a tale of adventure into a handbook to adventure'.

In its way *Swallows and Amazons* was as large a landmark of 1930 as *The Story of the Treasure Seekers* was of 1899. Other writers of the Thirties applied the same qualities of honest observation and informal style to stories about children in a recognizable contemporary setting. One remembers with particular affection Eleanor Graham's *The Children who Lived in a Barn* (1938), which showed children tackling problems of adult proportions and demonstrating good sense and persistence as well as a degree of good humour. Two almost forgotten stories by Monica Redlich were also concerned with contemporary realities. One of these, *Five Farthings* (1939), which drew a loving portrait—almost, in view of the holocaust to come, an *in memoriam* picture—of the City of London, was an early example of both the 'career' novel and the adolescent romance and an admirable example of both. This was outstanding in a decade of excellent book-design for its beauty of format, and Rowland Hilder's illustrations were perhaps the best he ever did for a children's book. *Five Farthings* anticipated by thirty years some of the most admired features of the children's novel of the Sixties.

If Monica Redlich looked forward, Noel Streatfeild and Kitty Barne were very much of their time. Both excelled in the portrayal of charming and idiosyncratic families; both showed sturdily individual children settling down to hard work. Both were unequivocally middle-class, like a majority of their readers. Eve Garnett's middle-class conscience was shocked by the squalor and heartened by the resilience of the London slums which she saw as a young student at the Royal Academy Schools. In *The Family from One End Street*, originally conceived as a picture-book, she found herself, almost against her will, emphasizing the comedy of working-class life, and this has probably given her book a longer span of life than it would have enjoyed as a social document. For a long time it stood almost alone as a 'proletarian' novel for children—although, to be correct, it never aspired to the tight construction, the detailed development of character or the complex study of environment which mark the true novel.

In pursuing new, and newly vitalized, forms of the novel, talented newcomers to writing for children tended to neglect one of the oldest of its traditions. Adventure was left largely to the production-line of the 'Reward'. Basil Blackwell tried the experiment of commissioning some of the best young writers of the age to contribute to his 'Tales of Action' and 'Tales of Two Worlds'. One of these young men, Rex Warner, even chose to write about the international drug traffic in an exciting and forward-looking story called *The Kite* (1936).

Few authors were tempted to follow this example. For the most part, those who preferred to write tales of strong action chose a period setting. The modern historical novel for young people, foreshadowed by a very few Victorian stories of which Austin Clare's *The Carved Cartoon* was perhaps the most seminal, was launched quite deliberately by Geoffrey Trease with a story about Robin Hood called *Bows against the Barons* (1934). This was not in itself a very good book. In his efforts to present a provocative and unconventional view of the Middle Ages, the young author protested too much; his peasants were uniformly oppressed and virtuous, his barons as monotonously wicked as Sir Jasper in the Victorian melodrama. Geoffrey Trease had, nevertheless, made his point; an historical novel for children might offer an original comment on history and draw parallels with contemporary society. His succeeding books drove home the same lessons with greater subtlety. L. A. G. Strong carried no partisan banner, and his historical novels were the more effective for their freedom from doctrinaire objectives. *Mr. Sheridan's Umbrella* (1935) in particular chose an unfamiliar theme and a period—the Regency—which on the surface lacked appeal to young readers. Strong poured into this unpromising bottle a sparkling wine composed of humour, romance and warm humanity.

In their very different ways both L. A. G. Strong and Geoffrey Trease emphasized the homeliness of history. They described people and situations which had modern parallels and were relevant to modern problems. In contrast, a young artist chose to show a past which belonged to itself alone.

*From* The Namesake (*see page 71*)

C.Walter Hodges' *Columbus Sails* (1939) was, physically, out-standingly beautiful in a decade of finely designed books. The author's own illustrations had drama and atmosphere and they were placed on the page with a rare instinct for effectiveness; they were balanced with restrained and dignified typography. All these excellences might reasonably have been expected of a man who was already outstanding as an illustrator. The per-fection of his prose came as a greater surprise. Rejecting equally modern colloquialism and 'Ye Olde', Walter Hodges told the story of Columbus's first voyage with timeless gravity. His was an artist's—or, more precisely, an architect's—style, building the story with careful artistry and calculated skill in the balance of sentences and episodes.

*A Traveller in Time* (1939) marks a halfway-house between history and fantasy. Alison Uttley, who in the rest of her work was to be mainly a master of delicate miniature painting, found in the memories of her own childhood material for a long and deeply felt historical fantasy. *A Traveller in Time* was in the tradition of E. Nesbit's 'Arden' stories. Penelope, who is perhaps a little like Mrs Uttley as a child, goes to stay in an ancient farmhouse in Derbyshire and passes, at first without realizing what is happening, into an Elizabethan 'Thackers' to become an observer, and to a small extent an actor, in the Babington Plot. No one—not even E. Nesbit herself—handled the apparatus of 'time' better. Penelope slips unobtrusively through the curtain which separates present and past, and the reader goes with her, fully conscious of the wonder of the ex-perience but quite without incredulity. As in all the best fantasies, the suspension of natural law is used not to evade reality but to provide an effective point from which to interpret reality.

There is something of this quality in Hilda Lewis's *The Ship that Flew* (1939), another 'time' story which falls short of the very highest quality only through uncertainty in the earlier chapters as to how seriously the theme is to be taken. When finally Hilda Lewis decides that hers is a serious and important matter, she writes with great sensitivity and power, although she never attains the grave, quiet sufficiency of Alison Uttley's prose.

In contrast, Patricia Lynch's great success in fantasy depends on her taking her seriousness lightly. In her finest imaginative stories—*The King of the Tinkers* (1938) and *The Grey Goose of Kilnevin* (1939)—there is a miraculous blend of homely humour and wonder. Mystery pervades the commonplace scene. 'This is very quare!' as the Ballad Singer says, facing a very ordinary inn-sign. ''Tis past all understandin'.' Patricia Lynch's fantasy is not explicit enough to be allegorical; the interpretation is left to each individual reader. Here is the heart of part of her success. The rest is the rough music of her prose which coaxes the reader into ready acceptance of extraordinary sequences of events. Of all the writers of the Thirties she spoke the most personal language, not merely Irish but Patricia Lynch Irish, a language which is tender, funny and richly memorable.

*The Hobbit* (1937), too, was at once serious and comic. Bilbo Baggins, hero *malgré lui*, is a character of high comedy, but the adventures to which he becomes reluctantly committed have heroic and at times tragic elements. The quality of J. R. R. Tolkien's original achievement has been a little obscured by the Tolkien cult which followed the publication of his long heroic fantasy *The Lord of the Rings*, to which *The Hobbit* is both the prelude and the key. Looked at in the isolation of 1937, *The Hobbit* is seen as a story of high adventure, with vividly imagined episodes, funny, grotesque, sad and noble, all sustained and given continuity by the writer's scholarship and his command of every detail of his created world, its topography, history and technology. It is not obviously, as the later trilogy is, allegorical in intent. It is concerned not with a struggle against the forces of evil but with a quest for treasure and for self-discovery. As a work of art—and it seems to demand measurement by the highest and most severe standards—it is distinguished by unity of mood. The episodes have a cumulative effect, rising to their climax in the Battle of Five Armies and the death of Thorin King under the Mountain. After the grave dignity of this latter scene, Bilbo's return to his house under the hill comes as a welcome and artistically acceptable relaxing of tension.

Bilbo Baggins, the Hobbit, is essentially a comic character, and several scenes in the book evoke laughter or the rich inward glow which is more rewarding than an audible laugh. The Thirties were indeed unusually productive of comedy. In particular they saw the arrival of three memorable and long-lived characters. Worzel-Gummidge, the endearingly un-gracious scarecrow created by Barbara Euphan Todd, owed much of his success to radio; the books, like the 'Toytown' stories of S. G. Hulme Beaman, had no great quality on the printed page, but they lent themselves precisely to presentation on Children's Hour. Professor Branestawm, however, was perhaps better to read than to hear. The plots of Norman Hunter's episodes about the ingenious but absent-minded inventor were too complex to fit readily into the idiom of radio, but Hunter's prose matched the dead-pan humour admirably; the reader, moreover, enjoyed the inestimable benefit of illustrations in W. Heath Robinson's best vein of crazy logic. Both Worzel and the Professor were characters of considerable stature; they transcended the books in which they appeared. The same is true of Mary Poppins. P. L. Travers' novels were curiously unsatisfactory, but the nursemaid heroine was an archetypal figure, one of those rare beings who go on living beyond the pages of the book.

A comic achievement which transcends these was J. B. S. Haldane's *My Friend Mr Leakey* (1937). Like Tolkien, Haldane was a man with a massive reputation in quite a different sphere of activity. Both as sociologist and as scientist he wielded great influence, and was sufficiently important to arouse the antagonism of other experts in his field. Mr Leakey was a scientist's creation, a magician whose magic followed strict rules. The episodes of Haldane's little book, casually as they are tossed off as the trifles of a great man, are strangely memorable, partly because of the writer's finely controlled imagination, partly for the exquisite precision of his style. *My Friend Mr Leakey* is a string of short stories, not a novel, but there is abundant evidence in it that Haldane's preoccupation with other and temporarily more important affairs deprived children of one of their finest comic novelists.

The best achievements of the war years were in comedy, too, Kitty Barne sought out, with characteristic sincerity and sharp observation, the comic, as well as the pathetic, elements in the strange social experiment of the Evacuation; her *Visitors from London* (1940) was not a particularly successful book by her own standards, but it explored with good-humoured shrewdness the dilemmas of the visitors and the visited. *Visitors from London*, in the thin War years, picked up a Carnegie Medal with ease. Eric Linklater's *The Wind on the Moon* (1944) romped home an easy winner too. Both this and Vaughan Wilkins's *After Bath* (1945) are private comedies in that they sprang, as some of the best and many of the worst children's books have done, from the need to entertain individual children. Although *The Wind on the Moon* was originally improvised in a desperate attempt to pacify the writer's children, Eric Linklater was too experienced a novelist to indulge in the irrelevancies and the private allusions of the extempore tale. *After Bath*, obviously originating as a bed-time serial—told after the bath—is less successful in eliminating the private language in which such stories are often told. Its frequent triviality, its appalling jokes, are the familiar pitfalls of the family tale. Both books rose above their origins, partly by sheer professionalism—for both writers were distinguished novelists at the height of their powers—partly by the discovery of unsuspected depths in apparently frivolous inventions. These farces of misapplied or mislaid magic both turn serious, almost, it would seem, despite their authors. They grew, their homely nursery settings notwithstanding, in war-time, and both are concerned fundamentally with themes—tyranny, endurance and sacrifice—which were staple commodities of their time.

For the rest, the years of the Second World War were not productive of fine children's novels. The political and the economic climates alike were unfavourable. The brilliant writers who had made a brave new world for children in the Thirties were engaged elsewhere. Occasionally an admirable picture-book rose above the limitations of poor paper and inadequate funds. The children's novel, which called for a more sustained creative effort and consumed more paper, awaited happier days.

# CHAPTER TWO

# *High Adventure*

'The best part of books is when things are happening'

THE PAPER-FAMINE which, almost as much as the writer-famine, limited the production of books during the war years did not come to an abrupt end with the cessation of hostilities. For several years books continued to appear in small editions on shoddy paper, and the contents often mirrored the dullness of the format. It was perhaps more damaging still that older books remained unobtainable, and there was a danger that at least one generation would grow up without access to a price-less part of its heritage. It is true that some publishers con-scientiously devoted part of their quota of paper to the most indispensable of the classics, but slightly lesser books, pre-war stocks of which had been victims of the London Blitz, were not to be found outside the libraries.

In times of shortage the first casualties are seldom the worst books. The 'Reward' with its familiar bulky, air-filled paper, its stereotyped plot, had burned as briskly as its betters in the fires around St Paul's, and it was never to be seen again in just its old form. Formula-stories continued to appear, however, looking a shade emaciated in their thin 'economy-standard' paper. A few new publishers, trying their luck in the brave post-war world, spent their quota on stories which took the old formulae of the adventure yarn and injected adrenalin into them. Peter Lunn was among the most interesting of these newcomers to the publishing scene. He used for the most part new writers and artists and gave to each book individual treat-ment within an identifiable house-style. These adventure stories have mostly vanished now, although some children who grew into their teens in the bleak days after the war may remember them with gratitude. At least one of the writers, John Keir Cross, survived the disappearance of the firm, to gain a different reputation on radio and to write more stories of high-powered action in exotic settings and richly colourful style. *Blackadder* (1950) is a good example of his robust manner.

Like many writers in the adventure tradition, John Keir Cross liked a period setting, something not too precisely identified but roughly in the eighteenth century of *Kidnapped* and *Treasure Island*. Some admirable work has been done in adapting the tradition to contemporary scenes and problems. Henry Treece made a reputation as one of the new poets of the war and later carved himself another name as a writer of historical stories and of anthropological romances. His tales of adventure represented what Graham Greene might call 'entertainments'. They were in some sort a relief from the deeply felt and closely researched stories for which he is likely to be best remembered, but he gave them the benefits of an exuberant style and bustling narrative pace. Readers of *Ask for King Billy* (1955) are unlikely to take it seriously, but they may still reasonably surrender to its excitement, enjoying the gross improbabilities and suspending disbelief for a time the more readily because of the contemporary scene and the clearly defined topographical background. Sober—and sometimes dreary—critics have handled Treece unkindly over these light-weight yarns; it might be argued however that there is a necessary, and not entirely unimportant, place in a child's development for the trivial time-passing story, and that it is all to the good that such books should bear the stamp of the professional writer. Treece might toss these books off light-heartedly; he was too good a craftsman to make them less than competent.

Another distinguished poet, Ian Serraillier, also entered this field. His first two stories, *They Raced for Treasure* (1946) and *Flight to Adventure* (1947), have plots which are well in the tradition of the 'Reward', with a small boy involved in man-sized adventures in wild settings. What sets both books above the tradition is the writing, which is clean and unfussy, while the improbable stories are neatly manipulated. With his third story of this kind Serraillier emerged as a fully mature artist. *There's No Escape* (1950) is scarcely more concerned with probabilities, but the realization of the theme is highly convincing. The writer departed from tradition in making his hero this time an adult, and he related the story and its setting to contemporary realities. The action may take place in Ruritania —or at least Silvania—but the country and its neighbours resembled in their topography and their political dilemma alike other Eastern European states at the time of the drawing of the Iron Curtain. The book has no very high aspirations. It is unashamedly a good 'yarn', using the conventional techniques of suspense and action, but using them honestly and always with respect for the reader.

To look for a higher parentage than the 'Reward' for *There's No Escape* brings the reader inevitably to Buchan. There is much of Buchan here, in the tone, the narrative technique with its rather stiff-upper-lippish narrator—brave, honest, not too intelligent—and its avoidance of the fundamental political and social issues, even its faint trace of snobbery. The comparison may even be deliberate, for Serraillier has a rich sense of humour and he may have indulged here a taste for parody. Unlike Buchan, he sustains his own interest in the story to the end, and he is perhaps more careful than his mentor with the technical detail of the action; there are neither short cuts nor loose ends. (There is the same competence and honest-to-goodness professionalism in C. Walter Hodges's strong and exact drawings.)

Peter Howarth's mission to Silvania, to rescue Dr Helpmann from the Yugs and to bring him and his scientific secrets back to the physical and political security of Britain, may have had its parallels in the situation of Europe after the war; Serraillier made no attempt to underline the comparisons, being content to tell his tale for all it was worth and leaving the reader to take it at its face or its inner value. When he turned next to a story of adventure, however, Serraillier had a richer theme and a deeper purpose.

*The Silver Sword* (1956) belongs to the adventure tradition in that it is essentially a fine narrative; it pushes the bounds of that tradition out as far as they will go. Serraillier had already proved his skill as an inventor of exciting contrived plots. There is no contrivance in *The Silver Sword*. All its episodes belong to the terrible history of Europe in its post-war chaos. The author selected them, matched them with vividly realized characters and clothed them in miraculously simple, dispassionate words. It is a book which one cannot read without profound emotional response and personal involvement, but Serraillier tells the story straight, never overstating the suffering, never adding his personal comment. It is an agonizing story in its very quietness; it is also a story of—in the words of its motto—'abiding hope'. Children's books in the mid-Fifties were still hedged in with taboos; writers were not encouraged to describe the realities of cruelty and pain. *The Silver Sword* deals with these things uncompromisingly. The story is one of tragedy and of heart-stopping tension.

It is in essence the story of a journey. A family of Poles, separated by the war, go to find their parents when the war is over. The quest takes them to Switzerland. This would have been a taxing experience for small children at any time, but the Balickis make their journey through a Europe devastated by war and disorganized by war's aftermath. They succeed, to have a credible reunion with their parents and to play a part in the making of the first Pestalozzi village. In summary it may seem that the solutions are too easy; no one reading the story to its richly satisfying conclusion can think that the author has indulged in short cuts or simplifications. The children tackle their enormous problems, growing with their experiences but becoming scarred by them too. It is the reality of the children, and of the adults with whom they co-operate or clash, which gives the book its piercing actuality. The touchstone of the story is not one of the Balicki family but Jan, the homeless, almost nameless boy who joins them for the journey. In one way or another each of the Balicki family has retained something from the days before the war, a fragment of belief in the human values which were lost among the ruins of the Warsaw streets. Jan has nothing, except a gaunt and savage cock and a box of treasures. He is sustained through the years of war partly by a genius for survival, partly by hatred. ' "Jan, can't you stop hating for one moment?" ' says Ruth Balicki when the little boy attacks the Russian soldier who tries to befriend the children. There is a remarkable episode when the children shelter in the house of a Bavarian farmer, and Jan is bewildered to find that the farmer's dead son had fought in the German army in Warsaw. 'That there could be any connection between these homely folk and the soldier in the photo was beyond his understanding.' It takes the agony of their long journey and the persistent goodwill of the Balickis to penetrate Jan's armour and expose his heart. Even the Balickis cannot do miracles, however. In the safety of Switzerland Jan still plays at firing squads and torture and steals the food and clothes which he no longer needs. Slowly he is edging his way towards a new life.

The essence of the traditional adventure story is that it has an ending. However convincing the development, the plot is necessarily contrived to build up to a climax and to move to a conclusion. *The Silver Sword*, the tension of its magnificent story notwithstanding, is not finally true to the tradition. It is an open-ended story. Jan and Ruth go on living and changing beyond the last page. There was room for a sequel, but Ian Serraillier was too wise to venture upon one.

The Second World War provided material for a multitude of tales in the tradition. It was the starting-point too for other books in which, as in *The Silver Sword*, the tradition became extended and transformed. Margot Benary belonged to the liberal tradition of Germany, temporarily eclipsed in the years of Nazi domination. She suffered for this personally during the war, and in the books which she wrote afterwards she showed in fictional terms the dilemma of the liberal in war and its aftermath. Her finest achievement, *The Ark* (1954), is more personal than *The Silver Sword*—understandably, for the author was closer than Serraillier to the bitterness and the anguish of political and military strife, and unlike him she had to take refuge in family love.

Essentially *The Ark* is a story not of adventure but of human relationships, and this is not the place to consider it in detail.

It was understandable that writers like Ian Serraillier and Margot Benary, who belonged to a generation deeply marked by the war, should choose to write obliquely about it. The next generation could view the conflict more dispassionately. One of the most striking of war books for children came from an Australian writer. Margaret Balderson surrendered to the strange appeal of northern Norway, and in *When Jays Fly to Barbmo* (1968) she showed this country of brief glorious summers and long dark winters in the grip of the Nazis. It was an extraordinary book for a writer to undertake almost at the outset of her career. Violent action is a comparatively easy subject for the writer; what is much more difficult to achieve is the proper timing of the preparation for this action. *When Jays Fly to Barbmo* is a quiet story which explodes suddenly into violence. The thrills are authentic and presented with real power. The reader is swept along on the tide of this narrative, but what he remembers in retrospect is the stillness of the Dark Time, the bitter cold night which works upon the mind like a disease, and the radiance of the returning sun. There is a rare depth, too, in the study of the young heroine Ingeborg, a complex, almost tormented character whose inner and outer conflicts are resolved when she discovers that the blood which so rebels in her against the disciplines of her orderly Norwegian home comes from her wild Lappish mother.

Because the story conveys without exaggeration the sufferings of a country under enemy occupation it may properly be described as a war story; because of the power and tension of the action it is certainly a story of high adventure; it is much more, a compassionate study of conflicting ways of life, and a tender and entirely unsentimental picture of a girl growing into womanhood.

The Fifties saw the emergence of a number of talented writers in the adult field who, running counter to the literary trends, chose to write novels with a strong narrative line. Two of the most successful of these turned also to the children's adventure story. Hammond Innes had already won spectacular success with tough and closely researched adventure stories when, thinly disguised as Ralph Hammond, he offered to young readers a similarly professional and stimulating yarn, *Cocos Gold* (1950). This was followed by *Isle of Strangers* (1951). Good stuff this, although one had the impression that Hammond Innes was a little too conscious of his audience, reining himself in and not giving of his full strength in these books. Not for the first, or last, time an adult writer of very great skill found himself ill at ease among children. Allan Campbell McLean, however, was completely at home with young people. If Innes was up-dating Buchan—a grossly simplified view of his achievement—McLean belonged to the Stevenson tradition, a tradition which includes *Kidnapped* and *The Master of Ballantrae* as much as *Treasure Island*. Where Innes took his readers to remote and exotic places, McLean, who had visited many parts of the world, was happiest in writing about Skye, a setting sufficiently familiar to make acceptance easy, sufficiently wild to give credibility to tales of violent action. McLean's debt to Stevenson is clearest in *The Hill of the Red Fox* (1955), but he is perhaps at his most confident in *Master of Morgana* (1960). This is a story of the salmon-fishers of Skye, a story which seems always to be about highly improbable treasure-hunting but which is resolved as a straightforward case of poaching. The reader does not feel cheated by the anti-climax, partly because the thrills are always convincing, mostly because much of the interest lies in the personalities. Not the hero-narrator, who is a necessary agent of the plot but hardly composed of flesh and blood. The principal poacher—called Long John—holds the interest longest, for his contradictions—he is almost as much hero as villain—and his careful avoidance of flamboyance. This is scarcely an 'important' book, but it is interesting for the evidence it offers of the persistence and the self-renewing strength of an adventure tradition and of its effectiveness in the hands of an expert craftsman.

It is not surprising that Hammond Innes and Allan Campbell McLean should turn to the adventure yarn for children, for it represents only one aspect of the tradition in which they chose to write. *White Eagles over Serbia* (1957) was less predictable. This is the only children's book of Lawrence Durrell, the manner and to a great extent the matter of whose adult novels was far removed from the world of the adventure yarn. It is a secret-service story and reads today almost like a parody. One has to remember that the formulae and the phrase, character and situation-clichés were less familiar in 1957.

Unlike Serraillier's *There's No Escape*, with which it has

some features in common, *White Eagles over Serbia* has an actual setting and situation—the Royalist plot against Tito, and the sympathies of the author, or at least the hero, are clear. It is undisguisedly a partisan story. There are some hazards in this, particularly with a young audience. Despite the excitements of the plot and the high-spirited narrative, the story does not on the whole wear well. Only in the sequence where the hero is alone in the mountains does it rise above the conventional, and here Durrell captures magnificently the sounds and smells of the wilderness. There is a stillness which increases the tension of the story and gives it an urgent authenticity which has nothing to do with the cloak-and-dagger extravagances of the plot.

*White Eagles over Serbia*, if not obviously or exclusively a book for children—it departs from tradition in having no child characters—was certainly a story of adventure. A curious group of stories published in the late Forties under the inspiration of John Lehmann were less amenable to classification. The first and probably the best of these was Roy Fuller's *Savage Gold* (1946). Some of the elements of the adventure story were here, an exotic scene and strong action, but there was an austerity of style and a complexity of thought which were alien to the tradition. Later books, Fuller's own *With My Little Eye* (1948), a kind of detective story, and P. H. Newby's *The Spirit of Jem* (1947), moved even further out of the mainstream. These were books which would stimulate little comment, and that favourable, today—a recent reprint of Newby's book was more warmly received than the original had been—because William Mayne and others have conditioned readers to oddities of character and stylistic virtuosity. In the Forties they were at least a decade before their time.

Lehmann sponsored these books, rather as Basil Blackwell had done before the war, as a deliberate attempt to inject literary distinction into stories for children. A different kind of sponsorship brought Norman Collins into the field. Collins, then a novelist at the height of his success and popularity with adult audiences, was invited to write a serial story for a new and revolutionary journal for children, *Collins'*, later *Elizabethan Magazine*. Norman Collins chose a traditional adventure theme for *Black Ivory* (1948) and gave it not only his highly professional skill in narrative but also an element of social criticism which was highly topical. *Black Ivory* is a story of the slave trade. Collins hid from his readers none of the brutality of the theme or the horrors of life at sea in the early nineteenth century. The book does not wear well in today's climate, but it has genuine historic interest because of its choice of subject and treatment, which afford further evidence of a spirit of experiment infiltrating the cautious world of publishing during the difficult post-war years.

*Black Ivory* put adventure and social comment, in that order, before history, but it was in addition an historical story, and many writers, then and since, have found it convenient to give their adventure a period colouring. One recalls the lively story-line and the unobtrusively authentic background of C. Fox Smith's books (*Painted Ports*, 1948), and Aubrey Feist's confident handling of a complex narrative in *High Barbary* (1950) and other stories, some of which were designed originally for presentation on radio. (Children's Hour, under the direction of Derek McCulloch and 'David' Davis, was then exerting an influence as powerful as it was beneficial on writers as well as listeners.) David Scott Daniell's books about Polly and Oliver (*Mission for Oliver*, 1953) were of the same kind and quality; they had lively, not too serious stories, but the historical background had been carefully researched and they were particularly good on the details of military life.

It is a long stride from the direct narrative and the innocent vision of these tales to the novels of two of the most able and controversial of today's writers, but Leon Garfield and Joan Aiken both belong to the tradition which chooses to put its tales of high adventure into a kind of historical dress while avoiding the restrictive gear of the historical novel. For both writers the period setting is essential. They trade in improbable situations and plots which would be intolerable in a contemporary setting, but which the reader gratefully accepts for the sake of the splendid readability of tales supremely well told.

Leon Garfield seems to have had no 'prentice period. His first book, *Jack Holborn* (1964), has all his characteristic qualities; indeed if one were to be unkind one might venture to say that he has gone on telling the same story ever since. The eponymous hero of this fine tale is a parish boy left in infancy in the porch of St Bride's, so getting his sustenance and his name from the parish of Holborn. As soon as he can escape from this wretched condition he chooses the different and more perilous miseries of life on shipboard. The *Charming Molly* falls to pirates, and Jack alone survives to enjoy the casually brutal companionship of the wolves who 'sail under the Devil's marque and their ships reek with blood'. There follow mutiny, shipwreck, jungle trekking, a slave-market and a great trial scene. The ingredients are all conventional enough. It is the author's expert chemistry—appropriately he is a biochemist by calling—which makes the unpromising materials react to produce tension and atmosphere.

Jack Holborn is sustained through great physical ordeals by the hope that he will discover his identity, and he sticks close to the mysterious Captain in the belief that when he has saved the latter's life thrice the pirate leader will keep his promise and tell Jack who he is. When the truth is made known—but not by the enigmatic Captain—it is unspectacular. Jack's mother is not a duchess but a treasure of a housekeeper to a foolish Sussex knight. In *Devil-in-the-Fog* (1966) the situation is reversed. George Treet, one of a travelling showman's brood, discovers early on that he is in fact the long-lost son and heir to a wealthy Sussex knight. He goes home to claim his inheritance and finds himself caught up in a sinister plot. At last it appears that he is not the heir, but that he has been called upon to play a part with innate professionalism.

What makes these absurd plots not merely acceptable but absorbingly fascinating is Garfield's craftsmanship. He has a gift for creating sharp larger-than-life characters, like Mister Solomon Trumpet in *Jack Holborn* and Mr Thomas Treet, genius and loving father who allowed his infant son to be scarred for life in return for payments down and to come, in *Devil-in-the-Fog*. He excels in equivocal characters, leaving the reader to puzzle through the course of a long story whether they are good or evil. More important than characterization is style. Written in conventional modern English, these stories would scarcely find a reader, let alone a publisher. But Leon

Garfield tells his stories in an extraordinary evocative language all his own (it is no more the language of the Eighteenth Century than Jeffery Farnol's equally artificial stylistic mannerisms were). Garfield hypnotizes the reader, wooing him with strange sounds and haunting circumlocutions into a willing co-operation. The words are like an incantation. Archaisms abound, and common words are disguised as unfamiliar contractions—'to've' and 'so's'. The pressure never eases. Garfield has remarkable skill in focusing attention on a situation or a character by a telling description. When Jack Holborn sees for the first time the agent of Nemesis—characteristically in the fog—'he never spoke nor nodded nor waved to any living soul, but stared and stared across the dirty sea as if he was looking for a particular wave.' Here the device is effective and functional, but at times it seems a form of self-indulgence or exhibitionism. Here is George Dexter (né Treet) looking at the portraits of his ancestors: 'God alone knows they were a corpse-eyed crew, who seemed not so much painted as grandly buried in their frames . . . as if, on the instant of death, they'd been hoisted up on the wall, ironed flat, and varnished against further corruption and decay'.

Leon Garfield's craft is at its most brilliant, and is most at the command of his theme, in *Smith* (1967). In this story of a 'sooty spirit of the violent and ramshackle town' and of the London underworld the stylistic mannerisms are comparatively subdued, and the story moves almost as swiftly as Smith, beside whom 'a rat was like a snail'. Smith is a fine creation, a most complex blending of apparent contradictions who, having survived for twelve years 'the small-pox, the consumption, brain-fever, gaol-fever and even the hangman's rope', is destined for greatness of some kind, and greatness of a sort comes not only through his sly swiftness but because of courage and even kindness. Smith's saviour is Mr Mansfield, the blind magistrate of whom Garfield paints a detailed picture based, presumably, on the reality of the eighteenth-century Sir John Fielding. In this book there are qualities lacking in most of Garfield's work, compassion and involvement. It is not just a masterly exercise in story-telling, but a book through which the reader shares in the triumphs and disasters of Smith and

*From* Smith (*see opposite page*)

his admirable sisters, Miss Bridget and Miss Fanny, Court Dressmakers—'Oo's to know the Court they was makers for was the criminal one at Old Bailey?'

There is something of the same virtuosity in Joan Aiken, another writer who dresses her fantastic invention in persuasive garb. Before embarking on her present course of pseudo-history Miss Aiken was a writer of short stories and she learnt a great deal in that most exacting of schools. Unlike Garfield she writes a direct, forceful prose with which she bulldozes the reader into acquiescence in her improbabilities.

For reasons which cannot readily be understood Miss Aiken has chosen to write about a might-have-been past. It is the Nineteenth Century and the reign of King James III. The Stuarts do not reign undisturbed: a ruthless underground movement favours the Hanoverian cause and works for the restoration of the Young Pretender Prince George. The Industrial Revolution has passed England by and the country is mostly rural and feudal. Wolves roam the woods and even come into London in hard winters. Neo-Jacobean England is more dangerous and less dull than the reality of history.

Miss Aiken moves in higher social circles than Garfield; one of her most important and genial characters is the Duke of Battersea, fifth in line from Sam Bayswater who was ennobled for supplying mince-pies to Charles II. Duke William is an egalitarian who squeezes time, between lecturing to the Royal Society and billiards with the Lord Chief Justice, for a game of chess with Simon, art student and part-time blacksmith. There is a gay informality about the Batterseas which contrasts with the dour sobriety of the Hanoverians. They live in a pink granite castle beside the Thames, designed to look 'like a great half-open rose'; when it is happily blown up by conspirators the Duke refuses to rebuild the monstrosity and the site becomes the Battersea pleasure-gardens. But the stories are not all of high life. Simon, the hero of *The Wolves of Willoughby Chase* (1964) and *Black Hearts in Battersea* (1965), may turn out to be the missing heir, but mostly he is the poor honest boy who makes good, while almost the most memorable and endearing of the characters is Dido, a dirty infant of the Bankside slums, as lacking in principles as in personal hygiene, whose courage is beyond all question. Miss Aiken has a keen ear for dialogue. She catches Dido's forthright cockney neatly. Ma forbids Dido to go to the fair as she has nothing fit to wear. When Simon offers to get her a dress she has no doubt about Ma's reaction: ' "Oh, it's dibs to dumplings she will [change her mind], if she gets summat for nix." '

Gratitude for Joan Aiken's high spirits and the gusto of her story-telling may make the reader value her rather beyond her worth. These are precious qualities, but they are not enough. What Miss Aiken lacks most grievously is self-discipline. Her stories gallop recklessly in all directions at once with never a touch of rein from the author. Grand yarns, they are too casual, even perhaps too full of self-mockery to be taken entirely seriously.

Here may be the place to consider briefly one facet of the complex craft of René Guillot. There have always been conflicting views of his achievement, some readers being alienated by his political opinions, others by a style which was sometimes as thick as treacle but less sweet. On one point there is a measure of agreement; despite the underlying complexity of his ideas he was at his best—and he was much too prolific a writer to keep always on the crest—a superb story-teller. Guillot was obsessed with a memory of the corsairs, the 'Knights of Fortune' who dominated the Atlantic and the Spanish Main in the seventeenth and eighteenth centuries, brutal pirates— Guillot was seldom disturbed by brutality—but also brave men and master seamen. Several of his books are concerned with their real and fictional exploits. In the novel which shows him at the height of his powers, *Companions of Fortune* (English edition 1952, original edition, as *Les Compagnons de la Fortune*, 1950), the corsairs have all been long dead, but their spirit lingers and their treasure-hoards haunt their descendants.

There is just enough of *Treasure Island* in *Companions of Fortune* to underline the enormous differences between the two stories. The opening period of waiting, the preparation for the voyage, the treasure-hunt: these stages of the stories are identical, but the pace and the tone of Guillot's narrative are worlds away from Stevenson's brisk and uncomplicated manner.

Guillot builds up his story slowly, savouring the dark atmosphere, a heavy foreboding almost outweighing the hopes of good fortune. Almost half of the book is spent in this way, before *Jean-de-Dieu* sails from La Rochelle with the Companions of Fortune aboard, heading for the hot coasts of Africa from which the source of Don Miguel's wealth, the black slaves, had come.

Africa was always René Guillot's particular passion. His heavy, sultry style matches perfectly the humid atmosphere of the jungle where Don Miguel's dead ivory and living gold lie waiting in the mud. So, through danger and hardship, the Companions of Fortune recover their treasure and are able to pay, in a surprising and highly satisfactory conclusion, the debt of their old captain.

Guillot was never an easy writer, and *Companions of Fortune*, which might be claimed as his best as well as his most characteristic book, is as difficult to read as any. It is partly a matter of style, of the ponderous and portentous sentences which Geoffrey Trease rendered most skilfully in an English version as doom-laden as the original. The ideas too, and the narrative with its slow pace and its many asides, do not make for easy reading. They are all, nevertheless, the essential matter of the book, and out of them Guillot created by main force a powerful and literally unforgettable story. The minority of readers, adult and child, who surrender totally to its forces guarantee for themselves disturbed nights, filled with dreams of the howling sea and the steaming river. It is one sign of a great book that it can haunt the reader for a lifetime, and by this criterion *Companions of Fortune* is a great book, a marvellous tale of adventure and a masterly piece of atmospheric writing.

In a tell-tale phrase Guillot speaks of the headquarters of the Companions as 'that house where everything was unusual'. It is the essence of Guillot's work that nothing is commonplace. In this he is exceptional among French writers, who have often taken particular delight in finding romance and adventure on the corner of the street. Of these Paul Berna has been outstandingly successful.

In this country Paul Berna's reputation stands firmly on the rock of *A Hundred Million Francs* (English edition 1957; original edition, as *Le Cheval sans Tête*, 1955). (I was astonished to discover recently, in conversation with a party of young French children, that his is not a household name in his own country.) *A Hundred Million Francs* is a story in the 'Emil' tradition in that it portrays children going about their own business in an adult world, not divorced from that world—as, for example, Ransome's children are—but living successfully alongside it. Like *Emil*, *A Hundred Million Francs* shows a classless rather than a proletarian society. The children and their parents are certainly all poor but not self-consciously so. Poverty is a part of everyday life like eating and playing. When the children, and their headless horse, help to solve the mystery of the missing haul from the great train robbery, the promise of reward briefly threatens the independence which their freedom from property gives them. The promise fades, fortunately. The gang would not have survived the assault of affluence. Besides, their parents would never have agreed. As Fernand's father said: 'It wasn't his way of earning money', and the kids had certainly enjoyed 'a couple of million's worth of fun'.

The book, like *Emil* and unlike the mainstream of adventure stories, shows not only a classless but a sexless society, or one in which no sex distinctions operate. Marion is a full member of the gang, earning the right by her forty-mile-an-hour rides on the headless horse and by losing a couple of teeth in the process, and consolidating her position by training her team of dogs for just such a crisis as the affair of the hundred million francs offers.

Kids outwitting a gang of professional crooks is a familiar theme, almost the most outworn of formulae and one which has produced some of the dreariest of all stories. Basically this is the theme of *A Hundred Million Francs*, but with significant variations. The children do not play a lone game; this is a combined operation between children and adults, and the courage and ingenuity of the former are in no way diminished by their calling on their parents and the police for help. The thieves are defeated by their own mean-spiritedness, by the professional skill of Inspector Sinet, and by Marion's love of animals which has given her the finest pack of crook-hunting dogs in France.

The book gives a highly convincing and satisfactory picture of society. Ultimately, however, it is the society of the children which gives Berna's book its unique quality, those Petits Pauvres for whom the street which witnesses their operations is happily named. Not since *Emil* have children been depicted with such spirit and unsentimental affection. Whether playing their break-neck games or hunting criminals, they are always credible, always high-spirited, never wholly serious. There is a splendid and characteristic moment at the very crisis of the story, when the Inspector is rounding up the crooks and hunting for their loot. Bonbon, the smallest and most cherubic of the children, is missing.

> 'The Inspector's foot chanced to kick open a big cardboard box. There, as though it were his coffin, lay a fair-haired, chubby infant, one arm raised, a huge revolver pointing straight at Sinet. "One move and you're a dead man," said Bonbon, closing one eye.'

For many children this book must have the quality of a wish-fulfilment, and this is partly the secret of its success. That children can be so self-reliant and have such dangerous fun, hindered not at all by the at-most mild opposition of parents— ' "One of these days, I warn you, you'll go and break your neck",' says Madame Douin casually—who are too busy to temper love for their offspring with admonition and restriction. Well-intended grown-ups have sometimes been appalled on reading about the headless horse which takes its riders headlong down the slum streets to the hazard of their limbs and the annoyance of sensitive neighbours, fearing that young readers will wish to emulate the feats of Gaby and Fernand. Children are more sensible. Joyfully suspending disbelief in enjoyment of a superbly told story, they know nevertheless that this, for all its persuasive credibility, is not their world.

Berna never matched the success of *A Hundred Million Francs*.

For worthy successors one looks elsewhere, and finds one such in a book which, for all its English character, had its origins in Paul Berna's France. One of the film successes of the Forties, when the French cinema was at its peak, was *A Nous Les Gosses*. This told a lively story about schoolchildren, clearly of the generation as well as the country of Gaby and Fernand, who interrupted their own tribal warfare to take on a gang of crooks. The poet Cecil Day Lewis enjoyed the film and was prompted to translate the story into a different form with an English setting.

*The Otterbury Incident* (1948) is memorable for its high spirits, for the swift sketches of real little boys (with line drawings of them by Edward Ardizzone at the top of his form), and especially for its style. Day Lewis used a boy narrator, and devised for him a brisk colloquial style which, in its artful heightening of the cadences of ordinary speech, is as good as anything of the kind since Oswald Bastable told us about the Treasure Seekers. The story is in outline almost a parody of the old-style 'Reward' in which little boys beat professional crooks. In the telling the absurd plot is given the illusion of realism by a skilful selection of details, and its improbabilities are masked by pace and brilliant timing.

*Line of Attack* (English edition 1959; originally *Les Chevaliers de l'Autorail*, 1958) also belongs to the Berna tradition. Michel Bourguignon lacked Berna's sparkle and his humour, but he was a master teller of tales.

The scene is Brittany. In the heart of the forest stands the Lone Tower, a ruined castle. It belongs by tradition to the village of Belmont, but on the very first day of the summer holidays a commando from Camarec occupies it. The two villages are hereditary enemies, and war is inevitable. It is a serious moment of history. 'The Belmontians were no barbarians voting an attack upon a defenceless neighbour, but men of good sense, conscious of the justice of their cause and anxious only that right should prevail.' The sentiments are elevated, the tactics down to earth. The Belmontians' strategy is based on the abandoned railway which runs through the forest; the technical expert, Junkshop, gets a diesel engine working, and the B.D.V. are carried by troop-train into the heart of enemy territory.

*Line of Attack* is, like *A Hundred Million Francs*, precisely

*From* The Otterbury Incident (*see page 43*)

framed to the needs of urban children deprived of adventure. Innumerable children, 'tied to their parents in some smart seaside town', have dreamed of just such a situation as this, in which their inventiveness and their bravery might operate free of the oppressive protectiveness of grown-ups. There are realists even in Belmont. The B.D.V. have to do without the services of 'three or four cowards, and over and above that the unfortunates who had parents so strict and unsympathetic as never to allow the slightest bruise or scratch to go unexplained'. *Line of Attack* is written from the children's viewpoint, taking the war, with its triumphs and disasters, heroism and cowardice, quite seriously; but the narrator's voice has in it always an essentially French note of irony. The soldiers may fight well, plan well, obey the laws of war; they are still not very big boys and girls. At the end of the campaign, when humanitarianism has prevailed, 'every so often Stumpy would roll up his sleeve and scratch the spot where a glorious purple bruise was beginning to show. He would have liked to keep the scar for ever'. It would have been easy, and very tempting, for Bourguignon to indulge in a sly, adult grin at the parent standing behind the reading child. He refrains, being content to tell his splendidly impossible tale for all it is worth. When the adult world catches up with the warriors at last and the law states its formidable case, the B.D.V. reply: 'We're too old to play tag!'

So many of the most distinguished books for children are disguised books for adults. *Line of Attack* is for children and for those rare adults who are capable of recovering their wonderlands.

Later exponents of the adventure-formula have been forced by changing tastes and the increasing sophistication of both writer and audience to leave the uninhibited world of Berna and Bourguignon, where the worst bruises can be displayed like the scars of an Agincourt veteran, in favour of more complex societies and the analysis of motives unsuspected by Gaby and Junkshop. In this changed aspect it is still a tale of children playing together. Even William Mayne made a characteristic and extraordinary contribution to the genre in *Pig in the Middle* (1965). For evidence of the change which came over children's literature in one decade, one might compare *A Hundred Million Francs* with Nina Bawden's *A Handful of Thieves* (1967).

'I'm trying to put everything down as it really happened', says Fred, the thirteen-year-old narrator of *A Handful of Thieves*. The method is hazardous, and indeed not strictly possible, but Nina Bawden does manage to give a convincing illusion of reality to a story of kids living in a city. Because this is fiction and not real life, play gets mixed up with the sternest facts to produce a story with its share of tension and drama. Its interest lies, however, mostly in its picture of a youthful gang and their relations with the adult world.

Fred and his friends become a handful of thieves. At first they are the Cemetery Committee, so called because 'Committee' is a more adult word than 'gang' and they are not babies, and they meet in a graveyard of old cars below the Death Wall of a disused motor-racing track. The activities of the Committee, at first childish enough, become broadened when Gran—she has the somewhat Cold Comfortish name of Blackadder—takes a new lodger. Sid, with that clarity of observation possessed only by the young, notices that Mr Gribble, 'a thin man with a thin, pale face and a long nose that seemed to quiver as he walked', has a fat man's voice. Mr Gribble is not what he seems ; he is, indeed, a professional preyer on old women, and Gran is his next victim. The Committee take on the job of hunting him and they succeed.

We have been here before. What puts life into this faded formula is Nina Bawden's skill in drawing recognizable children and her restraint in requiring of them no more than they can reasonably perform. Unlike the French children of *A Hundred Million Francs*, these are consciously aware of a debt to society, even if it is only the society represented by Gran. Unlike them too, they want to seem older than they are. At twelve, Gaby in Berna's story weeps at the loss of childhood and the feeling of getting 'sillier and sillier'. Fred and his friends would have found his attitude as incomprehensible as his tears. The social manners of the story are impeccable; all the children have the right instincts, and the frontier between them and the adult world is clearly demarcated. *A Handful of*

*Thieves* comes dangerously near to being a model children's novel, and such rarely prove to be working models. It is saved by the robust commonsense shared by the characters and their creator.

In Nina Bawden's work, and in a book like Antonia Barber's *The Affair of the Rockerbye Baby* (1966), a splendidly improbable and high-spirited account of villainy in industrial high places in America, the adventure formula is intact, but its character has been transformed. Action, the mainspring of the true adventure story, is giving place to a preoccupation with, on the one hand, sociology, on the other, psychology. Henceforward, while there would never be a shortage of hack writers on hand to give to the innocent the unsophisticated yarns of skullduggery and violence for which they crave, ambitious writers would think carefully before risking critical opprobrium by writing an undoubted tale of adventure.

# CHAPTER THREE

# To the Stars

' "Wouldn't you like to fly?" "Yes," said every one.'

THE DECLINE of the traditional adventure story left unsatisfied a very natural craving in both readers and writers for an exciting tale of action. To a small extent this need has been supplied by science fiction.

Mr Roger Lancelyn Green has explored the origins of science fiction in an entertaining book, *Into Other Worlds* (1957). For the purpose of the present study one might indulge in a broad simplification and say that the progenitors of children's SF were Jules Verne and H. G. Wells. Both took the science in their stories seriously, but Jules Verne was most concerned to invent a narrative packed with action in an exotic setting, while Wells was often preoccupied with the reaction of his characters to the scientific phenomena which he had devised. Both were story-tellers of a high excellence. Verne was primarily a chronicler, Wells a social novelist. Both have had their following among modern masters of SF.

The most Wellsian of the moderns—I am impelled, reluctantly, to leave such writers as John Wyndham and the John Christopher of *The Death of Grass* out of this discussion because, although their books have been taken over enthusiastically by young readers, they were originally conceived as novels for adults—is Donald Suddaby whose allegiance is most clearly demonstrated in *Death of Metal* (1952) and *Village Fanfare* (1954). Suddaby's technique here is, precisely as Wells's was, to assume a scientific situation—in the former book the sudden failure of all metals—and to show what happens as a result in an ordinary and easily identifiable community. *Village Fanfare*, the better book, offers a closely observed study of a Shropshire village under the dominance of a 'gallopin' 'airpin' of a visitor—or is it an army of identical visitors, 'reflections' from the future? The story might have been even sharper if it had been given a contemporary setting, but Suddaby, underlining his Wellsian affiliations, placed it in the Edwardian age and indulged almost to excess his pleasure in the bucolic charms of a village which, even when reeling under the impact of inexplicable events, is always delightful.

Despite the extraordinary nature of his themes Suddaby's stories are presented quietly and in matter-of-fact terms, and this is indeed their strength. In an earlier book, *The Star Raiders* (1950), he had attempted a more elusive theme and a more poetic manner, with interesting but not entirely convincing results.

The Wells tradition was followed mainly by writers who had serious literary pretensions, leaving Verne mostly to the pulp magazines and the revived 'Rewards'. One distinguished writer attempted an essay in the Verne manner; or, to be more precise, he wrote a strong adventure story with some Wellsian elements in it. David Craigie's *The Voyage of Luna I* (1948) was an admirable story, written with power and charm, its exciting episodes firmly directed by a creative imagination of high order. It was perhaps the best attempt, on either side of the Atlantic, to write a 'space' novel in the innocent post-war years before the realities of space exploration presented the SF writer with the intolerable situation that fact had overtaken fiction and left it far behind. When SF recovered from the shock it had to seek out a quite different network of paths to explore.

It was this abrupt change of direction which prompted some writers, who in a slightly earlier time might have been content to write mainstream SF in the old manner, to explore not the development of technology but its negation.

The future has always been a theme which exercises the imagination powerfully. In one of the short novels of which he was a master Wells looked at stages in the progress or decay of the world to the ultimate—or penultimate—vision of a tideless sea and a dead land. Two modern writers have chosen coincidentally to look at a nearer future, but one separated from the present by a huge catastrophe. It is not altogether surprising that Peter Dickinson and John Christopher should have hit upon much the same idea. Both, as sensitive observers must be, were conscious of the shadow of disaster thrown by the H-bomb and by abuse of the environment. In the event Christopher showed, in *Prince in Waiting*, a society rebuilding itself after a natural disaster, while Dickinson saw technological man overreaching himself as the agent of destruction. In the vision of both writers society reverts to its primitive condition. Not paleo- or neolithic. The England of *The Weathermonger* (1968) and *Prince in Waiting* (1970) is mediaeval. Dickinson's Englishmen turn on the machines which seemed to threaten their existence and destroy them, replacing the old civilization with a new—or perhaps an older—one based on the village unit and the unassisted work of hands. Christopher's society is a rather more complex one built around city states which are perpetually at war with one another. Technology has been banned too, not as a result of the instinctive revulsion of Dickinson's countrymen but by the deliberate establishment of religious taboos. In an earlier trilogy of novels John Christopher presented a somewhat similar theme from a different viewpoint and with rather more success. In *The White Mountains* (1967)—a powerful novel which had two less effective sequels—Europe, or most of it, is dominated by vast mechanical intelligences called Tripods. (These derive directly from Wells's *War of the Worlds*, but while Wells's Martians were destroyed by the bacteria of an alien world, Christopher's Tripods have triumphed.) The Tripods, after a violent invasion in which all the major cities were destroyed, master the survivors by an ingenious device. At puberty every boy is presented to a Tripod who 'caps' him, giving him a metal cap which fits neatly and permanently over his head and becomes a part of him. The ceremonial has all the appearance of a meaningless folk-ritual, but through his cap every man is controlled, quietly and unconsciously, so that his thought and personality can be moulded by the Tripods for ever. But not quite everyone is caught in this net. The emergence of a resistance movement produces the excitement and high adventure of *The White Mountains*. What sticks most in the imagination, however, is not the adventure but the pictures of the debris of a lost civilization which litter the lands over which the Tripods have dominion.

John Christopher's stories are distinguished by excellent writing and keen, original and logical thinking. The thought is subordinated to the writing in Peter Dickinson's three stories of England in its second Dark Age. In *The Weathermonger* Dickinson was not content only to paint a brilliantly colourful picture of a country which has developed certain instinctive skills to replace the destroyed machines; he attempted to explain his theme, and the explanation was sadly inadequate. In the two later books he confined himself to a smaller canvas and a shorter span of time, and the stories, freed of specious explanations, took wing magnificently.

Like Christopher, Dickinson is greatly affected by decay. The descriptions of London in the first stages of its decline which occupy the early chapters of *The Devil's Children* (1970) are sharply realized and profoundly disturbing; this, one feels, is uncomfortably near a possible reality. *Heartsease* (1969), the most tightly constructed of the three novels, shows England long after the cataclysm. Society has settled down to a Dark Age existence, content for the most part to live under a system of rough and ready justice and petty tyranny. Much of the action takes place in and around a Cotswold village, and this helps to concentrate the impact of the quietly grim story. Topography gives the book its unity. *The Devil's Children* is centred on the character of Nicky, a little lost Londoner who joins a party of Sikh immigrants in their search for a safe haven after the destruction of London. This child, armoured by her determination not to allow herself the soft option of love, is, in her strength and weakness, the most pathetic and the most deeply examined of Dickinson's creations.

Apart from the adventures and the occasional profundities of the character-drawing, much of the interest of Dickinson's achievement comes from his examination of society, whether the embryo manorial system of *The Devil's Children* or its matured counterpart in *Heartsease*. Society is at the heart of John Christopher's most consistently successful novel for young readers, *The Guardians*. This, another view of the future, shows apparently contrasting societies of town and country, the one a drab conformist society enlivened only by mob riots, the other a feudal system which seems at first to embody old-world graces as well as old-world inequalities. The climax of the story comes, with admirably controlled timing, when the hero discovers that these apparently separate worlds are in fact one, and that the destinies of both are in the hands of the Guardians, an omnipotent and omnipresent autocracy. It is a story somewhere between *Brave New World* and *1984* and in concept not less horrifying than either. Except that the hero is young, this is not especially a story for children, but in its disillusionment and its revolt alike it speaks the contemporary language of adolescence. Christopher is not greatly interested in personalities, and this keeps his books out of the first rank as novels. As an exciting and relevant social document *The Guardians* has not been equalled in recent years.

It is perhaps stretching definitions beyond comfortable limits to consider these novels of Peter Dickinson and John Christopher as science-fiction, although in their strict logical application of hypotheses they belong to the genre. The main development of science fiction for young readers has, in the past twenty years, followed two different paths, which one might call the innocent and the sophisticated. To the former category belong innumerable tales about small boys hitching a ride to Venus or foiling wicked plots against the peace of the Galaxy. These need not detain us. A number of far more professional writers have ventured into the science fiction field armed with little more than their literary skills. These include M. E. Patchett, an Australian writer best known for her success in evoking the heat of the bush and the beauty of animals, and Paul Berna, the doyen of French writers for the young. One of the hazards for the scientific amateur—it is often shared by the scientific professional—is that events will quickly prove him desperately wrong. When Paul Berna's *Threshold of the Stars* (English edition 1958) first appeared, as *La Porte des Etoiles*, in 1954 its speculations about the moon seemed highly improbable. It is now clear that all his guesses were wrong. This, however, is not a story which even the author could have taken quite seriously; it is a yarn about boys rather than about the Moon, boys getting into mischief and having dreams. Young Michael Jousse does not fly to the Moon at the end of the book; this is a bitter disappointment to him and to the readers, but he and they know that his hope had been only fantasy. He will still get there before it becomes 'full of nasty little men with fountain-pens in their breast-pockets.'

There is much of the same innocence, shrewdness and high spirits in *Encounter near Venus* (1968) by Leonard Wibberley. Wibberley's reputation rests on an extremely fine and deeply researched novel about the American Civil War. His approach to science is casual, or, to be more precise, he writes a space story out of his own exuberant fantasy, unfettered by considerations of probability. This does not make his book any the less enjoyable or exciting. If the science is innocent the writing is extremely sophisticated. In expressing his story so precisely in the idiom of the late Sixties the author courted disaster, for nothing ages more quickly than literary and oral idioms; but, if a year or two have outdated the dialogue, the sharp observation of lively and intelligent children has not.

There are moments of excitement in *Encounter near Venus*. The charm of the book comes from its gentler moments, from its skill in conveying purely physical pleasures like swimming —the children are able most conveniently to breathe the sea on the planet Nede because the water is 'super-saturated with oxygen'—and the prettiness of the lumens, light intelligences which feel 'like warm fur and ice at the same time' and which communicate with humans by Morse Code. The book is handicapped by having one of the more tedious of omniscient Uncles as its motive force, and it is enlivened by a creative imagination which never takes itself too seriously.

Sophisticated science fiction often regards itself with a seriousness which is literally deadly. In Hugh Walters's stories, which are sophisticated as to the science and innocent in their writing and characterization, didacticism is liable to break out at the more improbable moments; no crisis is so breath-stopping that it will prevent one astronaut from quizzing or instructing another about the technical reasons behind their dilemma. The entirely admirable sentiments conveyed by the stories, in support of international amity, co-operation and the interdependence of a team, are expressed in clichés of a gravity-removing banality; and the heroic young men by whose courage, skill and dedication space is conquered and the future of mankind assured fail to put on the garments of real personality. Partly this is simply an inadequacy of literary skill, the weakness of a writer who has a good tale to tell but who uses outworn words and concepts to express it; partly it is a weakness built into the nature of science fiction, and which only the rarest of masters can overcome.

Even within the formula of mainstream science fiction individual and memorable work can be done. Most of the best has come out of America, from writers like Alan E. Nourse, James Blish and Lester del Rey. When an English writer excels, as James Muirden does in *Space Intruder* (1965), it is because he, while keeping to the formula, chooses to express it in terms of people and places.

The two acknowledged masters of mainstream SF for young readers are André Norton and Robert A. Heinlein. Despite their almost parallel careers and their comparable status, their achievements have wide differences in style and manner. André Norton's strength lies in atmosphere. She gives a tangible quality to the most improbable invention by clothing it in vividly imagined detail, and her highly charged style—admittedly a little hard to digest in large quantities—evokes with equal success the terrors of darkness and the blinding glare of light. Hers is an astonishingly complete vision; she describes the topography and the sociology of new worlds as if from the life, giving them a kind of actuality rather like that of Tolkien's *Lord of the Rings*—although in no other way does she approach the breadth and range of his achievement.

André Norton tells a good tale, too, but here she is a shade derivative. For all the wonder of the settings, the action of her stories might almost be that of a Western. The strange worlds are often divided neatly into goodies and baddies, and the latter, after great hazards, bite the dust as convincingly as if they were redskins or rogue cowboys.

Here, however, is a writer who develops with each book; and the naiveties which made a good story like *The Beast Master* (1966, original American edition 1959) difficult to accept with unconditional seriousness, are being gradually purged.

*Dark Piper* (1969) has a concentrated power and, if the word is not unacceptable for an off-world story, humanity which marks a long stride forward. Her books continue to make difficult reading. An imaginative experience so completely realized can only be shared through the reader's total surrender, and not everyone is willing, or able, to follow her along some of her perilous paths. The inability to select which the writer showed in her earlier books, too, is an obstacle which not all young readers can surmount.

Almost alone among SF writers, Robert A. Heinlein has the self-confidence, the absolute mastery, which allow him to make fun of the medium. His smart, irreverent, wise-cracking young heroes give a solemn, inbred, often constipated literary form the sharp kick-in-the-pants it needs.

Heinlein's tendency towards frivolity has accelerated with the years and in some recent books—notably *The Space Family Stone* (1968)—American edition as *The Rolling Stones* (1956)—the jokes have almost taken over. In an earlier story, *Space Cadet* (1948, although it did not have an English edition until 1966), the wise-cracks are plentiful but the theme, the method of training a young man for service in the Interplanetary Patrol, is entirely serious and so is the treatment. The Patrol Academy, whose training includes the most violent and hazardous of assault courses, has built up—in characteristic American fashion—an historical tradition rather like that of an English public school. By an impressive convention every parade or exercise is carried out in the invisible presence of four long-dead heroes of the battle for Space.

Science fiction is inevitably didactic. The author cannot tell his story without putting it into its proper theoretical setting. With many writers, indeed most, this comes between the reader and his enjoyment of the story. Heinlein, although his scientific theories are complex, is a master of the art of painless indoctrination. His secret is that he shows his characters learning their lessons, and the reader shares in the educational experience. His interests range far beyond the mechanics of space travel. One of the most hilarious of his stories is largely a thoughtful examination of the phenomenon of identical twins. *Tunnel in the Sky* (1955, English edition 1965) shows his characteristic qualities at their best. This is partly about survival, partly about government. The hero is a candidate for a kind of super-Duke of Edinburgh award. With a hundred or so young men and women he is sent out to an unknown planet to survive for a few days. The operation is extremely dangerous even in normal circumstances—there are inevitably some deaths—and on this occasion the recovery procedure fails and the students are left on their own in the wild. It is a *Lord of the Flies* situation: that the solution is different from Golding's is partly because these are One Hundred Per Cent American boys and girls, partly because they have been trained for just such a situation and they have the mental equipment for survival. Heinlein shows brilliantly how each of the marooned youngsters reacts according to his background and personality, from the huge gay black girl Caroline who faces the unknown unarmed and half-naked, to Jimmy, a typical Heinlein creation, whose survival kit includes a pack of cards. Apart from the early chapters, which deal with the technique of getting into the wilderness, this is not a science fiction story at all but a tale of pioneering days. In it Heinlein, like all the masters of any literary genre, breaks out of the strait-jacket of definitions and writes a powerful, thoughtful and exciting story of adventure.

With Heinlein and his peers the terms of reference for their craft are constantly changing. Science fiction, so often disfigured by a clutter of scientific mumbo-jumbo, escapes on the one hand into high adventure, on the other into fantasy. In any other generation *A Wrinkle in Time* (1962, English edition 1963) would have been written, if at all, as a traditional story of the struggle between good and evil. Madeleine L'Engle took some of the ideas and some of the techniques of science fiction to the making of an extraordinary fantastic novel. In the event the mixture proved almost too explosive to be controlled, and the resulting story, for all its wit and occasional gaiety, failed to achieve total communication. *A Wrinkle in Time* remains an experiment, an uneasy blending of physics and metaphysics, but an experiment entirely in the spirit of the age in which it was conceived.

# CHAPTER FOUR

# The Abysm of Time

'She told us all about Becket, and then about St Alphege, who
had bones thrown at him till he died, because he wouldn't tax
his poor people to please the beastly rotten Danes.'

IT IS A CURIOUS CONVENTION of criticism that the
historical novel is *ipso facto* regarded as inferior to the novel
proper. This may be part of an even stranger belief that the
quality of a work of art is in inverse proportion to the labour
spent on it. The idea is that such a book as *A Man on a Donkey*,
which comes from a lifetime of study and a decade of close
research, must be less spontaneous and therefore less good than
one produced by the artist's unfettered fancy. Something of the
same concept is responsible for the idea that an instinctive
historical writer like Rosemary Sutcliff, who feels the past
through her nerves and her bloodstream, is somehow better
than an intellectual writer like Cynthia Harnett, whose
approach to the past is through her brain. Whatever the rela-
tive merits of the two writers, it is by their achievements, not
their methods, that they need to be measured.

Until ten years ago one might have said confidently that the
historical novel has been the outstanding achievement in
children's literature since the war. Earlier work, with a few
exceptions, had been tentative or apologetic. In post-war
England writers, stimulated by and indeed stimulating changes
in the method of teaching history in schools, found a rich vein
of inspiration in the re-creation and interpretation of the past.
As the old inhibitions of writers and the prohibitions of publishers faded, it became possible to portray historical figures
frankly, changing the old blacks and whites into convincing
and blending colours. Some writers found it rewarding to seek

in the past parallels to present dilemmas; others, dissatisfied with the worn formulae of adventure, discovered that history offered abundant opportunities for action-filled narrative. For a few, like Rosemary Sutcliff, there was no element of choice; they were themselves chosen by their own personal daemons to be interpreters of the past.

Geoffrey Trease had been the conscious inventor of the modern historical novel in the years before the war. His concern was to look at the past afresh, not through the screen of old text-book attitudes and judgements. In the immediate post-war world his work was taken up again both by himself and by a number of other writers, among them Ivy Bolton, whose *Son of the Land* (1948), a study of the Peasants' Revolt, was exactly in the spirit of Trease's first books. This was published by Basil Blackwell who had always been a practical advocate of a fresh vision in children's literature. Another publishing concern, Phoenix House, launched a series of historical novels entitled 'Pageant Books' which were intended to examine anew some of the conventional assessments on both political and social issues of the past, and which had such contributors as Trease and A. Stephen Tring (Laurence Meynell). L. Barringer's *The Rose in Splendour* (1953) was a good representative of the series; there were no surprises in this version of the Wars of the Roses, but its presentation of the horrors of civil war was—for its date—unusually ruthless. In this same decade Joan Selby-Lowndes wrote a pair of gentle stories about the social upheavals of Tudor England, which showed in human terms the economic and educational consequences of the destruction of the monasteries. *Royal Chase* (1947) and *Tudor Star* (1949) are among the best work of this undervalued writer. Hers was a middle-of-the-road view. For extremes there was Naomi Mitchison's sharp social comment in a very clever novel with fantastic elements in it, *The Big House* (1950), and Winifred Nolan's Catholic interpretation of the 'spacious days' in *Rich Inheritance* (1953).

Not all the historical writers of this age were extremists. Many were content to present familiar viewpoints of the past, and others, not much interested in original interpretations, turned to history for material for good strong stories about colourful personalities. From an attractive collection of books one might select Joyce Reason's *The Secret Fortress* (1949), which deals in traditional style with the last age of Viking rule in Cumberland, a theme later taken up by Rosemary Sutcliff, Ursula Moray Williams's richly colourful picture of the mediaeval road, *Jockin the Jester* (1950), another fine evocation of the Middle Ages by Christine Price, *Three Golden Nobles* (1953), and Violet Needham's portrait of William the Silent in *The Boy in Red* (1948).

These were some of the firm foundations of the modern historical novel. On them the greatest masters of the genre, Trease, Cynthia Harnett, Rosemary Sutcliff, Henry Treece, Ronald Welch, C. Walter Hodges and Hester Burton raised their more impressive edifices.

Geoffrey Trease is one of the best theorists among modern writers for the young. His principles are unexceptionable. His performance has not invariably reached up to his own standards; the bones of his political and social theories are apt to stick through the skin of his novels in an uncomfortable fashion. He was at his best in the decade immediately after the war. *Trumpets in the West* (1947) was written while the author was still in the Forces, and his affectionate pictures of Somerset and the London of Wren were painted among the hills of Central India. The book shows signs of its origins, as well as those of its writer's limited technical equipment. The writing is often naive and cliché-ridden, but the story is beautifully fresh, capturing the challenging spirit in the air of 1688. A year later a very much more mature book appeared. *The Hills of Varna* (1948) is a story of the Renaissance. A slightly contrived plot—plots have never been Trease's main strength—sends Alan away from the shelter of Cambridge into a world bristling as much with ideas as dangers. His journey is a treasure-hunt, but the treasure is not gold or such trash but the manuscript of a Greek satirical comedy lying forgotten in a Dalmatian monastery. Trease manages to share with his readers the intellectual excitement of the quest and its success as well as the more conventional thrills of piracy and banditry. He was less successful in telling the story of the origin of Alexis's play in *The Crown of Violet* (1952). He seemed ill at ease in Socrates'

Athens, and the attempt to make the young people of Classical Greece speak in a modern idiom is less happy even than an essay in 'tushery' might have been. (' "You know what Mum is . . . And I do think your old uncle is a dear." "He's a scream. Half the time he's scared stiff . . ." ') But clearly this was a book which had to be written, and there is some charm in the picture of Athens in its precarious heyday.

Trease's recent work is purged of the crudities of style and thought which mark his earlier writing, but he has bought this technical competence at a high price. The adventuring spirit has faded, and he no longer sparkles with a fresh vision. He still knows how to choose a good and original theme. His two stories about Garibaldi's Italy present, for English readers, an unfamiliar scene. The most satisfactory of his later novels is perhaps *The Red Towers of Granada* (1966). This has the handicap of an awkward plot, but there are admirable portraits of Edward I and his great consort Eleanor, and the author explores thoughtfully the status of the Moors in thirteenth-century Spain and their scientific skills. As always with this writer there is too much plot! The excellent ideas are constantly being swamped by desperate action.

Philip Rush belonged to the same school as Trease, sharing with him a teaching background and radical opinions. His stories were more conventional in construction than in viewpoint. His story about the Peasants' Revolt—*King of the Castle* (1956)—chooses an unusual approach to an overworked subject, but somehow convention breaks through and the story and its characters are largely stereotyped.

If Trease wrought the major revolution in historical fiction of the century, a change almost as far-reaching, if quieter, was achieved by Cynthia Harnett, who brought to the form a high degree of historical integrity and scholarship. Not for her, attitudes or points of view; she was concerned to build a story by synthesis, which would be as true to its period as research and disciplined imagination could make it. The result might have been accurate yet arid, had not the historian also been an artist. Of all the historical novelists writing for the young, Cynthia Harnett most resembles an architect, shaping a myriad of tiny details and fitting them together so that they all perform necessary functions and all contribute to an impressive and satisfying structure.

No doubt Cynthia Harnett's early training in art—her teacher was her cousin Vernon Stokes, a master of aquatint who also made books for children in which she collaborated— was important not only in enabling her to illustrate her own books—a capacity which of all writers the historical novelist most covets—but in helping her to keep her sense of scale, of the relationship between the whole and its parts. All her books have in common this conscious and fundamental structure.

It was entirely in character that Cynthia Harnett should start quietly. *The Great House* (1949) was only just a novel, in the sense that its plot was its least important ingredient. The action, such as it was, sauntered gently along, stopping frequently to enjoy the elegant, well-mannered landscapes of late seventeenth-century England, a tidy scene devised to set off the symmetrical houses and their immaculate inhabitants. It was a charming book, but it needed a discerning reader to see the strength underlying the charm. Cynthia Harnett allowed the strength to show clearly in *The Woolpack* (1951).

Nine years separate *The Woolpack* and *The Load of Unicorn* (1959), but the two stories have common elements apart from their concern with industrial history. Both deal with ages of violence and change, but both are essentially quiet stories, reaching their climaxes in stillness rather than action. The interest, indeed the excitement, derives from discoveries which the reader seems to make simultaneously with the writer. Intellectual excitement is not common in children's literature, but it is found here. One of the everyday miracles witnessed by those who have the privilege of bringing books to children is that of the child who has no obvious feeling for history and is certainly not intellectual, but who capitulates utterly to the discreet appeal of these books.

The main figures in Cynthia Harnett's stories are not of great interest; she sketches them lightly and pleasantly and makes no great effort to explore them in depth. Judged, as is not unreasonable, in the terminology of art, she is a genre painter, not a portraitist; her young heroes and heroines sit in the scene rather like the demure and neatly dressed people in a

Dutch interior. She is perhaps most effective in giving a swift impression of a great historical personage, like Caxton or Richard Whittington, who appears briefly, slightly off-centre of the scene. What engages her interest, and consequently the reader's, is not people but places and things. London in *Ring Out Bow Bells*, Burford in *The Woolpack*, Sulgrave in *Stars of Fortune* are not just places where the action, by chance or of necessity, takes place; they are essential agents in the stories. Most important of all, the author makes her story out of the ingredients of the time. All the paraphernalia of the everyday world is called upon to promote the action; the stories are as much practical handbooks as are Ransome's.

In a brief postscript to each book Cynthia Harnett gives the reader a glimpse into her workshop, showing the lengthy and exciting detective-work which precedes the writing; she shows, too—and this is the most individual feature of her work—in how strange a manner one discovery leads to another until all the dissimilar scraps come together and dovetail neatly.

Sound and even inspired scholarship may produce good history; it does not of itself make good historical fiction. Cynthia Harnett adds another ingredient to turn research into art—inevitability. Through these still, apparently leisurely stories a pulse beats, moving the action and the reader relentlessly forward to a climax. When the climax comes, it is rarely dramatic. It is not the trumpet-blast but the still small voice that marks the crisis; what matters most is not the unmasking of villainy but self-discovery. The supreme example of this comes in *A Load of Unicorn*, when the young hero, searching for the manuscript of Malory's *Morte d'Arthur* and for a key to the mystery of its author—a rogue and jailbird who wrote the elegy for the passing of chivalry—finds the answer in the white and gold of the Beauchamp Chapel in Warwick. The moment of truth is so brief that a careless reader might miss it, but it is the clue to the book and to this remarkable writer's craft.

There could be no contrast more sharp than that provided by the work of Rosemary Sutcliff. It would be absurd to suggest that she is a less careful researcher than Cynthia Harnett, but her methods and her results are entirely different. If Cynthia

Harnett's approach to history is essentially cerebral, Rosemary Sutcliff feels the past through her nerves. No other writer for children of any age or country gives so vivid an impression of just how it felt to live in Britain after the departure of the Legions or under the weight of the conquering Normans; these descriptions, one feels, are the work of an eye-witness. This extraordinary writer takes us by the hand and leads us into the barrack-room of a fortress perched between the Roman peace and the barbarian lands; a gentle woman so disabled that no movement can be made without pain knows exactly what it was like to swing an axe in the shield-ring and shares the knowledge with the reader.

There was little evidence of this power in Rosemary Sutcliff's first books. In *The Queen Elizabeth Story* (1950), *The Armourer's House* (1951) and *Brother Dusty-Feet* (1952), one found the charm of sensitive writing, careful domestic scenes of Tudor times, and a number of tenderly observed portraits of young people. The past—a century of desperate poverty and barbarous brutality—glowed in a golden light. It was a beginning which showed promise, but it seemed to be the promise of a talented writer of historical romance.

With her fourth novel—I discount her 'Robin Hood' book which belongs to a different phase of her work—Rosemary Sutcliff's writing underwent a change of a kind which has no parallel in children's literature, unless it is that of E. Nesbit's emergence from the chrysalis of her 'prentice work to the complete artist of *The Treasure Seekers*. Whatever the cause, Rosemary Sutcliff removed her rosy spectacles and took a hard look at the real world with its contrasts of wealth and harshness. *Simon* (1953) is a story of the Civil War dealing, as many others have done, with the conflict between personal friendship and public loyalty, but differing from others in its West Country setting and its concentration on the closing stages of the conflict. It is a fine story of action and of friendship, strongly written yet sensitive in its exploration of human weakness. Simon, the young supporter of Parliament whose greatest friend is a Royalist, is the first of a long gallery of portraits seemingly painted from the life. Some of the other characters are sketched in with the quick, sure touch of the professional writer, notably 'Fiery Tom' Fairfax, a favourite of this writer's for whom she was later to make an adult novel. *Simon* is a long story, although the skilfully controlled pace of its narrative keeps it moving. It is especially successful in the effective use of ironic 'throw-away' detail. For example, Amias, Simon's friend, hides the Colours of his Company in a foxhole after the Royalist defeat. It is a fine defiant gesture, but what of the sequel?

> 'The spring rains washed it into the ground, and next autumn a squirrel made a store in the folds, and then, after the way of squirrels, forgot the place. One of the nuts sprouted and took root, and presently there was a fine hazel sapling growing through the old Royalist Colours.'

After *Simon* there could be no turning back. Her next book —*Eagle of the Ninth* (1954)—is in some opinions her most successful, a very powerful story told with exuberance and strength, subtle but presented with a rare clarity. The complexity of thought which makes some of her later books difficult and the over-rich writing which sometimes mars them are not to be found here. Marcus Aquila, a young Roman officer denied active service because of a wound, goes north beyond the Wall to recover the lost Eagle of the Ninth Legion. Rosemary Sutcliff loves a good battle-scene, but here she is concerned with greater perils, with the terrors of loneliness and the enmity of unknown gods. For the Eagle is held by the priests of a warrior tribe in the highlands of Caledonia, and it has to be taken not in hand-to-hand fighting but from a burial-mound where darkness presses with physical weight. The author has written no finer pages than those in which Marcus forces back the powers of darkness by calling on the light of Mithras. Rosemary Sutcliff has explained how she came to write *Eagle of the Ninth* by bringing together two mysteries of Roman Britain, the disappearance of the Ninth Legion and the modern discovery in the ruins of Caleva of a battered Eagle. This may explain the genesis of her story; the conviction which each detail of the story carries is less susceptible of explanation.

The idea of Rome, of a civilizing bastion set against barbarism, is one which exercises a powerful influence on

Rosemary Sutcliff. It is at the heart of two lesser books, *Outcast* (1955) and a sequel to *Eagle of the Ninth* called *The Silver Branch* (1957). It is the motive force of the book with which, after many near-misses, she won the Carnegie Medal of 1959, *The Lantern Bearers*. This is a book of unequal quality, but its basic idea is deeply characteristic of the writer. The Roman legions are recalled from Britain and a young Romano-British officer, realizing at the last moment that his loyalties are at home, deserts and stays behind; in one of those grand symbolic gestures which Rosemary Sutcliff loves, he fires the beacon of Rutupiae as the legions sail away. 'It was his farewell to so many things: to the whole world that he had been bred to. But it was something more: a defiance against the dark.' Aquila becomes first a slave to the Jutish invaders, then a resistance-fighter. Like the secret messengers who pass through the occupied land, he is a Lantern Bearer, one of those who 'keep something burning, to carry what light we can forward into the darkness and the wind.'

Among other things *The Lantern Bearers* is a story about Arthur, another historic figure of whom Rosemary Sutcliff was later to paint a full-length portrait for adult readers. In a fine passage at the end of the book, when after a great victory the Lantern Bearers look forward to the darkness which will inevitably come, Aquila wonders whether the people beyond the darkness will remember them. His friend looks across to Arthur, a 'tall man . . . flushed and laughing, with a great hound against his knee', and says, ' "You and I and all our kind they will forget utterly, though they live and die in our debt . . . but he is the kind that men make songs about to sing for a thousand years".' The episode is one that only Rosemary Sutcliff could invent, and the language, with its incantatory lilt, is hers alone. At its best the Sutcliff style is flexible, eloquent and evocative, but it is often dangerously near to taking charge; it has a self-intoxicating quality.

Her search for the seeds of civilization took Rosemary Sutcliff into the remote past in a remarkable novel of pre-history, *Warrior Scarlet* (1958). In this she continued to pay her outstanding debt to Kipling, her chief literary mentor, who made the same journey more briefly in his 'Puck' stories. She feels very strongly the gulf between civilized man who draws strength from the tradition of his family and his legion and primitive man whose strength comes from the earth. The contrast is at the heart of the climax to *Eagle of the Ninth*. It is the essence of Rosemary Sutcliff's latest major novel, *The Mark of the Horse Lord* (1965). In this formidably difficult book the hero is a Roman, or rather a gladiator-slave belonging involuntarily to the Roman tradition, who becomes, first, the lord of a barbarous kingdom, then the willing sacrifice, the king who dies for his people. In his fatal dilemma Phaedrus listens to voices from a deeper past than that of Rome, and his solution belongs to the oldest of all traditions. This is a dark story, powerful and compelling for all that it is grossly over-written. In it Rosemary Sutcliff seems to be writing compulsively, as if for once she has surrendered to an external, or perhaps a deep internal, force over which she lacks control. It is her grimmest book—and Charles Keeping provided it with illustrations as grim and compelling—and it is potentially her finest. So stern a theme called for a disciplined approach, and the writer weakened the impact of the story by stylistic extravagance. If only she had matched its starkness with words equally bare!

In this book Rosemary Sutcliff moves within hailing distance of Henry Treece. Treece's death in 1966 at the age of fifty-five came as he seemed to be discovering his full strength. For years he had written at less than his best, producing possibly too many books, and these, for all their exuberance of narrative and unquestioned historical integrity, curiously unsatisfactory. In 1954 he had begun what promised to be a sequence of novels covering the great crises of English history. The project was never completed; this was inevitable and probably not to be regretted. He was side-tracked, by unrelated ideas which appealed to him, such as the pathetic story of the Children's Crusade with its bitterly ironic contrast between the holy innocence of the children and the cynicism of their exploiters—*The Children's Crusade*, 1958—and the emergence of gunpowder as a force in war—*The Bombard*, 1959; but apart from the initial ideas these books lacked distinction. Then he became obsessed with the Vikings, the pirates who founded kingdoms in the sun and propped up a crumbling

Roman Empire. This was a magnificent theme which might have kept any writer busy for a lifetime. Stories like *The Road to Miklagaard* (1957) are exciting enough, but they are never quite equal to the grandeur of the subject. There seemed always a sense of inadequacy, or at least of holding too much in reserve. Perhaps Treece, like other authors who work in the field of adult books, was inhibited by a vision of his young readers and tried, as the finest writers for children do not, to write for them rather than for himself. Certainly the adult novels he was writing at the same time, in which he retold the stories of the Golden Fleece, Electra and Hamlet, are brilliantly successful in just the way that the children's stories are not, in that they show an author clearly in control of his material and giving it the full force of his imagination, intellect and technique. Treece had started his literary career as a poet; in *The Green Man* the reader is aware of this, but *The Last of the Vikings* (1964), which has a subject almost as fundamental, remains obstinately earth-bound.

In his last year Henry Treece began to apply the lessons of his own mythological novels to writing for children. *The Dream-Time* (1967) was his last book. It was possibly not quite finished, for there are small hints in it of uncompleted revision. It is not entirely successful. It certainly opens a door through which we glimpse a different kind of Treece story, and one infinitely richer, wiser, more fundamentally poetic in concept, than anything which had gone before.

Even now it is difficult to evaluate *The Dream-Time* dispassionately. Apart from the pathos of its posthumous appearance, the theme and its handling still provoke controversy. The book may even be a failure; if so, there have been few more interesting failures during this century.

In one important sense *The Dream-Time* is not a historical novel, or even a story of prehistory. It is, as Rosemary Sutcliff wrote in a perceptive postscript, 'as though he were writing down a dream', a condensation of prehistory. The early stages of man's development are shown in parallel, so that one man, the artist Twilight who was once called Crookleg, is enabled to see, taste and reject them all before at last he finds a people who 'have something better than stockades' and who come out

*From* The Dream-Time (*see page 67*)

to meet him, laughing. It is an allegory of the birth of civilization, but an allegory told in very human terms. The terrible
chief of the Fisher Folk—Shark, Wander, the beautiful and
ruthless leader of the matriarchal society of the River Folk,
Big One the benevolent, inarticulate cave-painter, above all
Twilight and his enchanting little Blackbird who is clothed in
the elegant whirls and flowers of her tattooing—these are
people who, for all their remoteness and the strangeness of
their language and mores, engage our interest and sympathy.

The greatest problem in writing about the people of remote
times is that of communication. How can one convey convincingly the speech and thought of men whose word-patterns
and terms of reference are not only different but infinitely more
restricted by experience than those of the modern reader? In
*The Dream-Time* Treece was extraordinarily successful in
purging his words of modern concepts and colouring. Accepting
that his hero, Twilight, has the vision of a genius, he allows no
ideas or images of the modern world to creep in. The thoughts
of these people are deep and complex, arising from their concern with basic necessities like God and survival and fear, yet
the whole story is told with the utmost simplicity, almost
entirely in monosyllabic words; this is no artificial literary
device but an inevitable response to the demands of the theme.

Historical fiction in the post-war years has been especially
a province of English writers. A few Americans—like Harold
Keith—have found a source of inspiration in their own pioneering past, but never with the commanding success of Esther
Forbes's earlier *Johnny Tremain* (reintroduced to English
audiences in 1958). Elizabeth Borton de Trevino's biographical
story of Velazquez and his negro servant, *I Juan de Pareja*
(1966), was of the authentic quality. Perhaps the best recent
European work has come from Scandinavia (Poul Knudsen—
*The Challenge*, 1962), and Germany, where two major historical
novelists emerged since the war. B. Bartos-Hoppner writes
with passion and penetration about the confused provincial
history of Russia, overcoming a natural reluctance in her
readers by the ruthless power of her narrative and the ease with
which she wields her formidable scholarship. Hans Baumann
has a rather lighter task, for he writes for preference about

great world figures—Columbus, Kublai Khan, Vasco de Gama —but his closely argued stories, packed with authentic detail, are not easy reading, because the strong narrative line is inextricably woven into a complex philosophical pattern.

In general historical fiction for children has tended to be historical romance. Writers have chosen to interpret periods of history through the lives of invented heroes and heroines acted against the backcloth of historical fact, or, when they have taken historical personages as central characters, they have by selection and invention presented a romantic version of the truth. This is a legitimate approach to history, and the results are often excellent both as romance and as history. The historical chronicle is more rarely attempted. It is certainly more difficult to give interest and interpretation in depth to the chronicle which limits itself to people and a sequence of events which are predetermined by the known facts. The historical novelist reasonably leaves this to the historian. It is, however, possible to accept the rigid conventions of the chronicle and still produce an individual work of art, as readers of Hope Muntz's *The Golden Warrior* know.

The nearest to this in the field of children's literature is C. Walter Hodges's pair of linked novels about King Alfred. Hodges moulded the convention to his own will, selecting and inventing in order to underline the purpose of his story, but the books remain a chronicle of events rather than a novel. They are among the outstanding achievements of post-war literature for children.

Cynthia Harnett is a writer who happens to have the training and technique to illustrate her own books. A number of artists, pre-eminently Edward Ardizzone, have skill in handling words and provide texts to accompany their pictures. Alone among contemporary writers for the young, C. Walter Hodges is equally an artist in line and word. As an artist he is fluent and prolific, with a long list of illustrated books to his credit. He is the least prolific of writers, pondering a theme for years before it reaches a shape acceptable to him. The promise of a 'King Alfred' book appeared regularly in his publisher's list for many years until faith began to grow cold. *The Namesake* at last emerged in 1964. Even then it was only half a book, and readers had to wait until 1967 for the rest of the story in *The Marsh King*. In a revealing essay the author has explained both the delay and the nature of his solution, showing how the book which had evaded him for so long was in fact two books, each with its different creative solution. The essential difference between the two is symbolized by their narrators. In *The Namesake* the story is told by the Namesake himself, Alfred Dane-Leg who was disabled in a Danish raid in infancy but who, in an age of primitive surgery, still managed to survive and became the King's secretary. The Namesake is a chronicler, involved in events but seeing his role as a recorder of the truth as he has known it. The narrator of *The Marsh King* is concerned with events only through heredity; he is the son of a Danish father and a Saxon mother and so symbolizes the union of opposites which had been the great King's life-work.

The narrative technique mirrors the viewpoints of the two narrators. The Namesake, in old age serving the shrine of Edmund King and Martyr, is more than half a lifetime away from the events he records, yet he remembers with involvement 'the heart saddened . . . with all the memory of so long ago'. His King is a friend and he remembers the quiet informal moments as well as the battles and the peace conferences. There is a nobly imagined episode in *The Namesake* when the King—in a brief moment of peace—comes with his secretary and a few friends to Stonehenge and is moved to meditate on the meaning of history.

' "Every man is a part of the bridge between the past and the future, and must feel how it stretches out both ways before and behind him. Whatever helps him to feel this more strongly is good. By feeling this, God gives us to know for sure that we are not beasts and do not die as the beasts die. The beasts alone have no history behind them, and no future beyond their own unheeded deaths." '

With fine irony, Hodges follows this homily with a glimpse, as the royal party travels westwards, of 'a place called Ethandune . . . a hillside with a strange white horse cut in it . . . Save for ourselves passing and a hawk hovering, it was a deserted place, and hardly seemed worth a second glance.' The reader has to wait to the climax of *The Marsh King* for the crowning of the King's work by his victory upon this hill.

The narrative of the second book is more dispassionate. The narrator, half Saxon half Dane, moves through both camps and sees the King in hiding, Guthorm's treachery and his confusion in face of the inexplicable integrity of Alfred. When Guthorm at last realizes that Alfred is not dead but is indeed the Marsh King who is coming in arms against him, he turns his anger on to the grinning Norse gods who stand in his hall and throws them in the dust. It is a ludicrous scene, and he would only have indulged his fury in private. But there were 'watchers in the shadows', among them the Dane Skafti Olafsson who is to be father of the boy who grows up to tell the story. By such quiet touches Hodges preserves the integrity of the narrative. When the action passes beyond the narrator's experience, it is told in saga style. Hubba the Viking, last son of King Ragnar Hairy-Breeches, meets 'the end of his life's plundering' in the battle of Kynwit, and the author sends the old warrior home to Valhalla to the music of a savage war-lay.

The story of King Alfred is one of intermittent warfare and frequent battles. Hodges avoided the repetition which comes from a number of military set-pieces by rationing himself. Only the great final battle of Ethandune is described in detail. The battle of Kynwit becomes a lay, and Ashdown is overheard and not witnessed. Even the most blood-thirsty of readers—and it is a reasonable function of books to provide a vicarious outlet for this primitive appetite—grows tired when too many heads are cleft to the chin. This is a dilemma of all writers about the past, and especially of those who are attracted to military history. The undisputed master of this subject is Ronald Welch.

Welch—the pseudonym reveals the writer's origins but not necessarily his sympathies—is deeply concerned with the changing techniques of war and with such related subjects as military architecture, armour and heraldry. He gives a kind of unity to his work by relating it to the fortunes of a single family through many centuries. Such a device, however well-intended, can become a millstone, and it must be admitted that Welch is a very uneven writer; his uniformly vigorous story-telling notwithstanding, one becomes a little tired of the Careys at times. He is one of those writers, of whom there are many in the world of children's books, who wrote the best of their books too soon and were left with no choice but to stop writing or to go on emulating their own success.

Ronald Welch's first book stands apart from the canon. *The Gauntlet* (1951) is an exercise on a 'time' theme, not a historical novel. Peter, lost in the mist on Carn Eglwys, finds an iron gauntlet and slips briefly into the Middle Ages. Later he finds it again, and for a few weeks he lives the life of a young Marcher lordling of the thirteenth century. On the point of death in a skirmish with Welsh insurgents he escapes back to his own century. Or does he? The evidence is inconclusive. The author leaves the reader to decide whether Peter has lived the life of his own ancestor or merely had a particularly vivid dream composed of memories of what he has seen and read.

Like some other teachers turned writer, Welch clogged up his narrative with didactic passages. These are the stuff of a mediaeval page's education, it is true, but the devices creak uneasily and hold up the action. Yet *The Gauntlet*, despite its obvious weaknesses and its rather engaging amateurishness, is an interesting and occasionally a very fine book. The setting, half real half invented, is drawn boldly, and the details of mediaeval life, however clumsily introduced, are authentic and vividly described.

It is indeed a book of promise rather than achievement; curiously the promise was not redeemed in just this way. When Ronald Welch wrote his second book he chose direct historical narrative, with an unusual setting. An excessive number of writers have chosen as their subject the Third Crusade, and as their hero Richard Coeur-de-Lion. Welch used the same period for *Knight Crusader* (1954), but his hero is not a true Briton—as if there could be such a thing in the twelfth century—but a Knight of Outremer, the Frankish kingdom of Jerusalem. Philip fights in the disastrous Second Crusade, becomes a prisoner, escapes and is rescued by the Old Man of the Mountain, then joins Richard and fights in the battle of Arsuf. As if this were not enough—and indeed it is too much— he then goes to England and recovers his Welsh inheritance.

The contrast with *The Gauntlet* is greatest in the technique. Here is a highly competent piece of writing, the historical detail tightly integrated with the subject-matter, the narrative economical and very brisk. The battle-scenes are magnificently done, their sound scholarship firmly under the story-teller's control. The weakness of the book is apparent in the briefest summary; it desperately lacks selectivity. Welch was so keen to put all he knew and felt about the Crusades into his book that he dissipated his effects and left a string of loose ends. It is still his finest book and one of the most convincing and exciting pictures of warfare at a time when history was at a turning-point. As in later books he learnt more about the craft of novel-writing, Welch lost the keen edge of his enthusiasm and declined into a writer of scholarly, honestly prepared books from which the sparkle of a creative impulse had faded.

Welch, like Rosemary Sutcliff and Cynthia Harnett, was a writer whose interests lay almost exclusively in history. Barbara Leonie Picard came late to history after building a substantial reputation as a creator of invented fairy-tales, stories in the folk tradition but told with an eloquence and richness of fancy which gained for her comparisons—not altogether invalid—with Andersen. *Ransom for a Knight* appeared in 1956. It was a tour-de-force, a quite extraordinary achievement for one who had not previously written in this form and on this scale. It was a very long novel, running to more than 300 pages, and although there was no tedium it presented formidable problems of endurance and concentration for the young reader.

*Ransom for a Knight* is set in the England of Edward II. Bannockburn has been fought, and among those captured in the battle is a Sussex knight. The knight sends an appeal for ransom to his young daughter, but the message is so distorted after the long journey from Scotland that no one believes it— no one, that is, except Alys, who is ten. With a boy servant who believes in her if not in her mission, she journeys through an England teeming with rogues and bullies as well as kindly, considerate and interfering people. It is an appalling pilgrimage but it is successful. A thin, haggard and ragged little girl storms the castle of Glengorman and delivers the ransom to Lord Angus MacAngus.

There are two opposite hazards in a story like this. Either one simplifies the problems and describes a journey from which the dangers have been drained away, or one lays on the colours so lavishly that the narrative siezes up from overstatement. Barbara Leonie Picard steers skilfully between the extremes. No difficulties are evaded, as the two small travellers struggle on, encountering thieves and diseases and losing everything except hope. Yet all these appalling hardships are described quietly, almost in an undertone. In Miss Picard's skilled hands understatement becomes a fine art.

Detailed character-studies are not common in historical fiction; for the most part the writer is content with bold outlines for the principals and swiftly sketched impressions for the minor figures. Alys, however, has to dominate the action of a long story, and she is never absent from the scene. Hers is a masterly portrait, for she is never anything but a little girl, admirable but human, sustained through her ordeal by obstinacy as well as faith.

Many of the children's books which give immediate pleasure wear badly. The fresh flowers have faded by the time one turns back to them. *Ransom for a Knight* is still admirable after fifteen years, and admirable for the same reasons, because of the integrity as well as the excitement. And although the book arts have improved almost beyond measure in those years, it is still an outstandingly handsome book with line-drawings by C. Walter Hodges which catch confidently every nuance of the story.

*Ransom for a Knight* is concerned with people, not nations; the Scots come off as well, and as badly, as the English. Jane Oliver was a Scot, and not one to concern herself overmuch with impartial judgements. In most of her books she made a passionate statement of the Scottish position. When Bruce, in *Young Man with a Sword*, catches De Bohun 'on the blind side' (as Sellar and Yeatman have it) '. . . and maced him up for life' the reader of whatever nationality has been sufficiently conditioned by her special pleading to cheer heartily. Jane Oliver had one commanding strength as a writer; she wrote always from the side of the minority, and every right-minded reader is for the underdog. *Young Man with a Sword* (1955) deals with the return of Robert Bruce to Scotland, a magnificent theme culminating in Bannockburn (with no glimpse of Miss Picard's ransomed knight); *The Eaglet and the Angry Dove* (1957) is about Columba's conquest of Scotland for Christ against incredible odds; *Queen Most Fair* (1959) has as heroine Mary Queen of Scots who has the advantage, in fictional terms, of being beautiful and unsuccessful; *Faraway Princess* (1962) follows the fortunes of the pathetic royal family of Wessex who so signally failed to hold England together after the battle of Hastings.

These stories, soundly researched and utterly sincere as they are, are never entirely convincing. Partly this is a literary inadequacy; the books are competently written but they have not the high eloquence which wins a reader's total surrender. It is more important that the author accepts too readily the traditional conventions of the children's book. She seems to be reluctant to give all her strength in these stories, not because she cannot explore a theme in depth—there is no lack of power in her books for adults—but because she perhaps subscribes to the old-fashioned doctrine that one must extract from a child's diet the headiest drinks and the strongest meat.

Alongside the search for new themes and new angles writers continue to find interest in some of the favourite periods of historical fiction. The Civil War inspired Rosemary Sutcliff to achieve a personal revolution. It has had many other interpreters, including Barbara Softly's quiet and sensitive *Place Mill* (1962). Recently Barbara Willard has looked at the Great Rebellion and its aftermath from an unusual standpoint in *The Grove of Green Holly* (1967). The story touches national events briefly with the escape of Charles II from Shoreham aboard the brig *Surprise*. Charles has to adopt a disguise in order to get away safely, and an old stage-player helps by providing him with a new and slightly sinister face. This is an incident, if an important one, in the story; the main interest lies in the player himself, Gregory. Gregory Trundle, 'a name not unknown about the country in better days', had learnt his trade in London and, but for a prematurely broken voice, might have played Ophelia under the author's direction. But as he grew older the theatre declined in repute, and now the playhouses are closed and acting prohibited. Gregory, his head full of quotations but his occupation gone, kills time until the King should come again and trains his grandson Rafe to be the great player that he himself never was.

The old man dreams his dreams, and sometimes tries perilously to bring them to actuality, against the background first of a seaside inn in Sussex, then, after a final quarrel with the formidable Aunt Nags who rules the inn, its inhabitants and its clients, of the Wealden forest. Here is the grove of green holly where a play might be performed, and where indeed one is played out, but not as rehearsed.

Next in interest to the portrait of the old man is the iron industry of the Weald. Barbara Willard lives within the bounds of the old lost forest and has surrendered to the strange fascination of a landscape which was once the Black Country of England. Her picture of a forest community governed by its own laws and dedicated to its secret crafts is entirely convincing. Here historical fiction has become sound local history. After all the excitements of a well-marshalled story, what remains most clearly in the memory are pictures of an old man moving 'like a king' through the forest in the robes of Lear and of smoke rising from a forge where iron clangs on iron.

Writers looking for new subjects have turned increasingly to either end of the time-scale, to prehistory and the Dark Ages where imagination can eke out the meagre facts, and to the modern age. One of the best evocations of the remote past is Vian Smith's *Moon in the River* (1969) which looks, with a more conscious attempt at realism than Henry Treece in *The Dream-Time*, at the birth of a spirit of enquiry. Someone, somewhere, must have realized for the first time that a horse might be more useful as a steed than as meat. Vian Smith's pioneer lives on Dartmoor and suffers the persecution which is the lot of all innovators. What makes this book particularly memorable is that the author manages to communicate the thoughts of primitive folk who are necessarily almost inarticulate. The pioneer questions tradition, but no concepts from a more sophisticated age creep into his mind. J. G. Fyson, too, shows the dawn of revolutionary thought. *The Three Brothers of Ur* (1964) and *The Journey of the Eldest Son* (1965) are set in and around Ur in the second millennium before Christ, a time sufficiently remote for most readers but one of which the writer seems to have first-hand experience. She moves confidently through the crowded streets watching the strangeness and the ordinariness of the scene and people, noticing how similar naughty, lively little boys like Haran of Ur are to naughty boys of London. In the second book seriousness sets in, for the eldest son Shamashazir—who is Abraham—undertakes a journey which leads to spiritual revolution. When he returns, after many perils, 'there was a strangeness on him—a strangeness of the far mountains, the dusty roads and the wild forests, and the strangest of adventures'. With him he brings a new idea, that of the One God. The discovery of monotheism may seem an unlikely subject for a children's story, and it is a measure of Mrs Fyson's achievement that the idea is treated with complete seriousness yet communicated through an extremely exciting and human story.

The climax of the narrative of *The Journey of the Eldest Son* comes with Shamashazir's rescue of the chosen sacrifice of the Corn Dingir, for the children of Cain appropriately enough practise human sacrifice and the sons of Enoch abhor the custom.

A very remarkable book by an American writer, Harry Behn, shows the opposite side of this coin. *The Distant Lurs* (1963) is set in Scandinavia in a prehistoric time of transition, and the young heroine of the story, caught between the upper and nether millstones of opposing cultures, consents to be sacrificed for her people. Behn was influenced in writing his book by the discovery of Tollund Man, who had been ritually strangled in, perhaps, just such a crisis and had gone consenting to his death. The spirit of his nobility and resignation is at the heart of the book. Some adult readers have questioned the appropriateness of such a subject for a children's book, but in Behn's treatment there is no morbidity, only a sad and tender tale of love and death and of people at the mercy of events and of their own taboos.

Remote as Heather and her people are, we can understand

their philosophy better than we can that of the Norse warriors and the gods of Asgard. Many writers have, like Henry Treece, been prompted to write about the savage Northern heroes who ravaged northern Europe for centuries and about the Vikings who penetrated as far as Byzantium and America. The best words about the earlier invasions have been written by Rosemary Sutcliff. For the Vikings there is Pauline Clarke's *Torolv the Fatherless* (1959), in which a Danish boy sails the Swans' Road with a sea-king named Ali. Torolv is left behind in England after a raid and discovers the unexpected delights of a settled home. Then at the battle of Maldon he meets his own ship-companions again and is faced with a conflict of loyalties. This is a clever story, a little cerebral but deeply pondered and written with clarity and, in the battle-scene, with passion. The author's starting-point is the famous poem of the Battle of Maldon of which she provides a translation, and much of the story is in the spirit of the poem, with its insistence on courage and integrity and on the need to defend and avenge the Ring-Giver, and its constant reminder that Fate, which haunted the lives of these brave and industrious Anglo-Saxons, would inevitably change and blow away happiness like 'fleet clouds'. There is much tenderness in *Torolv the Fatherless* but little consolation.

This is a long but easily read book. Richard Parker's *The Sword of Ganelon* (1957) moves more slowly and is so packed with detail as to hinder comprehension. Parker, who has lived for much of his life in and around Thanet, makes brilliant use of the topography of East Kent in a story of Viking raids about 150 years before the battle of Maldon. There are exciting moments in the story, but the writer is at least as much concerned to give a detailed picture of the everyday lives of ordinary people. The book is packed with facts, perhaps to excess, and those who can stay the course learn much about the thought and beliefs of this remote age.

For both of these writers the Vikings are the enemy—in Parker's book shadowy figures who sail through the mist, in Pauline Clarke's gay and ruthless warriors. Alan Boucher is fascinated by their skill in navigation as well as their ability to sustain feuds through several generations. In a series of books, e.g. *The Wineland Venture* (1962), he follows the fortunes of hardy and harsh seamen who go ever westward in their hunger for land. His is a clear, unsentimental and scholarly view of these strange people. The most convincing picture of them comes, appropriately enough, from a Scandinavian writer, Erik Christian Haugaard. *Hakon's Saga* (1963; English edition 1964) shows a humane spirit which may be anachronistic, but this is an essential element in a story whose economy, sincerity and eloquence make it one of the most memorable of the century.

It is a bitter story. Hakon's father, Olaf the Lame, was 'king' of Rogen, an island of about two hundred people, until he made an enemy of Magnus Thorsen, the powerful lord of Tronhjem, by stealing his daughter. Magnus sends an army against Rogen, kills Olaf, and leaves the island under the protectorship of Olaf's treacherous brother Sigurd. In spite of this Hakon is still, in the eyes of the islanders, his father's heir, and Sigurd does what he can to destroy the boy. In a violent *coup d'etat* Hakon rouses the loyal Rogenese and recovers his kingdom.

The grim little story is told relentlessly. Life is harsh and there is no pretence. What sustains Hakon, and the reader, is belief in a better life. The islanders are pagans, but the slave Rark, whose loyalty is a vital factor in Hakon's success, believes in the 'new god'. When he kills the tyrant Sigurd he does not exult as a Viking might. ' "Never brag of having slain a man, Hakon. Life is holy, and even the foulest of men has once been a child and worthy of love" ', and Hakon is involuntarily sad because he has killed the equally vile Eirik the Fox. All the best historical novels are stories of change. The change in *Hakon's Saga* is a small one—a change of ruler in a tiny island—but it has importance because it represents a change of heart. The new Rogen will be well governed; it will also be a land without slaves. ' "That is everyone's birthright, his freedom, and the gods have only one message to us, that we must live." ' The message may seem oversimplified; the story, for all its brevity, is not at all simple. It has the naked splendour of great art.

It is a long way from Rogen and the Vikings to the modern

world, but the latter was for long hardly less familiar to the
historical novelist. Even the eighteenth century, apart from the
'45 and the battlefields, was largely alien ground until Margaret
Jowett chose to write her masterly story of theatrical life,
*Candidate for Fame* (1955). More recently Iona McGregor has
discovered material for stories of outstanding excellence in
post-Jacobite Scotland. In *An Edinburgh Reel* (1968) there is
yet another Jacobite plot toward, but this, if it provides the
pace for the story, is never very important. What gives the
book its singular charm is the picture of Edinburgh society,
surely one of the rare examples of advanced practical demo-
cracy in history. Christine, a delightful and very sensible
heroine, lives in the Lawnmarket, sharing a house with an
ancient judge, faded gentry and humble artisans, not to mention pigs. *The Burning Hill* (1970) has a slightly later date and
a country setting. In Iona McGregor's books social and
industrial history are almost equally matched and both are a
great deal more important to the action than politics. The
Burning Hill is an iron-mine. The Lindsays hope to rebuild
their family fortunes by exploiting the mineral wealth of the
estate. In this way they are hindered by labour troubles and by
their neighbour, a noisy self-made gentleman lately retired
from the East India Company who has planted new-fangled
flowering shrubs all over Burning Hill. The wealthy Captain
and the genteel Lindsays see mutual advantage in a match
between the Captain's boy Robin and pretty Jean Lindsay.
The young people dislike the idea (and one another) at first
because it was not of their own devising; then, as their affection
grows, the families fall out. The Burning Hill burns and with it
Captain John's beautiful shrubs. Here is matter for an
eighteenth-century comedy of manners. Even when the
Captain challenges the laird to a duel the comic mood continues; both gentlemen, although irascible, are essentially men
of peace, and each resolves to satisfy honour by firing into the
air. But the laird bungles it by firing with his eyes closed and
nicks the Captain. Captain John, in a fit of anger, shoots him
dead. The comedy has suddenly become tragedy. This is no
Romeo and Juliet, however; the feuding parents are the
sufferers while the young lovers marry.

There are many excellences in this book. No one conveys a sense of period more successfully and with more economical means than Iona McGregor. All the historical detail is in the narrative, so that the reader is never conscious that he is being taught an unfamiliar history-lesson. Despite the great interest of the background, however, this is essentially a story about society and about love. A few recent children's writers have dealt more sensationally with the theme of sexual love; Miss McGregor is content not to follow her young lovers into the bedroom, but she captures exquisitely their rapture and disillusionment.

These stories of the Scottish cultural revival, and Hester Burton's books about Napoleonic England, stand at a half-way stage, looking back to the old historical romance and forward to the modern social novel. With A. M. Hadfield's 'Williver' stories we are firmly in the modern age, following in careful detail—and with, it must be admitted, occasional tedium—the progress of a family in the Industrial Revolution. There is as sound an historical sense and more human interest in a slight and convincing Victorian story, *The Coal-Scuttle Bonnet* (1958) by E. K. Seth-Smith. Over a long working life Miss Seth-Smith wrote a handful of novels on widely varied themes and periods, always without sensationalism, always with distinction. Her characteristic qualities of understatement and quiet integrity, which have led to quite unjustifiable neglect, are at their finest in this little book. Miss Seth-Smith has no axes to grind.

Meriol Trevor had a dominating purpose in choosing to write about poverty in the great cities of Victorian England. Her earlier books for children had been disfigured by special Catholic pleading; by the time she came to write *Lights in a Dark Town* (1964) she was no less convinced a Catholic, but she had learnt to be a better novelist. Her definitive biography of Newman was still fresh with her, and in this novel she sets the story of the great reformer against its social background.

In *Path-Through-The-Woods* (1958) Barbara Ker Wilson tells another story of reform, about a young girl who defies Victorian prejudice by becoming a doctor. The structure of this highly original and intelligent book is based on a patchwork quilt, each piece of which is associated with a stage in Sophia Fielding's struggle. An artificial device of this kind may prove an uncomfortable strait-jacket, however useful it may be in pulling together the strands of a diffuse narrative, and *Path-Through-The-Woods* creaks a little. The author is a little too conscientious in name-dropping and in squeezing in the events of the day in order to establish her historical setting. A charming story, nevertheless, picking up the threads of its story together with those of the emancipation of women. Curiously, when the writer turned to a story of her own times and tried to recapture the events and emotions of the Second World War in *Last Year's Broken Toys* (1962), her touch was much less sure.

Gillian Avery's numerous and excellent novels of Victorian families might seem to call for mention here, but these are no more historical stories than the Victorian originals which were her inspiration. In them she is writing about people in society, and she needs to be examined in the company of her peers, the social novelists of today. E. M. Almedingen's tender studies of girls growing up in England and Russia are, on the other hand, essentially historical in their approach. The author, herself Russian born of English blood, is acutely conscious of the time-scale and of the pageant of world events against which her stories are played out. She based them on the journals and letters of her own family, and they have the depth and passion of personal involvement.

These quiet and moving stories of Anglo-Russian families lead to two of the most remarkable of all recent historical novels, which retell the story of the last days of the Russian Imperial Family through the voice of a young man, of Scottish, French, Austrian and Russian blood, who is an eye-witness of the tragic events. Two questions arise immediately in considering Stephanie Plowman's *Three Lives for the Czar* (1969) and *My Kingdom for a Grave* (1970): is this historical fiction or thinly disguised history? And is it for children? The publisher answered the second question, not altogether adequately, by giving it a new imprint: 'New Adults'. As to the first, it is true that all the major events of the two books are taken from authentic records; however the whole force and the poignancy of the story comes from the involvement of the young fictional narrator and his family.

The Hamiltons came to Russia, as others did in reality, through the failure of the Jacobite cause. By the end of the nineteenth century the Hamiltons were Russian except in name and in a certain cosmopolitanism which came from their travels and their European connections. They shared this international outlook with the Romanovs, but mixed blood seemed to give the Czar and his Empress an even narrower view. Through two long books Andrei Hamilton's hopes for the future of Russia fade, as do those of his friends, as his affection for the doomed Royal Family grows. The story—for the two books need to be read as one—has the classic tragic elements of terror and pity as well as the romantic element of a tragic flaw —in the Czar himself a host of flaws.

Pre-Revolutionary Russia is as remote from most young readers today as the Dark Ages. If they have any thoughts on the subject they are likely to be in sympathy with the revolutionaries who threw off the incompetent dead hand of autocracy. In her books Stephanie Plowman had therefore to overcome disinterestedness and antagonism. She succeeds— for it would be a mean-spirited reader who completed the story without emotion—by concentrating on the human elements of her theme. 'There will always'—says Andrei—'remain room for personal knowledge, physical, if you like—the remembrance of a perplexed tone of voice, the glance of imploring eyes, the touch of unseen lips on a hand wet with tears'. The Romanovs and the Hamiltons matter because they are people who bleed when bombs blow them to pieces. There are enough death-bed scenes here to satisfy a Victorian reader, and they are important. Miss Plowman's message seems to be that it is not death, but the dignity of man, that matters. The crime of the terrorists of Ekaterinburg was not that they murdered the Royal Family, who had nothing left to live for, but that they made dying a squalid and dishonourable business.

With Stephanie Plowman's elegiac novels, which come as near to greatness as any written within the child's range since the war, this brief look at the historical novel might have ended. Chronology, and a desire to complete the survey with a book which is at once happier and more obviously in the children's book tradition, demands some mention of Hester Burton's story of recent history—from the standpoint of today's children it is unquestionably history—*In Spite of All Terror* (1968). Hester Burton won a Carnegie Medal with a grave and beautifully written story of the struggle for freedom of expression in Georgian England—*Time of Trial* (1963). As a study of history and character this was wholly admirable, although a fundamental defect in construction—its impact was weakened by a sharp break in the middle—kept it out of the very highest rank. Her story of the early days of the Second World War has no such flaws. Mrs Burton was herself involved in the tragi-comedy of evacuation, and she puts herself and her family, in the thinnest of disguises, into the story; and for once the eye-witness is an expert witness with a keen sense of proportion but no Olympian attitudes. This story of a little girl who went into the country to escape the bombs glows with truth and compassion.

# CHAPTER FIVE

# Foreign Scenes

'In those hot longitudes, perhaps, the blood is always near
boiling point, which accounts for Indian tempers.'

THERE CAN BE FEW geographers, ethnologists or anthro-
pologists working in the field of children's books, compared
with historians. The historical novel has shown itself an admirable vehicle for ideas about the interpretation of history. Only
a small handful of writers have seen that a novel for children
is equally well adapted to illustrating the character of a country
and its people.

Plenty of books do this without design. Every story by a
French writer inevitably tells the reader something about the
French, whatever its ostensible subject and purpose. One of
the most interesting developments of recent years has been the
publication of picture-books for very small children which have
had their origins in almost all countries of the world. Illustration is very nearly an international language, and these books,
their brief texts presented in a score of languages, speak very
clearly of one nation to another. To a lesser extent—because
translation is still a major problem—children's novels from
places as different as Italy and Sweden have brought a little of
the quality of life in these countries into English homes.

Before the war only a few children's books from other
countries found their way into England, and these were not
necessarily always the best. English children formed their impressions of France from *Babar* and *Sans Famille*, Germany
from *Emil*, Italy from *Pinocchio*. During the past twenty years
conscious attempts have been made to select appropriate texts
for translation. The impetus came from idealists like Jella
Lepman and Richard Bamberger who believed that the peace

of the world might be served by children speaking together; it came too from a few publishers who saw that the translation of fine books could make good sense internationally and commercially. An invaluable contribution was made by the University of London Press, whose editor, Monica Burns, combined a sound business sense with sensibility and a flair for matching the book with its right translator. Eleanor Graham, and later Olive Jones, of Methuen's, had some of the same qualities and built up a list which was qualitatively at least the equal of U.L.P.'s. Many of the books chosen for translation had won awards in their own countries, and English readers became aware for the first time of such European prizes as Prix Jeunesse, Jugendbuchpreis, and Nils Holgersson Plaque, with their different standards and standpoints.

Probably none of these books was originally an exercise in international public relations. They were all books written to please children and in translation they still have the same objective. The national and racial qualities in a story are an additional bonus enjoyed by readers of the translation. Happily English children do not read a Paul Berna story in order to learn about France; they read for the joy of a good story told with style and gusto. Mostly they are not actively aware that they are reading a translation, and if they notice the foreign scene and atmosphere they take no particular note of it. But incidentally, in the process of reading for pleasure, they are being exposed to influences and suggestions which in time add up to a concept of France—or at least of Frenchness.

I have already looked (in Chapter 2) briefly at the work of Berna and Bourguignon. There are a few other French writers of this quality, notably Michel-Aimé Baudouy. His *Mick and the P.105* (1959; English edition 1961) is about a gang of boys who find an old motor-bike, repair it and then ride it, with moderate success, in a race. The leading spirit in this is Mick, whose family have written him off because he is a failure at school. It is a good story, told with economy and moderation, and it shirks none of the technical problems presented by the subject. English readers undoubtedly read it for its excitement and honesty. It is also a French story, and there is enough which is unfamiliar, in terminology, in the society and the attitudes of mind, to give it, for English readers, a certain strangeness of colouring which adds to the enjoyment of a tale very well told.

*Mick and the P.105* is just one book among many which one might choose for its liveliness and its French atmosphere. Others, in varying degrees, have similar qualities; Léonce Bourliaguet, who favours a Pyrenean setting, Etienne Cattin, who is fascinated by the railways of Eastern France, Paul-Jacques Bonzon whose stories are more violent and tragic, and Saint-Marcoux (who is Paul Berna's wife) who writes in a fine romantic vein. *The Honey Siege* is unusual among continental books in having started as a novel for adults and been taken over by the children; Gil Buhet's story of how an eccentric schoolmaster in Languedoc precipitates a rebellion among his pupils is essentially French—and of the South—in its humour and its leisured, relaxed narrative.

An equally identifiable French quality pervades Henri Bosco's books, although the effect is entirely different. *The Boy and the River* (1945; English edition 1956) is a slow, quiet story, as strange and elusive as a dream. The author says that 'all this happened a very long time ago', and the reader seems to see the action through the wrong end of the telescope, clear and bright but a very long way off. It is the story of Pascalet, a small boy who yields one day to the sweet lure of spring and runs away from his home and Aunt Martine to find adventure on the river. Here he finds Gatzo, who had been stolen by the gipsies, and for a few blissful days they live wild, eating food fished from the river and cooked on an open fire. 'Food of this kind gives to him who eats it miraculous powers', and the boys enjoy a marvellous oneness with the elements. The adventure ends not tamely, but with another miracle. This inimitable story is wonderful and difficult, not for all children and all moods, but for the right child—and adult; in a receptive moment its vision of freedom can be a formative experience. Only a Frenchman could have written it—although Gerard Hopkins's translation is marvellously successful—and it reveals more secrets about one kind of French landscape and one French household than could be conveyed in a hundred lessons.

Bosco is exceptional in the completeness of his vision and in the exquisite beauty of the language in which he describes it.

With lesser and varied success writers in other countries are telling stories which incidentally catch a little of the character of the land and its people. Margot Benary in Germany, Pacifico Fiori in Italy, Harry Kullman in Sweden—his *Secret Journey* (1957; English edition 1961) paints an unexaggerated picture of the terrors which a great modern city can have for a small boy trapped in its streets—Leif Hamre in Norway, Lotte Stratil-Sauer in Austria; these are all novelists who fill in the background of exciting stories with authentic and revealing detail.

Writers from the English-speaking world, too, are effective ambassadors. How many English children have a view of America made up of memories of Laura Ingalls Wilder and Elizabeth Coatsworth, of Elizabeth Enright and Eleanor Estes? These may not be complete or up-to-date impressions, but they serve as reliable foundations. Similarly a child's idea of Australia may be composed of *The Magic Pudding* with modifications from Eleanor Spence, H. F. Brinsmead and Nan Chauncy. None of these is actively engaged in 'selling' a country and its ways, but because the writers are fundamentally truthful the pictures they paint are—as far as they go—accurate in fact and spirit.

From this generalization one might except Nan Chauncy. Most of her books are concerned unequivocally with entertainment, and fine entertainment they are too. But Mrs Chauncy was not Tasmanian born—she emigrated with her family when she was a child—and she remained throughout her life an advocate, consciously interpreting the land and its people to those readers—the vast majority—who would never see her beautiful island. This is clear in the stories about Badge, the boy who explores the wilds and learns to identify himself with their creatures; the hero of these books is not Badge but Tasmania. In two books, and these her best, she acknowledges her mission openly. Almost every one of her stories has in it some mention of the aboriginal inhabitants of Tasmania who were all killed off, by bullets or kindness, in the nineteenth century. This was, for the best of reasons, an obsession with her.

A great crime had been committed by her race, and she felt the
need to make atonement. She did this by telling their tragic
story, first in an oblique way and then directly. *Tangara* begins
as a story of a lonely little girl who 'makes her playmates of
animals or anything'. But anything can happen in this land so
haunted by its past that even the church spire rises 'thin as a
blackfellow's spear', and Lexie soon finds a companion, a little
brown girl, naked, mischievous and friendly. Little children
manage to communicate with a minimum of words, and Lexie
and Merrina explore one another's small worlds delightedly,
experiencing such novelties as zip-fasteners and wombat-
baiting. It is an intensely happy time for both children. Lexie
is accepted by Merrina's tribe and enjoys their unaffected good
humour. Then, during a terrible storm, men with 'cruel white
faces' appear with guns and shoot down the helpless blackfellows. Lexie escapes from the nightmare, still not realizing
that she has had a vision of the past and that lively, gay
Merrina is a ghost. When she moves away from the blackfellow's country, these experiences are buried under layers of
new discoveries, to be unearthed years later when she comes
back to Blacks' Gully at a time of crisis and sees Merrina again.
In this final revelation she understands the meaning of the
tragedy which she had witnessed. She knows that she will not
see her friend again, 'not till the very end . . . when she calls us
to her little fire'.

This superb book moves the reader the more deeply because
the tragedy is told in personal terms and because it measures
past and present by the eternal yardstick of love. In a later
book—*Mathinna's People*, 1967—Mrs Chauncy told the whole
story of the aborigines and presented it in chronological form.
This is only a little less effective than *Tangara*. More than half
of the book is concerned with the story of Towterer, the last
chief of the Toogee who led his people against the white men
and then, when there was no more hope, to the deadly sanc-
tuary of the settlement on Flinders Island. There he waited
long until the Old Ones came at last to call his spirit home.
Towterer's daughter was almost the last of the aborigines. She
was caught up in the reaction created by the bitterness of the
blackfellows' tragedy, and she was taken into Government

*From* Tangara (*see opposite page*)

House, renamed Mathinna, spoiled and cherished. There she learnt to write. The last words of a letter of hers which has survived are: 'I am very glad'. They provide a brief moment of consolation in this heartbreaking story, before the Old Ones come for her too and she escapes her fate to 'run free with the wind . . . over the long beaches of the West'.

Nan Chauncy adopted, and was adopted by, Australia in childhood. At about the same age Meindert de Jong left Holland and settled in the United States. In middle age he began to write a book about his native village, which he had not seen for thirty-five years. It should have been a sentimental picture coloured by an adult's nostalgia for a past which never really happened. Afterwards Meindert de Jong went back to Holland on a visit. Most of the country bore no resemblance to his memories or his imagination, but in his own village nothing had changed. Untouched by the years and by a world war, Wierum (or Shora) still sat snugly under the dike with its white cottages, its church and its schoolhouse, just as the child had last seen it in 1918. It was a miracle as remarkable as the writing of *The Wheel on the School* out of the scattered memories of a distant childhood.

*The Wheel on the School* (1954; English edition 1956) is, long before its time, a conservation story. When Grandmother Sibble III was a little girl storks used to nest in Shora; they have not been seen since, although villages all around are favoured. The children of Shora see what can be done to attract them. What starts as a modest extra-curricular exercise becomes an obsession and then a source of adventure and great danger. But at last, all is well; two storks set up house on the great waggon-wheel which stands perilously on the schoolhouse roof.

This is such a delicate wisp of a story that the slightest wind of criticism would, one might imagine, blow it quite away. In fact, however, it is a sturdy story, firmly anchored to the realities of life in a small community. Part of Mr de Jong's success comes from his manner; he has a most engaging throwaway style which shows how keen and exact an ear he has for the cadences of speech and with what skill he heightens them to make them acceptable on the printed page. For the rest, the great charm of *The Wheel on the School* is that it gives a complete picture of a village so small that one can get to know each house and its inhabitants intimately. The children of Shora are of the universal stuff of childhood, and children of all races will see themselves mirrored in this glass; and yet they are also clearly Dutch, with idiosyncrasies of behaviour and tradition which come from their homeland.

Ten years later, when Meindert de Jong knew what the real Shora was like, he wrote another story about his home village. *Far Out the Long Canal* (1964; English edition 1965) is a longer story which looks more closely into the motives of its characters. There is charm as well as honest observation in the story of poor Moonta, who wanted so much to be able to skate that he went to bed with his ice-skates on. The picture of a happy and united family is refreshing. Yet the author adds nothing further to a reputation established once for all by the earlier book.

It is notable that, in general, the under-developed and the developing countries have not yet produced indigenous literature, or at least none which has achieved a market outside its own country. Those writers who have so far emerged in the struggle for independence, economic viability or plain survival are too busy with more immediate tasks to devote their energies to the entertainment of the young. There is one distinguished exception to this generalization. The children of Jamaica have a most eloquent spokesman in Andrew Salkey— and it may be significant that he writes from the relatively detached standpoint of London where he has lived for many years.

Andrew Salkey is a chronicler of natural disasters. *Earthquake, Drought, Hurricane*: his list of titles is a catalogue of the hazards familiar to those who live in tropical countries. Yet, however violent or harrowing the subject, he is always restrained, with his eye more on the human than the natural elements. He is fascinated by people's reactions to crisis. In *Earthquake* (1965) his story is mostly about echoes of the great earthquake of 1907, awakened by a few minor tremors— scarcely more spectacular than the surface shiver in *High Wind in Jamaica*. The earthquake is a memory in Gran' Pa's mind. The foreground is occupied by three small children absorbed in serious play. Their desert island, just a stone's throw from Gran' Ma's back door, has an unexpected visitor, a Rastafarian named Marcus. (Rastafarians are Back-to-Africa Jamaicans and preachers of a creed of peace and love, almost hippies of the black world.) It would have been easy, and indeed popular, to turn Marcus into a figure of fun. Funny he certainly is, but he is perfectly serious too, and so is the author. Even Polly, who at first thinks that Marcus looks 'cute and silly all at the same time', grows to love him. *Hurricane* (1964) has a more direct narrative, but here too there is no hurry. More than half the story is told before the hurricane hits Kingston. There is the same shrewd observation of human behaviour in this book and the same unsentimental enjoyment of family life. The same eccentrics too; here the place of Marcus is taken by Mother Samuel who preaches death and repentance in terms which the islanders can well understand. When a girl student heckles her, she retorts: ' "You'd better go right back to Mona and do your last homework. Your Maker will mark it in heaven, if you repent. If you don't, the Devil will!" '

The admirable stories speak out boldly on behalf of the people of Jamaica, the more effectively because there is no overt social criticism in them. Mostly the poorer countries have had to find alien spokesmen. Bolivia has a lively advocate in a German writer, Gunther Teustel, whose *José* (1963; English edition 1965) gives a convincing brief account of the poverty and high spirits of the Andean Indians. It is an affectionate portrait, as warm with sentiment as it is free of sentimentality, and the tone is matched by a host of masterly drawings by Hans Baltzer. A lesser story of Argentina, *Chucaro, Wild Pony of the Pampa* (1958; English edition 1959), appeared first in the United States and has a Hungarian author. Francis Kalnay knows horses better than people; his account of the training of a wild pony has the stamp of authenticity, and he gives a clear picture of the horse-orientated society of the pampa, but as a human story *Chucaro* is a little thin.

India has always attracted the writer. The combination of an ancient civilization with a precarious economy produces situations which appeal strongly. On the whole the Europeans do better than the residents, for example, Taya Zinkin, who as a journalist knows contemporary India intimately. Her 'Rishi' books are carefully documented. They are full of the incongruities which make up Indian life. She writes with real affection and understanding, but the stories are self-consciously didactic. A Danish writer, Marie Thøger, does this better. In *Shanta* (1961; English edition 1966) she is just as eager to teach the European reader about India and about the ways in which her ancient cultures survive in the modern world, but for her the theme and the personality of her young heroine are inseparable. In finding about Shanta's growth to womanhood we learn about Shanta's India, a land as full of contradictions as Rishi's although Marie Thøger, unlike Taya Zinkin, is not much concerned to show India's movement towards an industrial society.

A little between these two approaches comes Aimé Sommerfelt's *The Road to Agra* (1959; English edition 1961), which is beyond question a finer book than either. This Norwegian writer has got right into the Indian scene and into the minds of two Indian village children, a remarkable feat of imaginative understanding. A very small girl Maya, like so many Indians, is going blind with trachoma; she is a bright little girl, pretty and spirited, but she is doomed. There are too many handicapped people in the sub-continent for much sentiment to survive. Most of the villagers are opposed to Maya who is clever enough to occupy one of the few precious places in school. Three hundred miles away, at Agra, there is a hospital and eye-specialists. So Maya, who is seven, and her big brother Lalu, who is thirteen, walk to Agra. On the way they encounter some kind and helpful people and others who are antagonistic, indifferent or criminal. When at last they reach the city two men trick them out of their pitiful handful of rupees, as a subscription to the 'Society for Fighting Blindness', and the hospital, which looks to the children 'as big as a mountain range', is guarded by a bullying Sikh porter who regards it as his duty to keep patients away. The dignified despair of the children is utterly convincing. At this moment fate enters in the guise of a 'dusty grey jeep' in which are 'Miss Norway', 'Mr U.S.A.', 'Beautiful Mrs India', and Peter, who is in every sense a great

Dane. These are representatives of international health organizations, and Lalu is at last able to lay his burden on stronger shoulders. The heroism of this story is uncomplicated and the telling is appropriately simple. The author knows how to grip the heart with a few monosyllables: when Lalu has handed over to the doctors, he asks the lovely Indian Dr Prasad to write a letter home, so that ' "Nani will know that the thin branch called Lalu has not cracked on the road" '. The essential India is here: poverty, greed, elephants, bullock-carts, All-India Radio and the Five Year Plan, and ordinary people going about their business.

Some distinguished books belong partly with stories of other lands, partly with the historical novel. Roderick Haig-Brown's remarkable *The Whale People* (1962) describes a way of life which, although immemorial, has ended, and the same is true of Harold Keith's story of Red Indian life, *Komantcha* (1966). The former, however, is a serious ethnological study in fictional form and the latter, although more in the spirit of historical romance, looks closely at the racial characteristics and customs of an Indian tribe.

It is, in fact, very difficult for a children's writer to combine successfully an absorbing story with an accurate and detailed examination of a contemporary way of life. Many of the books which are most successful as fiction—Fritz Muhlenweg's great *Big Tiger and Christian* (1954) English edition 1954—deliberately look backwards to an age which is past. This is to some extent true of Fay King's *Friends of the Bushveld* (1954) which manages to describe South African life in most loving and authentic detail, with only the barest hint of Apartheid in the fate of Bansela, a Teller of Tales, who has to work in the mines; and so does P. H. Nortje in a series of clever but fundamentally unsatisfactory stories (*Wild Goose Summer*, 1959; English edition 1964).

The most successful writers about Africa have avoided dealing with the mixing, or segregation, of races. *Bemba* (1957; English edition 1962) deals with the Congo after independence. Andrée Clair is French and knows the country well; in this book she shows the interweaving of new ideas and ancient beliefs among a proud and enterprising people. A German writer, Herbert Kaufmann, has been even more successful in getting into the hearts of strangers. In *Red Moon and High Summer* (1957; English edition 1960) he tells a story of the Tamaschek tribe of the Sahara, who are usually known in the West as the Tuareg. He based the book on a journey which he made in the Sahara in 1957 and illustrated it with his own photographs—a device which gives added authenticity but is otherwise not altogether satisfactory.

*Red Moon and High Summer* is a long and discursive book, not easy to follow but immensely convincing in its individual episodes. Kaufmann was very skilful in his rendering of dialogue (and the translator, Stella Humphries, is equally successful in catching its cadences). There are some memorable portraits, too: Mid-e-Mid the poet, 'a skinny, ugly boy with green eyes, a snub nose, and hair like a hedgehog's spikes'; Abu Bakr the bandit, who has no friends and guides his life by a crude philosophy (he tells Mid-e-Mid: 'You think that just because you are an honest lad, there is justice in the world'); Tiu'elen, High Summer herself who is more lively and free-spoken than is quite proper for a Tamaschek girl; Ajor Chageran, Red Moon, the prince's son and the rising star of the tribe. The book tells a stern story of love and revenge and of tribal customs based on principles which are alien to western people but which are applied with grim logic. The ways are strange, but the wisdom which lies at the heart of the story is universal. It is the wisdom that comes from suffering which makes Mid-e-Mid's heart grow bigger than his head—as the idiot Kalil puts it—when he has lost High Summer, and it is for the idiot that he sings his finest song:

> 'Sun! oh, sun! Our life, our sister,
> Spin a circle round our hearts'.

So the poet goes singing through the desert, while Red Moon and High Summer raise a family. They call their first child after him;

'and when the baby kicked and crowed in her lap, she said, "He has the strength of his father, Ajor, and he has his forehead too. But he has Mid-e-Mid's beautiful voice".

'And because the women round her nodded, she believed it herself. Only Takammart said, "He squarks like a cockerel, and has as many teeth as my father Intallah, and he has none at all." '

Herbert Kaufmann's book falls short of the very highest excellence only in a certain difficulty of communication; the story and its motives alike are not easy for young readers to comprehend. Among books which interpret the life of other countries it is surpassed only by two small books by R. Forbes-Watson which also have African settings. Of these, *Ambari!* (1952) is a gay, light-hearted story of high adventure, *Shifta!* (1954) a grim ruthless story of revenge. They are markedly dissimilar in mood, but they share a fine clarity of expression and remarkable penetration of the mentality and motives of primitive people.

*Ambari!* is a tale of the East coast. Its principals are two delightfully naughty, spirited boys, Ali and Juma, whose homes, clothes and speech are African but whose philosophy is that of naughty boys of all ages and climes.

' "Fishing is a man's work, school is for children, so fishing comes before school", said Ali.

"That's it", said Juma with great conviction. "The time for school is when the tide is wrong for fishing." '

On the day when, as on all other days, Ali was awakened by Joogoo the cock greeting the dawn from a roost on his chest, there was no school, because 'the daughter of Kingi George has had a son', and so the two boys go fishing and drift into very bad company and grave danger. They return safely and take part in an impromptu celebration, marred only by the boorish behaviour of the school bully, Squidface.

'Poor Squidface! He did not realize that travel broadens the mind. Before he knew what had happened he was on his back in the dust . . . with the two returned travellers almost quarrelling for the best seat on his body, his chest, for pummelling his unlovely face.'

This happy little story is told with great gusto and in terms of the utmost simplicity. One of its many charms is the dialogue which abounds in curious inversions: ' "There is profit of what kind of a sort in reading and writing?" ' Although Europeans come into the story, and indeed play an important part, race is not a factor in it. The children and their families live to themselves in a relaxed, uncomplicated society.

Complications, or perhaps a philosophy so simple and single-minded that to Western eyes it seems to produce complications, enter into *Shifta!* This lacks the spontaneous charm of *Ambari!* But it is a book which leaves a profound impression. Here is none of the gay fecklessness of the coast. The desert Somalis are nomads who lead a hard, bitterly unrewarding life in conditions of appalling privation. As if nature has not done enough to them, they are subjected to periodic raids by the Shifta, savage and merciless tribesmen who steal their camels and slaughter all who oppose them. *Shifta!* is the story of a raid and its aftermath, and of one boy, Farah, who helps to save his tribe and avenge his family, and acquires the traditional stoicism of his people.

Some Western critics have been disturbed by the violence in the story and by its emphasis on the necessity for revenge. This is to judge it by social rules to which it does not subscribe. By its own standards the story is consistent and admirable. The most remarkable feature of the book is not the action, which is exciting and swift, or the characters, who are subtle and keenly observed, but the desert setting. Farah and his family live in one of the cruellest environments in the world. The desert is harsh, barren, unlovely, at least as seen by Western eyes. To Farah it is home and it is beautiful.

'Now that the simple tasks were over, Farah had time to notice that the shimmer of thin, hot air had ceased; every leaf, grain of sand and blade of grass was crystal-clear and full of colour. A gentle, drifting wind, still warm but with a promise of delightful coolness, was caressing his body. A feeling of well-being and appetite came over him like magic.'

It is for this land, as well as for his family and his camels, that Farah fights.

R. Forbes-Watson wrote his two books many years ago, and he wrote them without self-consciousness. Today's writers might choose similar themes, but their interpretation would most probably be more calculated and more selective. Their view of the sea and the desert would be coloured by symbolism or by social awareness. Their books would be profoundly different, but they would be unlikely to be better than Forbes-Watson's. His quiet, restrained artistry and his deep understanding and great love of the (in Western eyes) primitive folk of whom he wrote produced two small books of lasting quality.

# CHAPTER SIX

# *Laughter*

'It did really cheer Father up, and you cannot always do that
. . . even if you make jokes, or give him a comic paper.'

THE FAVOURITE EVERYDAY reading of all children is
called a comic. The contents may, by design or ineptitude, not
be funny, but the name persists. Before the present insidious
trend towards education affected even this literary underworld, comics were, at least in intention, comical. They
attempted to feed one of the basic appetites, the craving for
laughter.

Although humour is so fundamental a necessity of life,
there are few really funny books for children. Humour is incidental to many books—it is for example an element always
present in William Mayne's work—but it is seldom the dominant ingredient. Looking back through the century, one sees
only the thinnest scattering of books which give a completely
topsy-turvy view of society. Outstandingly the most conspicuous of these is *The Magic Pudding.* Norman Lindsay's
inverted picture of Australia is more than forty years old now,
and its jokes are still as fresh as ever, because they are consistently imbedded in reality and because the language in
which they are expressed has the inevitability of poetry.
Norman Hunter's stories of Professor Branestawm and J. B. S.
Haldane's of Mr Leakey wear well, too, the one for the seriousness of its crazy logic, the other for its precision and scientific
accuracy. Dr Dolittle is another who survives, because Hugh
Lofting took his own comic concept quite seriously. If there is a
golden rule for the writing of funny stories for children, it is that
they should be serious. These jokes are not to be laughed at!

Today's climate is not particularly favourable to humour.

Our self-conscious concern for Children's Literature either as a vehicle for social theory or as an art form gets in the way. Humour is spontaneous, however hard the humorist may sweat to put his spontaneous idea into the right words.

There is, I believe, no modern counterpart to *The Magic Pudding*. The nearest is *Uncle*, J. P. Martin's continuing series which began to appear in 1964. These stories of a wealthy and highly cultivated elephant come from a consistently comic view of life, but they seem to me to suffer from a fundamental failure of communication. Like many other stories which began as improvizations for the amusement of individual children, they remain private rather than universal. The discursiveness too is a sign of their origin; a ruthless revision might reduce each book by a third. A more serious defect, and one which pervades the books, is a slack use of words. Bare, taut prose is an essential vehicle for humour; clumsy, ill-formed phrases tear a hole in the fabric of the story through which laughter runs to waste.

Mr Leakey has one obvious descendant and an acknowledged one. In a note to *The Adventures of Chunky* (1950) Leila Berg agrees that Professor Haldane got there first. Chunky is a bright boy and the child of scientific parents. His adventures are all concerned with science and with the establishment of scientific truth. When something odd happens to Mrs Spriggs's pigs, she appeals to Chunky for an explanation.

> 'Chunky began to look very important. But he remembered just in time that scientists never pretend to know anything they don't really know. So he quickly stopped looking very important, and looked ordinary instead.'

Like *My Friend Mr Leakey*, this is a string of stories, not a novel, although it gives a close-up of character and sets the episodes in an identifiable society. This, and the science, give distinction to a book which uses a throw-away style almost to excess. The fun is in the invention rather than the expression; the first time that Mrs Spriggs says, 'Cut my legs off and call me Shorty!' and 'Hop in my pocket!' is fine, but the joke wears thin. Chunky is mainly situation-comedy, but the situations gain an unusual degree of actuality from the science. When

Chunky and Mike clean the typewriter with Friar's Balsam the situation is a commonplace of comedies about unsuccessfully helpful children; Chunky knows—or thinks he knows—that Friar's Balsam contains ether which will dissolve the dirt, but the typewriter grows a beard from the hairs of the cleaning-brush. 'They were so thick and close together that Chunky had to take a comb from his pocket and part them down the middle to see the typewriter at all.' It is a logical step to call in Joe the Barber, but who could have predicted that the typewriter's beard would remind Mrs Spriggs of her late-departed?

No modern writer has matched the self-absorbed nonsense of the 'Professor Branestawm' stories, and while the original remains so persistently lively there is no need for imitators. The same idea—of an idea blown up to ten times its size and then applied quite seriously—lies at the heart of *Pippi Longstocking* (1945; English edition 1954). Astrid Lindgren's books are the outstanding masterpieces of much-larger-than-life portraiture. In Pippi she embodies all the dreams of small children who weave fantasies about total freedom from adult supervision, enormous physical strength, escape from the conventions of a civilization invented by grown-ups. Pippi lives alone except for a horse and Mr Nelson the monkey. She sleeps with her feet on the pillow. She dresses as she pleases, which means that when she is at home her black stockings sag and have holes in them, and on the South-Sea island where her father is King she has a bit of cloth wound around her middle—and lovely she looks in Richard Kennedy's pictures. She says what she likes, being rude only when she meets rudeness in others. She has enough for her needs and to entertain her friends. Great strength enables her to carry her horse when he is tired and to deal effectively with bores and villains.

This is great fun, and that might be enough. It would not sustain Pippi through a whole series of books. Pippi, however, is not a simple exaggeration. There is considerable subtlety in this portrait, so that the reader is constantly being surprised. When, in *Pippi in the South Seas* (1955; English edition, 1957), her friend Tommy falls into the sea and is attacked by a shark, Pippi deals roughly with the shark, while Tommy scrambles ashore.

'Pippi went to him. She behaved very oddly. First she lifted Tommy in the air and then she hugged him so hard that he nearly lost all his breath. Then she let go of him suddenly and sat down on the rock. She put her face in her hands and wept. Pippi wept. Tommy and Annika and all the Canny Cannibal Children looked at her in surprise and alarm. "You weep because Tommy nearly eaten," suggested Momo. "No," said Pippi sulkily, wiping her eyes. "I weep because poor little hungry shark not have any breakfast today." '

At the end of the same book, when the children are safely back home, Pippi declares her firm resolution not to grow up. But when Tommy and Annika are going to bed, in their own home, they get a glimpse through the window of Pippi sitting alone gazing into the candle-light. Whatever happens, 'Pippi would always, always be there.' But can it be that Pippi, who does just what she likes, is lonely? The question remains in the air.

The purely comical story cannot sustain a full-length portrait because no one is exclusively funny. Falstaff grew too big for his comic frame and, put into a farce, he was no longer himself. Notwithstanding the gales of laughter in the Pippi books, she is constantly threatening to turn serious. Character is therefore a hazardous ingredient of the comic novel. Christianna Brand is wisely careful, in *Nurse Matilda* (1964), to keep her central figure a caricature, though a convincing one. Nurse Matilda is one of those archetypal figures who have had a place, from time immemorial, in the legends of some favoured families. Mrs Brand could no more have invented her than the Brothers Grimm could have invented Rumpelstiltskin, or Homer Hector. Nurse Matilda is, not only by profession, somewhat in the mould of Mary Poppins; where P. L. Travers explored her creation in depth, Christianna Brand is concerned mainly with comic anecdotes centred on her formidable mistress of the nursery. Nurse Matilda, who engaged herself to the Brown household, is a terrifying sight, with 'a nose like two potatoes' and 'one huge front Tooth, sticking right out like a tombstone over her lower lip'. She is also tough, and she needs to be. Mr and Mrs Brown's uncountable children are very wicked. Even the Baby stands at the front gate, 'pleading, "Alms for ge lovey Aggy!" ' and holding out the little nursery potty to passers by.' Nurse Matilda has drastic remedies for their ills, even invoking the aid of the domestic staff in the great Battle of the Porridge-Soaked Socks. When the seven lessons have been learnt, and the children want, but no longer need, Nurse Matilda, she goes away to a needful household, leaving as a memento her Tooth. Perhaps *Nurse Matilda* is out of place in an examination of the children's novel, but children's literature would be immeasurably the poorer without this timeless, unforgettable book.

The essence of humour is incongruity. A child slipping on a banana skin excites no laughter, for children spend their time falling over; it needs the silk hat and the striped trousers to produce the prototype of all physical jokes. In all funny books the laughter comes from the juxtaposition of incompatible elements. Nurse Matilda exercising discipline is not funny because that is her job; she is funny because she gains control by letting the children carry their wickedness to excess. The strange humour of *The Twenty-One Balloons* (1947; English edition 1950) derives from pairing a great natural disaster— the explosion of the island of Krakatoa—with a most elaborate and precisely described artificial society. There is nothing intrinsically funny about a cataclysm; but what if the disaster concerns a Gourmet Government and a civilization in which technical ingenuity has been stretched to the limit to achieve minimal results in terms of human welfare? The absurdity of *The Twenty-One Balloons* is intensified by its sobriety. Never once does William Vene du Bois lose his gravity; he takes himself, his invention and his audience entirely seriously. The adventures, and the marvellously detailed drawings in which the author showed how they actually happened, are in fact not funny at all, nor is the exquisitely mannered prose; it is the idea which is fundamentally and deeply comic.

One of the oldest vehicles for humour, as for satire, is the animal-story. Human dignity and human folly show up well when dressed in animal-hides. Uncle, in J. P. Martin's books, only looks like an elephant, but in that guise he attracts the attention more than he would in human form. Walter R. Brooks's curiously appealing stories—*Freddy's First Adventure* (originally *To and Again*, 1928; English edition 1948)—are no more about pigs than is *Animal Farm*, but they make use of the piggishness in man and the manliness in pigs to make valid points. This is true, also, of Margery Sharp's charming stories about Miss Bianca, the brave and talented mouse (*The Rescuers*, 1959, and others) and of E. B. White's *Charlotte's Web* (1952). Miss Bianca and the members of the Prisoners Aid Society over which she presides are all mouse, and Miss Sharp is meticulously consistent in keeping them to scale. The mechanics of their daily lives and their journeys—Miss Bianca habitually travels on duty by Diplomatic Bag or in a Rolls, but for the great adventure of the Diamond Palace she goes with the rank and file by public transport, the municipal dust-cart —is worked out as carefully and honestly as the economy of Mary Norton's *The Borrowers*. But the mouse society is a miniature of the everyday world, and the author makes gentle fun of convention by presenting it in mouse-guise. The stories have all the authority that a highly skilled novelist can give them. The touch is perfect, light as a feather—or a mouse's whisker.

Another successful adult novelist also writes about animals. Emma Smith's heroine is a guinea-pig. Although a highly domesticated animal, Emily—like the Mole in a very different book—tires of housework and longs to travel. In *Emily's Voyage* (1966) she goes to sea in a ship captained by a poetical hare and with a crew of rabbits and a cargo of fireworks. Emma Smith is not much bothered with scale. Her creations are humans under the skin; they have the adventures that humans might have and their faculties are human. The book would lack distinction were it not for the beautifully under-written style with its gravity and restraint and for the very fine illustrations by Margaret Gordon. It is funny only in retrospect.

Then there is Paddington (*A Bear Called Paddington*, 1958, and others). In common with some other readers, I thought on first meeting Paddington that he was a little too Poohish to be original. This first impression was unjust. Paddington shares with Pooh only his bearishness—and this superficially, for Pooh has sawdust under his pelt—and a certain sententiousness of speech. The humour of Paddington is largely visual; it is not what he is but what he does and how he does it that is funny. The books owe as much to Peggy Fortnum for her drawings as Milne's do to E. H. Shepard; she not only captured the bear's appearance, his shagginess and his deplorable hat, but his movements in a number of fluent action-pictures. The stories in fact would lose nothing by being translated into the terms of the film; the fun lies in the action and the dialogue, not in purely literary qualities. In general the writing lacks distinction and there is no attempt at development. Paddington is a creation of the same kind as Worzel Gummidge; he has become a part of the folk-lore of childhood, not because he appears in a great or even a particularly good book, but because there is something in his personality which lodges permanently in the imagination.

Humour is often a matter of situation. Paddington is funny because Peruvian bears are not commonly found in middle-class English households. In *The Magic Bedknob* (1945) Mary Norton introduced a witch of modest attainments into English village society; much of the fun of this book—which is very much more than a comic novel—comes from this basic incongruity. Miss Price could pass for a member of the Women's Institute—indeed she is ideal for the office of Honorary Secretary although she lacks the indefinable quality which would make her a good President—but she is a witch. There are witches, too, in *The People in the Garden* (1954) and the many sequels in which Lorna Wood examined in greater detail the career of the Hag Dowsabel. The Hag cannot sustain her charm throughout, but the first book is, in both senses, enchanting. It is the story of Caroline who is eight, staying with Great-aunt Sophia, and bored. The only remarkable thing about Great-aunt Sophia's house is that it is large, but all around magic is at work. The gardener has a green thumb—bright emerald—and can make weeds leap out of the ground. His cat, Sootylegs, smokes a pipe. His daughter, Vanilla, makes wings with feather-stitching. Nearby lives the Hag Dowsabel in a hut with hens' legs, which is convenient when flitting. The fun would be diminished if everyone was magical; but poor Mrs Pettigrew, the gardener's wife, disapproves of all the goings-on and laments that she did not after all marry Perkins the carpenter. The invention in this story is lively and the fun innocently sophisticated. When Caroline flies on gardener Bill's back and lands in France they dine at the Duchesse de Berri on happily unidentifiable food served by toads to the accompaniment of music by the Giddy Grasshoppers (their stage-name; they are really the Brothers Cicada). These jokes are perhaps predictable; more unexpected is an Old Crab on the beach who sings 'Rule Britannia' and yearns for Margate. In this happy book, whose gaiety is always of the right pitch and never becomes shrill, Lorna Wood brought the traditional apparatus of magic into a contemporary setting without self-conscious anachronism. If her Hag is not quite as funny as she herself finds her, the whole society of the Garden is beautifully managed.

The highest art of the humorous writer is to create a truly comical and consistent society. Natalie Savage Carlson achieves this in her 'Orpheline' books. The basic humour of these is that orphans are by tradition sad and these are the Happy Orphelines. In their crumbling institution—as Josine tells a reporter proudly: 'We live in a slum with mice and the walls all broken down'—they are haunted by only one fear, that of being adopted. In *The Happy Orpheline* (1957; English edition 1960) Brigitte makes sure that she is too wicked for any potential foster-parent to want her. In *A Brother for the Orphelines* (1959; English edition 1961) Josine, the smallest orpheline, insists that Madame Flattot adopts a baby who is left in the bread-basket 'instead of bread'. But this is a girls' orphanage and Coucky—as Josine calls the baby—is chubby, coloured and beyond question a boy. Natalie Savage Carlson, an American writer who knows France and French ways, writes with an effortless lightness of touch. It all seems easy, but so vivid a picture of an interdependent society of children and adults cannot but be the work of a disciplined and very skilful writer. The dialogue is especially fine, capturing the fine inconsequence of children talking and of the logic of men like the merry-go-round man. When he was a boy he had always said when he felt miserable: 'When you are a big man you shall have a merry-go-round.' Now he is big and he has one, and he is sick of it. But he cannot sell it. ' "How can I sell the merry-go-round that I promised to a poor, unhappy boy?" '

There is a brilliant comic study of society in Manfred Michael's *Timpetill* (1937; English edition 1951). This is the society of a small Swiss town, so precisely imagined that it would be possible to compile a directory on the authority of the text alone. The children of Timpetill are a troublesome lot and at last their parents can stand them no longer. They walk out, leaving the children to run the town for themselves. There is anarchy for a time, and then a moderate party asserts itself and puts the town to rights. The parents return in due time, to find that the dissidents have been tried and sentenced—to peeling potatoes. Timpetill is its delightful self again and St Matthew stands erect once more on his pedestal in the Goat Market. *Timpetill* is a book in the 'Emil' tradition, like *Emil* deploying a large number of clearly defined characters in a precise environment, although lacking *Emil's* distinction of style. It is a very funny book, although the comedy may be more apparent to adult than to child readers who, like the narrator, will rightly take the situation and its resolution entirely seriously.

Nearly all completely humorous books are anecdotal, like *Professor Branestawm*, *Paddington*, and *Nurse Matilda*. The integrated novel ranges more widely; however funny its fundamental idea and individual episodes, it will burst the bounds of conventional humour and spread out over a larger field of emotions. This has happened conspicuously in the realm of the adult novel; Dickens passed quickly from the episodic conventions of *Pickwick* to novels which were certainly funny but also romantic, sentimental and tragic. In the present decade the children's writer who illustrates most convincingly the comic genius of English literature is Helen Cresswell, and she is very much more than a comic novelist. Even in *The Piemakers* (1967) and *The Signposters* (1968), which are certainly comedies, she is not content merely to make the reader laugh. The ideas behind these two books are identical; they are concerned with craftsmanship as a guiding force in life. The crafts —in the one pie-making, in the other checking and renewing signposts—are more mundane than one might expect, and they are pursued beyond normal limits. Herein lies the incongruity which produces comedy. Arthy Roller does not only make pies

*From* The Piemakers (*see opposite page*)

fit for a king; he makes them big enough for the King, and the Court, and the whole society of Danby Dale, so big that the pie-dish sails down river with four Dalesmen on board and it takes twenty to haul it ashore. When the pie is at last baked and brought before the King, 'it was impossible, a miracle under that blue sky ... It was seen and yet impossible to believe.' Even the piemaker is overcome with awe at his own achievement. When the pie has been shared out, some of the people of Danby Dale take their portion home in a handkerchief, to keep for ever 'like a pressed petal'. A joke as big as this becomes no longer humorous but heroic. The rest of the book—characters, setting, writing—is to match. The Rollers of Danby Dale are related to reality, but it is a reality heightened and enriched by art. The scale of the story is worked out with exquisite accuracy, so that, despite the monumental absurdities, the reader is compelled to suspend belief.

There is fun in *The Piemakers*, but, despite the destination of the pie, there are no belly-laughs. The book produces the warm glow, not the loud guffaw. There is also, as in all the finest humour, a hint of sadness.

> 'Where is beauty?
> Gone, gone.'

said Walter de la Mare. He was not thinking particularly of pies, but they are a case in point. As that loyal Roller wife, Jem, says:

> ' "When I saw them trimmings, a shiver went up me right from my toes. They was *beautiful*, Arthy. I shall never forget them trimmings as long as I live."
> ' "But the texture, Jem," Arthy persisted . . .'

Like the great craftsman that he unquestionably is, Arthy is not satisfied with perfection; neither, I suspect, is Helen Cresswell. Her search for some mystery beyond laughter continues.

# CHAPTER SEVEN

# Magic Casements

' "Our carriage is a fairy one, drawn by griffins . . ." said Noel.
The little girl looked at him very queerly, and said "That is
out of a picture-book." '

HELEN CRESSWELL's move, predictably, was from humour
to fantasy. In her world the larger-than-life society of *The
Piemakers* is only a step away from the off-world mystery of the
Greeneyes who haunt the fringes of the everyday scene of *The
Nightwatchmen* (1969) and yet another to the poetic fantasy of
*The Outlanders* (1970). Humour and fantasy have always been
closely allied, both being based on an extension of the natural
order. Humour depends on an exaggeration of nature, fantasy
on a suspension of natural law.

Many fantastic novels are essentially humorous. The great
master in this field, as in so many others, was E. Nesbit, who
had a fine instinct for the ruthless logic of fantasy. In *Five
Children and It* the fantasy comes from the Psammead who has
the power, and the obligation, to grant wishes; the humour
comes from his maliciously literal interpretation of the wishes.
When Robert wishes that he was bigger than the bullying
baker's boy he is—many times bigger. This formula is a
favourite with many modern writers, notably with a self-
confessed disciple of E. Nesbit, Edward Eager. In *Half-Magic*
(1954) the agent of magic is a nickel which Jane finds. It is an
ancient coin—not a nickel at all, in fact—and in its long life its
magic has worn thin. Now it is only able to manage half a wish.
(The same idea occurs, in reverse, in Ada Harrison's *The
Doubling Rod* (1957).) Mother discovers this short-change magic
first. During a social evening with Aunt Grace and Uncle Edwin
she is desperately bored. The holiday snaps of Yellowstone

112

Park are dreadfully like those of Glacier Park last year, and Aunt Grace's conversation is as predictable. She wishes to herself that she were at home. Mother had happened to borrow a nickel from Jane's dressing-table for her taxi-fare home, and instead of being at Aunt Grace's or at home she finds herself halfway home. The magic works within mathematically strict limits. It takes some practice to operate it successfully, and during the learning Carrie the cat half-talks, the iron boot-scraper dog comes half to life, and the children find themselves in the middle of the desert. (Mark wished that they were on a desert island and the magic could only cope with the first half of the request.) The wishes, and their interpretation, become more sophisticated. Katharine beats Sir Lancelot, Jane turns into Iphigenia, alias Little Comfort, in an episode which is pure Nesbit.

Edward Eager keeps strictly to the rules, and this is an essential of the good fantasy. Magic does not break out uncontrollably all over the scene but follows its own basic laws. This gives *Half Magic* its tight construction and its peculiar satisfaction. The fun is brisk and consistent, both in the main stream of the story and in its incidental events. In a hilarious episode in King Arthur's days which later turns serious, Katharine (who is temporary custodian of the coin) loses her temper with Morgan le Fay and wishes that she would 'go jump in the lake'. Had she been thinking carefully she would have said 'Go jump in two lakes'; as it is, the lovely Morgan le Fay falls in a pond and sticks firmly in the mud.

There is the same consistency in the application of new laws in *The Flying House* (1947). Uncle Ben invents a gas called Jeddium. This is considerably lighter than air, and Uncle Ben is experimenting with balloons. He is a good inventor but less successful in practical matters. When testing the gas cylinders in the house he ought to have taken more care of the key which controls the supply. The gas flows into a balloon stored, inadvisedly, in the attic, and the house takes to the air. Flying houses are not likely, and the reader is required to accept C. Walter Hodges's basic improbability. Thereafter no further concessions are needed; the story follows its logical course to a satisfactory conclusion.

Although an agreeable idea, *The Flying House* is not particularly original and it would have been forgotten but for the writer's beautifully controlled prose and the artist's precision of his detail. It is impossible for someone who draws as well as Hodges does to think sloppily, because his imagination and his draughtsmanship go hand in hand. The absurdities of *The Flying House* are credible because the author gives them, and not only in the illustrations, visual credibility.

Humour is not enough. However gravity-removing the individual episodes, comic fantasy is apt to become serious. It does in Nicholas Stuart Gray's *Grimbold's Other World* (1963). Before turning to the novel Gray had made a substantial reputation with a series of plays—the most considerable contribution by any one writer to the children's theatre—based for the most part on traditional tales and using such familiar stories as Beauty and the Beast as the launching-pad for independent exploration. In *Grimbold's Other World* his story is original, but it is closely modelled on the folk-tale. Muffler the goatherd is a foundling and it is clear to every reader that he will prove to be a member of a royal family. In a series of adventures in the 'Other World' of night he fights evil and rescues a friend from a violent end. The matter of the story is familiar but the interpretation is quite original. In a fine conclusion the action moves towards the revelation that Muffler is the lost prince. It seems that Muffler's goats will lose their master. But the lion-headed Bargas, who is the key-witness and who cannot lie, knows that

> 'all of truth is never known;
> only bits and pieces show.'

Bargas identifies Jeffery, not Muffler, as the prince. It is strictly true, so far as it goes; Jeffery is a lost prince, 'lost in the other world five hundred years ago'.

If the theme of *Grimbold's Other World* is entirely serious, the treatment is often delightfully light. The dialogue, as one would expect of a dramatist, is lively and closely related to character; in moments of high emotion it smells a little of the stage, but it will turn abruptly and make fun of its own solemnity. Always the words are at the service of a lofty theme, the necessity for freedom. As Grimbold, the cat who roams the Other World, says of the hounds who fear him in the night 'It's just the way they see me in the night-kingdom they have forgotten. To them I represent all that they've lost of freedom and magic. Fancy selling this for a bone and a pat!'

Gray is also, like a good dramatist, an expert in timing. Early in the story Muffler earns the gratitude of Madam Nettleweb, 'a tiny, tattered, ancient lady' who has some skill in magic. She gives him the choice of outgrowing his dreams and living a happy normal life, or of paying the price for magic. He chooses magic. ' "It would cost me more to outgrow my dreams" '. Magic enables him to 'talk with all living things—in their own language, and by daylight'. Will this work? Back on the mountain-side with his flock 'Muffler took a deep breath of the fine air and slid the silver ring on his little finger.

"Where you bin?" said one of the goats.'

Nicholas Stuart Gray was to write other stories of magic, at least one—*Over the Hills to Fabylon* (1954)—perhaps more important, but his light eloquence was at its best in this magical story of the wonders of the night world through which Grimbold stalks with gleaming black fur and bright green eyes.

Grimbold is the largest and fiercest of the cats who prowl or doze in the realms of magic. Carbonel is smaller and, despite his royal origin, more approachable. Barbara Sleigh's *Carbonel* (1955) has lasted longer than many more pretentious books because it tells a good story with quiet competence and it never overreaches itself. When he was a mere kitten Carbonel, who is a Prince of the Blood Royal, was stolen by a witch. When this detestable Mrs Cantrip retires, she sells Carbonel, for three farthings, to a little girl who devotes herself to freeing the cat from his servitude. The action takes place in a cathedral city and this background is sketched neatly. What gives the book its special distinction is the fine observation of behaviour and particularly cat behaviour. Carbonel is drawn beautifully, yawning 'so that she could see his magnificent white teeth and his pink tongue, frilled like a flower petal, between', or settling into Rosemary's lap 'like water in a bowl'.

Barbara Sleigh's witch is a malicious creature. Even in retirement, when she runs a sweet-shop, she cannot refrain from giving her customers stomach-ache. Miss Price is a witch of quite another school. In Mary Norton's expert hands Miss Price is wonderfully real and complex. She rides into *The Magic Bedknob* (1945) on a high bicycle, visiting the sick and teaching the piano. 'In all the village there was none so ladylike as Miss Price'. Only Paul notices that she also rides a broomstick and he doesn't mention it to anyone, preferring to keep his 'nightly joy' to himself, and holding back the news from Carey and Charles until Miss Price is sufficiently proficient to be shown off. For Miss Price is a learner-witch. What she finds most difficult is wickedness, although she has her moments when the children notice how very long and yellow her teeth are. The adventures which follow when she gives the children the magical charge which makes their bed into a flying-machine are in the Nesbit manner, partly funny, partly terrifying. In a sequel—*Bonfires and Broomsticks* (1947)—the bed takes them into the past and into more horrifying dangers.

Mary Norton, as she proved conclusively a little later with her books of the Borrowers, is a master of detail. Not for her a half-imagined context. The two stories about Miss Price are exquisitely written, and the portrayal of character is done with tenderness and understanding, but what puts these books in a class apart is the actuality. In *The Magic Bedknob* Miss Price and the children go by flying bed on a visit to an uninhabited South Sea island. Unfortunately it *is* inhabited—by cannibals. In her deepest distress, with a savage's grip upon her, Carey sobs 'People should be careful what they write in encyclopaedias.' Miss Price and the local witch-doctor engage in a contest of skills. Miss Price wins a struggle to control the broomstick, but the witch-doctor thinks he can trump this ace with a knife. Miss Price then turns him into a frog. Mary Norton gives an eye-witness account of how she does it.

> 'She held out her two arms towards the witch-doctor as if to ward him off with the broomstick. He stopped, with knees bent, about to jump. Then he seemed to shrink and dwindle. He sank downwards into his legs as if the heat of the fire was melting him ... Every part of him was shrinking at the same time ... The witch-doctor melted into a tiny blob of gold, a tiny yellowish object, barely distinguishable upon the sandy ground.'

Eager, Gray and Mary Norton all acknowledge their debt to a tradition of fantasy. Honor Prime's achievement was original, or at least she took a different tradition—that of the animate toy—and bent it into a quite new shape. *Moonface* (1961) is not on the surface a fantasy at all. When Helena was unhappy because she had left her toy mouse Matthew behind when she packed for her holiday, Father came to her bedroom to comfort her. While he talked he picked up her old vest and absent-mindedly tied it into a knot. Helena held the lump of vest into a moonbeam. 'She looked intently at it. "Who *are* you?" she said.'

The vest had become Moonface, 'a great round face like the moon' and little else. Moonface is inanimate. He is never more than a vest tied in a knot, and, after his adventures, a very dirty one. Yet he exercises a powerful influence over his owner. Or does he? Is all that happens a series of homely coincidences interpreted by an imaginative child? Honor Prime wisely does not answer the question, leaving an enchanted reader to his own conclusions. Certainly things happen to Helena after she acquires Moonface. Her words, for example, go their own way. She is an articulate child with an appetite for new words. When Moonface looks at her 'out of the eye you couldn't quite see' they get quite out of hand.

> ' "And don't look so undependent. Can't you look one bit sorrish? I looked alwheres for you . . . Oh you *are* a respongie-bubblety." '

The place to consider *Moonface* might seem to be with other books which explore the strange recesses of the child's mind, and this certainly is one aspect of the book. So clearly, how-ever, does the reader see the action through Helena's eyes that the final and lasting impression is one of magic. Moonface develops a mind of his own and an ability to influence fate. How else can one explain his escape from the pebbly prison which Helena builds for him in the sand? How else the mystery of his recovery when helpful adults unknotted him and gave him a much-needed wash? As Helena says: 'You knew just what to do.' Helena is not alone in rejoicing at his restora-tion, even if he is 'a flewing thumpillious diskappearish supper salting amtriphlewbious bertibrake'. The book, with its sequels, is a masterly study of childhood and, still more, an imaginative work of outstandingly original quality.

For every child, if only for a brief time, a favoured toy lives and goes adventuring with him. The child grows older, and the toy freezes back into its original wood or felt or plastic. But what of toys which have been exposed to the creative fires of genius? Would they not receive a lasting charge of energy, enough, carefully stored, to last for a century? This is the thesis of Pauline Clarke's *The Twelve and the Genii* (1962). The Morley family move to a farmhouse on the moors near Haworth. Max, exploring the attic, finds a loose floor-board and rescues twelve wooden soldiers 'from a living death'. These are the Twelves, the wooden soldiers which the Reverend Patrick Brontë—in an uncharacteristic moment of generosity —bought for his family, and which enlivened the dullness of Haworth Parsonage. It is arguable that these toys focused the genius of the Brontës for the first time, and that *The History of the Young Men* and the other childish writings inspired by the Twelves contained the seeds of the Brontë novels. If toys can inspire genius, may not the Genii in return give life to the toys? It is a wonderful idea, one of the most brilliantly original in the whole range of children's literature. It would be too much to hope that the realization might be as brilliant. Pauline Clarke brought to it intelligence and formidable technical equipment, but she was not herself one of the Genii. Fascinating as the story is, and however skilfully she marshals the Brontë facts and builds them into her narrative, the book never quite rises to its theme.

The greatest contrast to both *Moonface* and *The Twelve* is provided by Russell Hoban's powerful and shatteringly disturbing fantasy, *The Mouse and His Child* (1967; English edition 1969). This too is a story about toys, but here the toys are divorced from their human owners and left to fend for themselves in a harsh world. Russell Hoban had previously been known, at least in this country, as the writer of shrewd and tender texts to his wife's picture-books. They were no preparation for the blockbuster of *The Mouse and His Child* which, whatever its ultimate status, was one of the most revolutionary books in the whole history of children's literature.

The book is about toys. Toys have their moment of glory when they are cherished by children. Then they wear out, or break down, or are superseded by new favourites, and are relegated to the dustbin. This, one might think, is the end. Russell Hoban shows that it is indeed a beginning.

The mouse is dressed in blue velveteen trousers and patent-leather shoes. He is powered by clockwork. He holds his child by the hands and, when wound up, dances around swinging the child in the air. It is an attractive toy, and not surprisingly it is sold after only one day and night in the shop. In this brief time the child forms impressions and affections which, like those of a human child, stay with him through his life, of the dolls' house which offers a vision of home, and of the elephant, also clock-work, who declines to be his mama. ' "Really", she said . . . "this is intolerable. One is polite to the transient element on the counter, and see what comes of it." '

The mouse and his child are sold to careful parents and obedient children and so survive four Christmases. On the fifth the child is so overcome by nostalgia that he breaks the rules and weeps 'on the job'. The family cat is disturbed by this unusual occurrence and knocks a vase right on top of the toy, smashing it. So the mouse and his child are thrown away and begin their appalling odyssey.

This is a long, closely argued, difficult book. It is full of a savage humour, irony, satire—a rare manifestation in child-ren's books, drama and near-tragedy. The world of toys is as bitter and ruthless as the human world, and Hoban pulls no punches. The reader who keeps up with his agile imagination weeps and laughs on adjoining pages. A relentless logic under-lies the apparent inconsequence of the episodes, and at the end the reader realizes with astonishment that there have been no loose ends and no waste.

The toys remain toys. They suffer and rust but cannot bleed. Their initiative is limited by their own mechanical limitations; they can act only while their clockwork functions. Behind them comes Manny Rat. Manny is a major creation, one of the very few full-length portraits in post-war books for children. He is a nightmare figure, a gang-leader, a mechanical genius, smooth-spoken and grotesquely humorous, motivated by pure malignity. He is horribly credible and in a strange way almost lovable. Although type-cast for the villain, he comes near to being the hero, or at least the anti-hero. When he stands at bay in the dolls' house in the magnificent climax of the story, and realizes that a prophecy is being fulfilled—the Frog had said, long before, 'A dog shall rise; a rat shall fall', and the attackers carry their assault-force in a tin can which once held Bonzo Dog Food—he is a ratty Macbeth in his despair and his courage. A lesser writer would have let him perish in defeat; Hoban allows him one more fling, then, softened but not—one thinks—reformed, promotes him to the rank of Uncle Manny. It comes perilously near to a sentimental conclusion, but not quite.

What does all this mean? The author is wise not to be specific. As Crow says of the play *The Last Visible Dog* which his Caws of Art Experimental Theatre Group is to perform:

' "It's a play with a message."
' "What's the message?" said Mrs Crow.
' "I don't know," said Crow. "But I know it's there, and that's what counts." '

It is a commonplace of all writing about children's literature that nearly all the most lasting books are fantasies. This may be partly that the 'realistic' story dates more easily because it deals with contemporary problems and values; when these change the book rests on its intrinsic merits, and these may not be strong enough to sustain it. The fantasy stands outside time; it is concerned with universal problems and eternal values and so is less affected by temporal changes. The oldest of all stories are folk-tales. The circumstances which prompted them originally, in a peasant's hut or the hall of some primitive king, have vanished out of mind, but they survive and speak clearly to the modern world because they are miniature fantasies, illustrating eternal truths in the terms of a timeless story. The writer of fantasy, however sophisticated his literary equipment, returns to the earth from which he came for his themes and his materials. Fantasy tends to be the medium for a writer who has some important message to deliver, for the poet, the moralist and the philosopher.

It is obviously the medium for allegory. Formal allegory, in which each character is a personification and each incident a symbol, is out of fashion, and a good thing too; but there is room in children's literature for the allegorical romance in which the story is told at two levels, the surface and the allegorical. Professor Tolkien's trilogy of *The Lord of the Rings* —which I reluctantly exclude from this study because only in the sense that all the best books are for everyone is it a book for children—is a great tale of adventure which is also a moral allegory. The 'Narnia' books of C. S. Lewis too can be read on these two levels, and so can Lloyd Alexander's stories. On a lower plane, but not as low as some critics have been inclined to place it, is Elizabeth Goudge's *The Little White Horse* (1946).

*The Little White Horse* is a sentimental romance. This is a precise, not a pejorative description. Miss Goudge, like the highly competent and successful novelist she was, had no compunction about playing on the reader's emotions and she did so very well indeed. The little book is brilliantly written and extremely readable. If one sometimes yearns for a touchstone, some yardstick of normality by which to measure all these delightful oddities, this is to judge the book by standards which it does not itself acknowledge. *The Little White Horse* has attracted much adverse criticism in later years; it has also given much pleasure. I regard it with a very personal affection; it was the first children's book which I read on return to civilian life. I recall clearly the satisfaction which it gave then, and I have received the same pleasure in many more critical re-readings.

The book is an allegory of the war between good and evil. This was personified, long before the story starts, in the quarrel between Sir Wrolf Merryweather and Black William, but it is not a simple matter of blacks and whites. Sir Wrolf was mainly good and William certainly evil, but Sir Wrolf was greedy, arrogant and an aggressor. The war goes on, in a modified form, into the action of the story. Maria, the enchanting heroine, is a Moon Princess who may perhaps resolve the quarrel, but she is also a young woman of character, and not all of it good. She spills just one tiny drop of acid into the syrup of the romance.

The setting is an important agent in *The Little White Horse*. Miss Goudge took an actual Devon landscape, purged and idealized it, and then brought its charms vividly to life. She was served well by the illustrator, C. Walter Hodges, who gave her scenes and characters the colour and personality which she had imagined and added a little tartness of his own.

*The Little White Horse* is partly concerned with self-knowledge. This is an important subject, and Miss Goudge treats it with becoming seriousness. Jane Langton hides her essential seriousness behind a featherweight gaiety. In two books—*The Diamond in the Window* (1962; English edition 1969) and *The Swing in the Summerhouse* (1967; English edition 1970)—she explores the personalities of her principals through the medium of funny, witty, wise and exciting adventure stories. The books invite comparison with those of the greatest writers of comic fantasy, E. Nesbit and Mary Norton, not because they are in any way derivative but because they have a comparable vitality and inventiveness.

Like E. Nesbit's, Jane Langton's stories are deeply concerned with places. The Hall family—Aunt Lily, Uncle Freddy who is 'not altogether sound in his mind', Eleanor and Edward P. Hall, alias Trebor Nosnibor (he habitually talks backwards), the future President of the United States—live in Concord, Massachusetts, a town haunted by Thoreau, Emerson and the Alcotts. Among all those neat white board houses theirs—'a little like the Taj Mahal'—looks 'like an exotic tropical plant in a field of New England daisies'. It is a house made to breed wonders, and marvellous and very dangerous adventures come in the course of the children's quest for treasure, which turns out to be a search for self-knowledge and wisdom.

*The Diamond in the Window* is a singularly perfect book, with an entirely satisfying conclusion. It took great courage to embark on a sequel, yet *The Swing in the Summerhouse* is as good as the original book. Again, this is a moral tale embodying precepts which would have been acceptable in a Victorian children's book but the interpretation is individual and there is a fine balance between humour and high seriousness. Above all, both books are about people, brilliantly sketched caricatures like Mr Preek and his secretary Miss Prawn, proud citizens of Concord—the glorious heritage of the Prawns is the memory that her 'own dear grandfather put Henry Thoreau in jail'; jolly surface portraits like the impossible Oliver Winslow who has caused trouble 'ever since he had discovered as a baby that everything he touched came apart in his hands', and loving portraits in depth. These include not only the Halls but Georgie, the little girl from next door who will be five 'pretty soon' and whose tragedy is that she cannot read yet or tell what's two and two. Georgie wants to know 'everything there is in the whole world', and Uncle Freddy helps her towards her heart's desire by unveiling the mystery of two and two and teaching the dictionary from either end, one word each night beginning with *abacus* and *zygolic*.

The allegorical element, buried deep in Jane Langton's books, is closer to the surface of *The Land of the Lord High Tiger*. This little book may seem to be an offshoot of C. S. Lewis's 'Narnia' stories, although I believe that in composition, though not in publication, it antedated them. Roger Lancelyn Green is a major authority on early children's books. He has perhaps read too many of them to be entirely original, and *The Land of the Lord High Tiger* is undisguisedly derivative. It owes something to Masefield's *The Midnight Folk* and to Lang and George Macdonald. There are echoes of *Alice* and a hint here and there of Mrs Molesworth. But if the books is pastiche, it is lively pastiche with a bustling action and verbal dexterity. Much of the dialogue might appear in double-quotes, and there are some terrible puns—'Whoever heard of a Princess in blue serge? Only school girls and tidal-waves have serge on them!'—of a kind dear to children.

Roger Lancelyn Green's story is the familiar one of the boy and girl who come from the world of humans to purge a magical kingdom of its enemies. In his case the kingdom is a comical one, and one never takes too seriously the plight of King Katzekopf the Conqueror or the evil magic of the Black Wizard. This is as well, because Roger and Priscilla do not seem to be of the stuff of heroes (the book in fact has the marks of an improvisation, made up for the bed-time amusement of a real Roger and Priscilla). A writer is in difficulties when he attempts to make a story of this kind serious and convincing because, however old and hallowed the convention, the reader will not readily accept that an ordinary child out of the everyday world can play *deus ex machina*. This is a fundamental weakness of the 'Narnia' books. Despite C. S. Lewis's persuasive prose and the many excellences of the stories, one balks at the idea of a group of schoolchildren, not notably brave or clever, becoming kings and queens in a magical world. Peter and Susan are so terribly commonplace, yet if one cannot believe that they will rule in wisdom and holiness the whole massive edifice of the stories falls to the ground.

With this basic—and inevitable—weakness goes another and a less predictable deficiency. The style is uncertain and uneven. There seems to be no mean between the elevated heroic speech of the Narnians and the flat trivialities of schoolboy—and public-schoolboy at that—English. The stories embody, on occasion, an oversimplified public-schoolboy code. There is no great tension in the conflicts because there is insufficient subtlety in the issues for which each side fights. Black and white make effective contrasts, but the eye soon yearns for some gradations of tone.

The story of Narnia is that of *The Land of the Lord High Tiger* writ large, and writ too with much greater vitality and inventiveness. C. S. Lewis said in defence of his work: 'our superiority (over children) consists . . . partly . . . in the fact that we are better at telling stories than they are', and his is a case in point. He was one of the great story-tellers. Whatever one thinks of his ethics or his sociology, no one need resist the appeal of a tale supremely well told.

Whether or not C. S. Lewis conceived his 'Narnia' books as one whole, in retrospect this is what they are seen to be. The chronological sequence is not immediately easy to find, but the writer had classical authority in starting in the middle. Later he showed—in *The Magician's Nephew* (1954)—how it all started, in a slightly uncharacteristic Nesbitish introduction. *The Horse and His Boy* (1954)—in some ways the best single volume—stands apart from the sequence.

Lewis himself denied that the books were an allegory, and in the literal sense they are not. They are heroic romances with allegorical features. Aslan the lion is a type of Christ; the

Biblical parallels to the Crucifixion and Resurrection in *The Lion, the Witch and the Wardrobe* (1950) are undisguised, and the stable in *The Last Battle* is clearly symbolic. The White Witch is a personification of evil, and Edmund plays the part of Judas. The parallels are not pushed too far. Lewis's pre-occupations with theological and ethical problems were too profound to be put aside, but he was too good an artist to let his ideals ride him as, for example, Kingsley's did in *The Water Babies*.

Lewis turned to children's books fairly late, and he did so not so much to entertain individual children of his acquaintance, or to make money, but because the children's fantasy was the right form for the books he wished to write. The choice was more deliberate than is common among writers, but it was inevitable. In no other form could he have been so direct, so free to indulge his fancy and his exuberance. Fantasy allowed him too to invent strange and memorable characters, not so much human or even human-Narnian, but animals like Reepicheep the heroic mouse and semi-human creatures like Puddleglum the Marsh-wiggle, and—perhaps less acceptably—conventionally brave and noble unicorns, centaurs and eagles who talk in an exhaustingly elevated style. The books are indeed a muddle, fascinating, absorbing, sometimes genuinely moving but never so irresistible as to override criticism. Some books one loves as much for their weakness as their strength, but not Lewis's. Yet in the end the uneasy memory of moments like Jill, in the tragedy of *The Last Battle*, cheering on her team with cries of 'Oh well done. *Well* done!' like the Captain of the Fifth at a hockey-match are blotted out by the great moments, the coming of Spring to the frozen land in the first story and that magnificent apocalyptic moment in the last when the Time-giant, at Aslan's command, 'stretched out one arm . . . across the sky till his hand reached the Sun. He took the Sun and squeezed it in his hand as you would squeeze an orange.'

Lloyd Alexander's Celtic romances lack the magnificence of Lewis's vision and the depth of his bathos alike. They share with the 'Narnia' books a preoccupation with the nature of evil and the necessity of sacrifice. This is presented in the terms of this world and of a vaguely historic time. Alexander, an

American linked in spirit and blood to the Celtic world, has been much influenced by *The Mabinogion*, which he uses on the whole more freely than Alan Garner. There are powerful episodes in *The Black Cauldron* (1965; English edition 1967), but it is rather more important that there is also fun, a rare element which seldom manages to fight to the surface of the heroic fantasy.

Laughter is quiescent in Alan Garner's first book, *The Weirdstone of Bringamen* (1960)—another story devoted to the struggle with the forces of evil, here commanded by the Great Spirit of Darkness, Nastrond. This was a remarkable first book by a young writer but hardly a successful one. The narrative is confusing and confused, always whipping itself into a further frenzy of activity. The terms of reference are Norse rather than Celtic, and the Norse gods were always a complicated lot. There are some fine moments, mostly marred by a turgid style. Where the book excels is in the use of an actual landscape whose topography plays an essential part in the action and in relating the nightmares of the story to commonplace figures of the everyday world. When the two children make their perilous journey through the homely countryside below Alderley Edge, the agents of the evil one who lie in wait for them include two hikers, Mr Hodgkins the commuter, and, unkindest cut of all, Harry Wardle who is 'all reet'.

This skill in harnessing the modern scene and its inhabitants was more marked in Garner's *Elidor* (1965) where the magic starts to work in Piccadilly, Manchester. It is not chance that when Roland spins the wheel which operates the index to a street plan it comes to rest at Thursday Street. For Thursday Street has disappeared into a heap of rubble in a slum-clearance scheme. And why is an old street Musician playing his fiddle among these inhospitable ruins? From this confusing scene, strange yet typical of a modern city, the Watson children are shot into 'a magic land and full of song' where Malebron of Elidor holds back the night. The children—it seems improbable—have been sent to 'bring back light to Elidor'. It is never quite clear why. As in the 'Narnia' stories, the weakness lies in casting such commonplace children as the agents of destiny.

The scenes in Elidor are unconvincing. The book picks up when the children return to their own world with their Treasures. In Elidor these were a spear, a golden stone, a sword and a chalice; back in Manchester they turn into a bit of iron railing, a stone from a demolished church, a wooden sword and a cracked cup, but they retain their magic potency. Much of the interest lies in Garner's use of technology, not to explain away but to make the magic credible. The Treasures, buried in the Watsons' back garden, ruin reception on television, start the family car, and make Mrs Watson's washing machine churn all night with the plug out. These are effective devices, but neither they nor the clear presentation of the Manchester and Cheshire scene and its inhabitants make the central theme sufficiently important to justify the book.

Garner reached maturity in *The Owl Service* (1967). Here the real and the magical worlds are very close and there is no awkward transition between them. The characters, too, are acceptable, and their social problems in the everyday world are relevant to the main theme.

The Welsh valley is, as the Welsh boy Gwyn sees it, 'a reservoir . . . The power is always there and always will be. It builds up and builds up until it has to be let loose'. The agent in its release is an English girl, Alison, who owns the house in the valley. She is the electrical connection, and the battery is a dinner-service stowed away in an attic. This has lain dormant for many years, until Alison sleeps in the room below—she is ill and this may have had something to do with it. Power is let loose in the valley with startling results.

This valley was the setting of a story in *The Mabinogion*, the bitter, intensely human story of Gwynion the magician who made for Lleu a wife out of flowers. She betrayed him with Gronw, causing the death of both her lovers, while she was turned into an owl. The passions released by this tragedy are still running free in the valley. Alison sees that the innocent formal floral decorations on the Owl Service can be made into owls. On the wall in the ancient original house, now an outbuilding, there is a crudely concealed painting of the flower-wife Blodeuwedd. She is very beautiful, but the flowers which surround her have claws where petals should be. The conflict in the nature of Blodeuwedd between flowers and owls, beauty and cruelty, is echoed in the storm which sweeps the valley at the climax of an extraordinary story.

Wisely, Garner does not make his theme explicit. The clues are scattered throughout the action but the reader is left to pick them up as he goes. What gives contemporary meaning to the ancient tale is that it is played out by modern people whose personal problems are curiously connected with the old drama. On the one hand there is the English family, step-brother and step-sister, one deserted by his mother, the other learning to live with a kind, rich, not very clever step-father. They are united in what Gwyn calls 'the all-year-round cultural pursuit in your family . . . Not Upsetting Mummy'. Mummy herself, a formidable and sinister force contained within the framework of an English Lady, never appears in person although her shadow lies over the action. Opposite them stand the doom-ridden Celts, Nancy who was once beautiful and in love with an Englishman, Huw Halfbacon, the crazed lord of the valley who loves her and is not allowed into the house, and Gwyn their son, a brilliant unhappy boy trapped between opposing cultures.

Garner draws a disturbing picture of a modern scene in which timeless forces are at work. A similar situation is at the heart of William Mayne's first and most successful essay in fantasy, *Earthfasts* (1966). Mayne is so skilled in discovering fantastic elements in the real world that formal fantasy would hardly seem a necessary part of his art, but *Earthfasts* is clearly a story which had to be told. So immediate and corroboratively detailed is it that it is tempting to believe that the author, who lives not far from the scene, was a witness of these strange events.

*Earthfasts* is a Swaledale story. Relics of the past lie thick in this land and folk-memories are long. In such a landscape there is no incongruity in a story which brings together a neolithic stone circle, an eighteenth-century drummer-boy, and the kind of boggart who, given the right combination of circumstances, is likely to pop up in any century.

The drummer-boy comes first. Legend has it that a drummer went into a hole in the rock in Richmond Castle in search of

King Arthur's treasure and was never seen again. Two typical Mayne boys, David and Keith, clever, articulate products of the twentieth century and the grammar school, hear a drumming noise beneath the ground of Haw Bank. The earth stirs, and out of a crack shines a thin flame with the noise of violent drumming. ' "I wasn't so long", said the drummer. "But I niver found nowt." '

Nellie Jack John, the drummer-boy, went underground in 1742. Two centuries passed like an hour and the drummer comes out into a world of mechanical marvels. He ignores these, being more concerned with keeping an age-old date with his lass in the town. But Kath is dead and forgotten and they set the dog on him. Nellie Jack John came from Eskeleth in Arkengarthdale, and he goes there next, marching in soldierly fashion by the river.

> The only change since his day was the chapel itself, and he looked at it once, and then at the houses. He tidied himself, sounded a rattle on the drum, and walked up to the second house.
>
> He opened the gate, walked over the flags, patted a chintz cat on the head, and opened the house door, and went in.
>
> Thirty seconds later he was out again, without his cap, and that followed flying through the air.
>
> 'Out of it you cheeky besom,' said the woman of the house . . . 'You hikers are all the same . . .'

Rejected by an unfamiliar world, Nellie Jack John goes back into the ground. At the last moment his resolution weakens, for he is 'arfish of the dark', but David gives him his bicycle lamp, and the drumming fades away under Haw Bank.

It is a masterly and touching short-story, and that might have been enough. The emergence of the drummer-boy, however, had started, or been a symptom of, a series of supernatural phenomena. Up on the moor the Jingle Stones begin to move, sending up a bow-wave of turf in their path. A twenty-foot-high giant walks on the moor. In Mr Watson's farmhouse a boggart, a Yorkshire poltergeist, gets to work. All the pigs in the area disappear, and a wild boar makes havoc of Garebridge Market. It is mysterious, a little funny. Then, quite suddenly, it is tragic. Keith and David, out on the moor, are struck by lightning and David vanishes, his body presumably vaporized by the shock. The story moves to its climax in King Arthur's hall deep under the castle rock—the one fantastic episode which fails to convince. The end comes more satisfactorily with Nellie Jack John, reconciled to another age than his own, happily salving sheep for Mr Watson.

This strange story is not less strange but is less confusing than the synopsis. There is an odd inevitability in the sequence of events. Mayne gives actuality to the most improbable episode by relating it to an environment and a society evoked in every detail. Innumerable little touches contribute. After David's disappearance his friend Keith grapples with the man-sized mystery, but he is still just a small boy. Haunted by the strange cold-flamed candle which came out of the hill, he still 'went back to the shops, and bought toffees. His mother was a marvel at jam, but no good at toffee at all'. The famous Mayne style, which in earlier books was so exuberant and uncontrolled, is here unwontedly disciplined. He no longer chases the hares of his private fancies, but devotes the exquisite sentences to furthering his theme. Marvellous, wonderful, haunted by a deep sadness, it is still often a funny story. The boggart of Swang Farm is one of Mayne's most delightful creations. Immediately before the lightning strikes David and Keith there is a charming episode at the farm when the boys have a demonstration of the 'good little fellow's' capacity for mischief, and David discovers that he has a way with boggarts.

> He found a chair nudging him behind the knees, and he sat down. Then he thought a cat had jumped into his lap, but there was nothing there when he looked. . . . 'He likes me,' said David. 'Do you think it'll follow me home?'
> 'Oh,' said Mrs Watson, 'I wouldn't like to see it go, no I wouldn't.'

No wonder the Watsons needed Nellie Jack John's company when the boggart went back to its long sleep under the bedroom floor.

*Drumbeats* (1953) has a theme which might have commended itself to William Mayne, although he would certainly have developed it along lines far different from those favoured by David Severn. David Severn had started his writing career as the author of a series of open-air adventure stories some way after Ransome. From these dangerous channels he had escaped, in a strange, not altogether convincing, story on a 'Time' theme, *Dream Gold* (1949). In *Drumbeats* he followed a similar line of thought with much greater confidence.

*Drumbeats* is set in Dulvercourt, a co-educational progressive school, a place quite unlike the appalling and unbelievable institution over which C. S. Lewis spilled his prejudices in *The Silver Chair*. Dulvercourt is a school founded on sound modern principles, but it is dealing with ordinary human animals, who have to kick over the traces 'even if there aren't any traces'. One of these was Hubert Seligman, a brash and insensitive Dulvercourtian who left in 1931 and joined a scientific expedition to Africa. On this he stole, in his stupid schoolboy way, a sacred drum from an African tribe and sent it home with his scientific specimens. The expedition was lost, and the drum sits in the school museum at Dulvercourt as a memorial to Hubert. One of the pupils is Oliver, a musician who tries out the drum and finds that it has a will of its own, forcing him to beat out complex rhythms which enable him, and the children with him, to have a vision of the African jungle and the doomed expedition. The idea is a familiar one, but Severn gave it an original turn. The fate of the expedition is reflected, in a slightly distorting mirror, in the life of the school. This idea is worked out brilliantly so that suspense, which might have been lost through too precise an application of the theory, is maintained to an exciting conclusion. The principal questions remain unanswered.

Technically the book is of great interest. With a theme of this kind there is a danger of repetitiveness; one journey into the past may, in its mechanics at least, be very much like another. Severn presents each drum-session in a slightly different way, and the final vision is shown only through the reactions of those who experienced it.

The supernatural element in *Drumbeats*, fascinating as it is, would not in itself have sustained a long book, nor would a story about the children of Dulvercourt have been of more than passing interest. It is the combination, the skilful dovetailing of two such improbable partners, which makes the book memorable.

Style, so vital an element in creating the atmosphere in which fantasy can breathe, is not David Severn's strong point. It is the essence of *The River Boy* (1955), a strange and beautiful, fantastic story by Theresa Whistler. Mrs Whistler had worked with Walter de la Mare, and there is something of his mastery in the slow building-up of atmosphere—although Walter de la Mare would have built on stronger foundations and suffused the story with his own warm humour. *The River Boy* is about Nathaniel, a lonely boy who finds his *alter ego* in a boy reflecting his own image in the river. The river boy dives upwards out of the water to join him in the exploration of an idyllic landscape. Their journey is one through childhood, and it ends when Nathaniel meets the sea. He is suddenly afraid of the unknown dangers awaiting him on his voyage and turns to his companion for reassurance. But childhood is over and the river boy has left him. 'To-morrow he had a new journey before him', and he has to make it alone.

The story is told with great beauty. Nathaniel sees his new-found world with bright innocent eyes. The most ordinary things are new to him and evoke a delighted response. When a moorhen scuttles ahead of him, ' "She looks like the district nurse in a hurry", he thought, "with her black stockings" '.

*The River Boy*, closely as it observes the natural world, has something of the quality of a dream. There is a different dream-like feeling in *The Tinsel November* (1963), a hauntingly evocative story by Julia Rhys. Emma, a lonely little girl—psychiatrists would have no difficulty in explaining why so many of the human agents of fantasy are lonely—lives in an old house-turned-office which 'smells of solicitors'. Down the road is Alfredo Minotti, specializing in Italian dishes, and in the kitchen is Guy washing up. Outside in the dark cold lurks a small figure, pathetic rather than frightening. He is looking for Columbina, who disappeared long ago. His name is Arlechino, and he brings with him the fine magic and the comedy and pathos of the Commedia del Arte. Fortunately Aunt Elizabeth, who does the cloakrooms at Lyons Corner House, 'believes a lot of things that other grown-ups don't', and she is a useful collaborator in the quest for the missing members of the marionette troupe.

*Petrouchka* has shown that puppets who have no hearts to break may yet suffer heartache, and the plight of Arlechino and his scattered companions matters greatly, to Emma and Guy and the reader. The 'peculiarly small' people are very real, their elegance beautifully contrasted with the faded charms of Well House. When Arlechino comes to Guy's birthday breakfast—on 5th November of course; it has to be breakfast because of homework and washing-up—it is only fitting that he should drink the Best Sicilian. The brilliance of the marionettes brightens a life for Emma which has previously been shadowed by Mr Povey's moods—Mr Povey is the solicitors' clerk and the ogre of Well House.

Environment plays an important part in *The Tinsel November*. At the heart of the story is Well House with its forgotten escape-route to the church next door. It provides a little world for the marionettes, not always a haven but a place apart with a self-contained community. Many writers of fantasy have found satisfaction in the idea of a little world, either an invented world or a part of the real world cut off from the rest.

One of these worlds is Vogelsang in Margot Benary's *The Wicked Enchantment* (English edition 1956). Vogelsang is a German city. It is not obviously detached from the rest of the world, but through many centuries it has gone its own way, living for the most part contentedly beneath the shadow of the great Gothic cathedral. People from other towns say 'We are all a little touched', but the Vogelsanger madness is of an agreeable kind and the ghosts who haunt the town are mostly 'nice and respectable'. But evil comes to Vogelsang; to be precise, it comes from within the town, from the forgotten vault beneath the cathedral where Earl Owl of Owlhall rests uneasily. (The parallel with Nazi Germany is implicit.)

One of the first to suffer is Anemone who lived happily with her widowed father and her Kerry Blue terrier Winnie-the-Pooh until the household was polluted by a new housekeeper. Ilsebill makes marvellous dumplings, but she and her son Erwin ruin life for Anemone. The fine old household routine of

'Dust under the beds and sunlight in your heart' is replaced by incessant cleaning and polishing and the destruction of every living thing which has found shelter in the house. When Winnie is next on the list for disposal Anemone runs away from a house which is no longer home and takes refuge with Aunt Gundala.

Ilsebill—did Margot Benary, who had been brought up to a heritage of German folk-tales, deliberately choose the name of the fisherman's wife whose self-destructive ambition dominates the greatest of the Grimm tales?—is only one manifestation of the evil abroad in Vogelsang. A new Mayor has been elected—no one knows why—and the Town Hall is in turmoil. Moreover one of the Foolish Virgins has disappeared from the West Front of the cathedral together with her attendant gargoyle. The regime becomes more and more oppressive until the Mayor makes two orders which strike at the heart of Vogelsang's way of life. All birds are to be handed in at the Town Hall, and there are to be no Easter Eggs this year. Aunt Gundala leads a great resistance movement, and in the Battle of the Easter Eggs the Mayor is revealed as Earl Owl of Owlhall, escaped from his tomb, and the councillors turn back into a flock of crows. Best of all, Ilsebill reverts to her ancient role of Foolish Virgin and the repulsive Erwin is reinstated as the most hideous gargoyle on Vogelsang Cathedral.

Margot Benary adopted an appropriately Gothic frame for her story, with an extravagance of style and numerous side-chapels and pinnacles of episode and sub-plot. The book has its share of Teutonic sentimentality too, but the general impression is, like the cathedral, of a unified and harmonious structure. The little world of Vogelsang, in turmoil or at peace, is the true hero of the story.

Clive King created a little world in *Stig of the Dump*. (The book had an unusual bibliographical history, being issued first as a paperback in 1963 and not achieving hard covers until 1965.) Clive King's story is based on a remarkably original idea. The author spent his childhood in a Downland village in Kent where, as is common in the area, there was a chalk-pit near his house. Into this everyone threw unwanted rubbish. Might not someone find the raw material of an environment in the refuse of civilization? Out of this thought sprang Stig, who has survived—who knows how?—from the Stone Age and has made a home in the dump. Barney finds Stig by falling through the roof of his house. Culturally a small boy and a neolithic man are much of an age, and Stig and Barney get on very well without the need for a common language. The boy is understandably fascinated by a domestic economy based on the misuse of household articles; the man welcomes an appreciative and unfussy companion. If Clive King could have left the story there, it would have been the perfect expression of a wonderful idea. But the writer felt the need to provide action and a climax, and when Barney and Stig leave the little world of the pit to take part in the ritual erection of a Great Stone Monument, creative imagination flags and credibility is blown away on the Downland wind.

*Stig of the Dump* was Clive King's first English book. He had previously published two books in America and one of these—*The Town that Went South*—appeared in an English edition in 1969, ten years after its original publication. In this book he combined happily his affection for England with knowledge of the world which his job—he worked for the British Council—had given him. The story concerns another little world, this time the Ancient Town of Rye, lightly disguised—but neither author nor illustrator tries hard—as Ramsly. The hill-top town, complete with Mayor and Corporation, old ladies and shopkeepers, Vicar, policeman and Gargoyle the cat, breaks away from the mainland and drifts out to sea. Gargoyle is the first to discover what has happened and he does not approve. ' "People are always changing things". ' However he and the rest of the population quickly adapt. When H.M.S. *Incredible* attempts to rescue them, Able Seaman Slippers, who hopes to see his words 'It's all right, Puss. The Navy's here!' in headlines, gets a severe bite from Gargoyle, and Operation Noah's Ark is a dismal failure. Only one of the Ramsly Sea Cadets agrees to be rescued; long afterwards when he was an Admiral he 'used to boast that he was the only man in the Navy who'd had a warship sent to his backdoor to ask him to join'.

The breakaway of Ramsly apart, there is no fantasy in this book. It is situation comedy of a high order, written with scrupulous regard for the rules. It ends magnificently. As the town drifts south its inhabitants—or passengers—gradually desert until only Gargoyle is aboard when Ramsly comes to rest at last in the Antarctic pack-ice. Steeple Rock on the maps is an ice-pinnacle encasing the church spire, and here Gargoyle sits. 'It was no place for a cat', and so he joined a polar expedition. 'You probably remember the picture in the newspapers: "First Cat to Reach South Pole".'

Another fantasy without magic, if one excludes the pervasive magic of the creative imagination, is that of Moominland. The supernatural in the Moomin stories—as for example the Ghost called the Horriblest—is treated derisively. Such things may exist but they are not to be treated seriously. Fantasy in Tove Jansson's work consists of the creation of another little world inhabited by creatures whose way of life and emotions have their parallel in the everyday world but whose physical form is roughly animal. The Moomins themselves are a little like hippopotami but not much; they look in fact like Moomins.

*Finn Family Moomintroll*, chronologically the second book, was the first to reach England in 1950. In it Tove Jansson described a Finnish landscape of water and forest and peopled it with a society of creatures some of whom, like Snufkin, are approximately human in form, a few like the Muskrat have their counterpart in the animal kingdom, but most inhabit Moominland exclusively. It is a land where natural hazards abound but where there is always the compensating security of a happy home. After every adventure Moominhouse stands open with the comforting presence of Moominmamma within. In a world of alarming changes she is a constant factor; even when, through a misunderstanding with the Hemulen's hat, Moomintroll becomes the 'King of California'—with all his fat parts turned thin and vice versa—Moominmamma alone sees the essential Moomintroll through this monstrous disguise.

Miss Jansson's instinct is for the episode; indeed some of her very best work—in *Tales from Moominvalley* (1963)—is in short-story form, capturing briefly and unforgettably the essence of such situations as The Case of the Invisible Child. (The child faded away in face of hostility and indifference, but

*From* Moominland Midwinter (*see page 138*)

became visible when angry or amused.) Most of the books are strings of stories, highly amusing and consistent in sustaining the atmosphere of a strange land, but not aspiring to the novel's complex structure or evolutionary narrative. *Comet in Moominland* (1951), however, is a single long adventure story which is given force and direction by an impending disaster. Perhaps the writer's most considerable achievement is *Moominland Midwinter* (1958). Moomins very sensibly sleep out the cold Finnish winter in hibernation. But once, a little past New Year, Moomintroll awakes to a 'new world in which he didn't feel at home'. It is a silent white world, apparently deserted; but Moomintroll in his wanderings finds that others too cannot sleep, including the appalling Little My, and Too-Ticky who thinks about 'things one can't understand'. Too-Ticky hibernates—or fails to hibernate—in Moominpappa's bathing-house. 'In the summer it belonged to a daddy. In winter it belongs to Too-Ticky'. In this strange world of snow—'You think it's white, but at times it looks pink, and another time it's blue. It can be softer than anything, and then again harder than stone. Nothing is certain'—Moomintroll has adventures with new friends and discovers an ancestor. The snow acts as a unifying factor to hold the strange story together.

Tove Jansson's little world consists of hills, valleys, forests and sea; Lucy Boston's is a house and its immediate surroundings. The enclosed magical world of Green Knowe has inspired a series of novels, all of them marvellous although not all concerned with magic.

The case-history of Mrs Boston and Green Knowe has no parallel except that of E. Nesbit and Well Hall. Unlike E. Nesbit, Mrs Boston came to her new home at an age when one is usually thinking of consolidation rather than new ventures. But neither Mrs Boston nor Green Knowe is usual. There can be no doubt that Mrs Boston's home did not merely provide her with a setting for her books; it pushed her whole life in a new direction.

Unlike E. Nesbit who had written, not very well, from childhood, Mrs Boston was not a writer when she moved into her Huntingdonshire manor-house beside the Great Ouse. Her inspiration dates from her discovery that encased within the framework of a dignified Georgian mansion lay an infinitely older house. As she dug the Norman masonry out of its enclosing plaster, she released the stored-up memories of centuries, and these became the raw material for her act. She wrote an adult novel about the house—E. Nesbit did the same in *The Red House*—but she soon found that the children's fantasy provided the best framework for what she had to say.

The first two 'Green Knowe' books are, if you like, ghost stories; at least the children who come shyly and teasingly to play with Tolly have been dead for centuries. The fact is not very important. When Mrs Oldknow tells Tolly, without fuss or preliminary preparation, that Toby, Alexander and Linnet all died in the Great Plague, he is for a moment appalled. 'He felt the world had come to an end.' But Mrs Oldknow in her infinite wisdom quickly puts the tragedy into its perspective. ' "After all," she said, "it sounds very sad to say they all died, but it didn't make so much difference. I except the old grandmother soon found out they were still here" '; and Tolly, listening, watches a marble rolling towards him, picks it up and finds it is warm to his fingers.

Mrs Boston has learnt her craft as she went along. The first books, masterly as they are in atmosphere and in understanding of human values, are loosely constructed. They build up erratically to their climaxes. The writer reached full command of her material in the fourth book, one in which there is, in the strict sense, no fantasy. In *A Stranger at Green Knowe* (1961) the story of the little Chinese boy Ping's strange affinity with Hanno the escaped gorilla—two displaced persons who both find asylum in Green Knowe—is told with great concentration and intensity. There are no loose ends, and the story eases only for momentary relief before driving on to its harshly inevitable conclusion. From this excursion Mrs Boston returned to the magical world in *An Enemy at Green Knowe* (1964). Here the kindly spirits—living and past—of the ancient house are faced, not by fire or flood or wild animals, but by uncompromising evil in the person of Dr Melanie D. Powers of the University of Geneva. Her proper designation is not Melanie Delia Powers but Melusina Demogorgona Phospher, a 'spirit of another sort'. The account of how Dr Powers beseiges Green

Knowe, letting loose some of the Plagues of Egypt on the defenders, is frankly terrifying, prompting some adult readers to wonder to what extent one is justified in scaring children out of their wits. The real terrors of 'An Enemy' are of another kind, and they are outbalanced by the enduring and triumphant goodness of the book. Melanie is defeated, not just by white magic—although this helps—but by the intelligent courage of two small boys, which reduces her from a controller of demonic powers to a crumpled, empty woman who scuttles about aimlessly like a hen.

There is no room for two Mrs Bostons in children's literature; her only peer in the creation of little worlds is Mary Norton whose world is smaller still and, though not less perilous, is threatened not by pure evil but by natural hazard and foolish malice.

Originality is not in itself necessarily an important element in children's books. Most of the basic themes and forms had been devised by the end of the first decade of this century, and writers have, in general, been content to exercise their originality within an existing framework. Only rarely is a writer visited by an entirely new idea. There is nothing new in little people; folk-tales are full of them and Lilliput has appeared in literature many times since Gulliver first landed on its shores. But the idea of a miniature society living alongside and on our own came to Mary Norton out of the blue—or, as she says, out of her childhood memories of a myopic world seen at very close range.

' "There's rules, my lass, and you got to learn" ', says Pod, and what makes *The Borrowers* (1952) outstanding among fantasies is that Mary Norton knows her own rules and abides by them. The harshness in parts of the story, which distressed some readers, comes inevitably from this recognition that an author is responsible for his creation and cannot take short cuts or easy ways out. The Borrowers, as the boy who discovers them sees prophetically, are doomed.

Borrowers live behind the skirting-boards or under the floor, in the nooks and crannies of our civilization. They are responsible for all the daily petty losses which we suffer. When such things as needles and thimbles disappear, they are not lost or stolen, they have been borrowed. Pod, Homily and Arrietty—even their names are borrowed and underwent transformation in the process—are Clocks. They live under the floorboards behind the great grandfather-clock in the hall, within easy reach of the kitchen for food and fuel. Pod is a master-borrower who borrows farther afield for luxuries, visiting—in his young days—the dining-room, 'taking a nut or sweet from every dish, and down by a fold in the table-cloth as the first people came in at the door' and walking on the quilt of the bed where Great Aunt Sophy lies with only Fine Old Pale Madeira for comfort. All the details of life beneath the floor are drawn to scale with consistent accuracy. The Clocks are resourceful and ingenious in turning every unconsidered trifle to account.

Disaster comes because they break the rules. On her first borrowing expedition Arrietty is 'seen' by a small boy who befriends the tiny people and, during a brief golden age, supplies them with all their needs and more. It is magnificent, but it is not borrowing. Pride of possession goes to all their heads, and they overreach themselves. The Borrowers are 'seen' not by kindly boys or drunken old ladies but by the stupidly malicious housekeeper. The exquisite life that they have built up with so much labour is destroyed. And the Borrowers . . .? In a brilliant coda Mary Norton leaves their fate in doubt.

Unfortunately the book was so vastly successful that the writer had to go on with a string of sequels, following the escaping Borrowers into new out-door adventures. There are excellent inventions in these books, and no one would grudge Arrietty's hard-won bliss with the virile and resourceful Spiller, but the original book, with its finely conceived introduction and conclusion, is perfect and needs no appendages. There is no magic in *The Borrowers*. Once the basic thesis is accepted, the book follows its self-imposed rules logically and with no concessions to sentimentality. It may not be strictly a fantasy at all; it certainly possesses in a high degree all the essentials—concept, development, character, environment, social criticism—of the novel.

# CHAPTER EIGHT

# *Open Air*

'In the country the most interesting events occur quite freely,
and they seem to happen to you as much as to anyone else.'

ARTHUR RANSOME INVENTED, or at least gave convincing
and consistent form to, the story of holiday adventure at the
beginning of the Thirties. Seventeen years and a World War
later he wrote his last words on the same subject. The twelfth
of the 'Swallows and Amazons' books, *Great Northern?* summed
up his work most admirably. At the same time, while he continued to refuse most resolutely to be the pioneer of a new kind
of children's book, he foreshadowed some of the development
to come. *Great Northern?* is a watershed-book between two
differing concepts.

The Ransome books are conspicuous among fictional series
for the development of character from book to book. The
children grow steadily, even if their physical growth is not
according to a conventional time-scale. Even allowing for a
winter holiday and a spring or two, John and Nancy would
have been too old to join so uninhibitedly in the adventures of
this voyage of *Sea Bear.* They grow, lucky children, not by the
year but in experience and resourcefulness. There is not more
than a half-dozen physical years between the children of
*Swallows and Amazons* and those of *Great Northern?,* but the
latter are emotionally and practically much more mature.
Physically they are frozen halfway to adulthood, at an age
when adventure needs to have an objective, but when the
sheer animal delight of activity in the open air is still fresh.

Ransome wrote the first books for actual children and he put
them, with an occasional change of sex where necessary, into
the books. By the 1940s these children were grown up and he

no longer used live models. The fictional children had developed an independent life and led their creator along new paths. The first books had been about manufactured adventures. The children might be caught up in the realities of forest fire and sailing and climbing hazards, but basically they were making-believe. Halfway through the series in *We Didn't Mean to Go to Sea*, the adventures became real. In *Great Northern?*, although Dorothea still reads romance into the events of every day and the others continue to invent—sometimes tiresomely —their own derogatory names for the owners of the land on which they play, the essence of the story is not play at all but real earnest.

In 1947 the theme of *Great Northern?* was novel. To many readers it then seemed strange that so much should be made of a piece of ornithological research. Today no one would be surprised that the Ship's Naturalist should go to extraordinary lengths to protect a rare breeding bird and that his friends should support him to their own discomfort and potential danger. Today however there would be no story. Dick, a responsible boy whatever one may think of the others, would call in the R.S.P.B. to maintain 24-hour watches and there would be no need for decoys and red herrings. The idea of the book, if not the execution, is very modern. It is a story about conservation. The methods may be deplorable but the objectives are essentially admirable. It matters greatly that the Great Norther Divers should rear their clutch of eggs on a remote Highland loch, and innumerable readers have echoed Dick's joyful 'Gosh! oh Gosh!' when the stolen eggs are restored, still warm, to their parents.

No one evokes better than Dr Ransome the ecstasy of being free in the open air in wild places. He does it without fuss. There are no detailed landscapes, no paintings of dawn and sunset. The children get on with what they are doing, and the reader shares their deep physical and spiritual satisfaction in their activity and its fulfilment. There is no 'fine writing', only plain, exact words conveying concrete images. One knows precisely what is happening and how it comes about.

There were two valid criticisms of the earlier Ransome books. The more important was that the books showed an incomplete society, one in which children lived apart from the adult world and in which they were seen only on holiday. We know, it is true, what the Amazons were like at home when they became Martyrs, but the mind rejects the thought of them at school. *Great Northern?* does not really answer this criticism. Uncle Jim (Captain Flint) comes into the story more than he did in previous books, but he still has the habit of opting out of responsibility. The other adults are villainous like the Egg-Collector—it is characteristic of the author that he is reluctant to call adults by name—or obtuse like the Highland Chief. The other criticism, which may be an intrusion from the adult world, is that the children are too unbearably competent. One longs for a little human fallibility. In *Great Northern?* Ransome allows them to be beaten at their own game. The Gaels literally run rings around them, giving them an unforgettable lesson in fieldcraft.

Because Ransome's children are so often engaged in serious practical business they may seem to be lacking in humour and normal high spirits. They rarely play the fool, but their enjoyment is always clear. They have a marvellous time and they know it. Their humour springs not from fantasy but from a practical acceptance of the real world. There is an admirable and typical passage in *Great Northern?* when the egg-collector, having failed to cozen Dick into helping him, tries to buy Captain Flint with his 'long narrow cheque-book'. When Captain Flint's fury threatens to choke him,

' "Spit in the water," said Nancy. "You'll feel better".'

From the start Ransome inspired disciples, including two schoolgirls Katharine Hull and Pamela Whitlock who paid the old Master the most sincere of compliments by imitating the very essence of his manner. It was surely Ransome's example too which prompted a flood of family stories and holiday chronicles during and immediately after the war. Of these the 'Crusoe' and 'Warner' stories by David Severn and the sailing adventures devised by Aubrey de Selincourt were the most distinguished. In retrospect one sees the thinness of the invention and the shallow observation which the writers' high spirits at first obscured. Certainly in the hard 'economy-standard' years immediately after the war they seemed to shine like beacons, and so did Virginia Pye and M. E. Atkinson. Both Severn and De Selincourt may in fact have been deflected from their own bent by the attractiveness of the Ransome formula and both found themselves later, the one in remarkable stories of fantasy, the other in historical biography. M. E. Atkinson was in a rather different class. She was perhaps not influenced directly by Ransome so much as by the spirit of the times which, in wartime and war's aftermath, demanded both the security of the family and the luxury of adventure without real danger. Her 'Locketts' were initially one of the best of fictional families, their personalities and their interrelationships convincingly drawn. From the start, however, their desperate quest of adventure was tiresome. The plots were manufactured instead of springing from the consequences of character and environment. The books went on, too, rather too long; the reader tired of the Locketts before the author did. Some of these strictures apply to Virginia Pye's stories, too, but she was sustained by a rich sense of humour.

The best holiday story since Ransome came from a writer who was too old to have come directly under his influence and who, one suspects, served a literary apprenticeship under a greater master, Richard Jefferies. Not that there was anything of the nature mystic about Roland Pertwee; his is the Jefferies of *The Amateur Poacher*. He reinforced his bookish theories with much practical experience. He was no doubt the prototype of Old B in *The Islanders* (1950), who, being now too fat to follow his favourite pursuits, enjoys them vicariously through the activities of three boys. Under his patronage Pat, Toby and Nick have a marvellous desert-island holiday in Devon where, with the help of a generous amount of jetsam such as might come the way of genuine castaways, they live rough, feed the wolves, fight a few battles with savages (gypsies) and generally enjoy themselves immensely and with profit to their characters and their souls.

Like Ransome, Pertwee is interested in how things work. There are no easy short cuts in *The Islanders*. The boys do nothing which is beyond their strength and ingenuity and cunning, granted that they have the few tools so thoughtfully and discreetly provided by Old B. There is, for example, the little matter of the Flying Goat. Having annexed a mobile milk-supply, they are faced with the problem of getting her across the river to their island refuge. Toby rigs up an aerial railway out of rope, wire and an old scooter-wheel. The result Pertwee lets us see through the eyes of Old B and his man-of-all-work Vellaby, concealed on the road above.

> ' "Lo-tammy-I! They little hellers is 'anging she."
> Mr Beckett had his glasses up again and was roaring:
> "I'll have 'em on the night train. I'll have the skin off their backs. I'll . . . Well, look at that."
> It was a surprising spectacle, for suddenly the hanging goat made a swift aerial passage across the river, into the arms of a naked boy.'

When Roland Pertwee came to write *The Islanders* he had a lifetime of working in the theatre behind him. He had no great literary pretensions, but he knew how to express character through dialogue. He establishes the personalities of his three principals quickly and clearly; each represents one facet of the complete out-door boy, and together they make an admirable team. Pat, who had freedom of choice for his companions, had chosen not obviously but well. Pat is the most interesting of the boys. Because he lives with Aunt Avis, who would like to holiday in Switzerland with her friends but who is prepared to stay at a hotel in Eastbourne for the boy's sake, he has had little chance to develop his latent field-craft and has been forced to satisfy himself with books and dreams. Old B's proposal launches him into reality, but he still finds that books and dreams are useful in tackling the problems of the wild. Toby and Nick, future doctor and actor respectively, seem to be neatly drawn types at first, but they too grow with their experiences, discovering unsuspected depths within themselves.

*The Islanders* is unusual among holiday stories in presenting adults who are neither clowns nor boors. There is the Master of Stag Hounds whom some writers would have felt obliged to draw as a noisy fool, but Pertwee, a lover of field sports himself, shows that he can be a good naturalist and a man of human understanding—this much to the confusion of Toby who thinks 'how strange it was that people who you would expect to be hard and cruel . . . could be thoughtful and good-natured'. Even Captain Gerrity, the villain if there is one, is not all black and shows a just-credible right instinct at the end of the trial-scene which makes the splendid climax of the story. What gives this book its unusual distinction is that it breaks its self-imposed bounds. The boys who, begin as desert-island castaways, become part of a complex and interdependent community.

So good a story was bound to have sequels, and these, although adequate, did not advance a reputation made once for all by a remarkable single achievement.

Both Ransome and Pertwee were good naturalists whose books reflected their concern for wild life and its survival in a changing world, although by a familiar irony both were also field-sportsmen dedicated to a ritual destruction of life. Many writers have been concerned to study the relationship between men and animals, a few with the more difficult task of examining animals living for themselves alone.

The fictional animal story proper has always been a minority book. When it is treated seriously it imposes very great demands on both writer and reader, until ultimately, in such a book as *Salar the Salmon*, it becomes utterly authentic and practically unreadable. Few writers have followed Henry Williamson along his chosen track and fewer still have written thus within a child's range. Of these 'BB' (D. J. Watkins-Pitchford) was the most effective, and his best work was done before 1945. Among recent writers Helen Griffiths is closest to this tradition, and hers is work—beyond question of high quality—in which I have been unable to take personal pleasure.

'BB' belonged to the Jefferies/Williamson tradition in developing a philosophy of nature in which man does not regard animals as merely servants or food. For Williamson at least man is almost always the enemy. René Guillot was obsessed with the idea of the spiritual affinity between men and animals. This has its clearest expression—I speak relatively; Guillot was never the clearest of writers—in *Sirga* (1951; English edition 1953). Sirga the lioness and Ulé the

African are born on the same day. Both mothers confidently expected to bear twins; instead man and animal enjoyed a fellowship akin to that of brother and sister. When they were babies they shared the same dish of milk. Whatever the probabilities of the situation, Guillot gives conviction to his invention by the remarkable accuracy and vividness of its detail. Here is Sirga the cub learning to drink out of Ulé's calabash:

> The baby lioness was clumsy. She had been accustomed, while her mother still had milk, to nestle into her fur, clinging with her front paws as she sucked and making a cosy place where her little paws could play in her mother's soft coat. She would have liked to suck now. She was waving her paws about and floundering in the calabash, getting splashed all over with milk.

Guillot excels too in casual, throw-away details which bring a scene vividly to life. Kru (the snake) 'went along like a tape-measure measuring the road, folding and unfolding himself from head to tail.'

If Guillot belongs to any tradition other than his own, he belongs to Kipling's. The seriousness, the respect for animals, the recognition of a law of the wild which governs the society of animals and which the wiser humans recognize, these are the stuff of *The Jungle Book* and of *Sirga* and *Sama* alike. And although Guillot's strange style is his own, there is in it something of Kipling's sententiousness and his incantatory lilt.

Guillot's are essentially stories of the wild. Animals and men live in the jungle and obey its laws. The law embodies grim justice; in *Sama* Oworo the monkey tells with approval the story of the queen who saved her people by throwing her baby daughter to the hippos. A few white men, like Marlow who deals in ivory yet makes a nature reserve, obey the law. In general, however, civilization is evil. 'Even when an animal kills . . . it is innocent . . . Wild beasts and elephants die under man's law. Men are not innocent'. For Sama the elephant civilization means the living death of the circus where animals cling precariously to their dignity. In the ring 'the tigers began to climb on their stools as usual, full of contempt, with an air both nonchalant and noble, like lords in slavery'.

Rutherford Montgomery is neither as passionate nor as provocative as Guillot. His books belong to the tradition of Jack London and James Oliver Curwood and, like them, he writes of the northern forests of America. In *Mister Jim* (1952) his hero is a grizzly bear of the Rockies. Mister Jim is a character. He has, if not a sense of humour, certainly a sense of fun. He combines great strength with a rather endearing incompetence; he is a hunter of only average ability. We should enjoy getting to know him and watching him about his endless business of eating. 'Mister Jim picked the cricket off the ground, holding it between the points of two of his claws like an oriental using chop-sticks.' Observation as keen and precise as this is admirable, but it does not make a novel. What makes the story is that Mister Jim is only partly a creature of the wilds. As a cub he had been brought up by Two Grey Hills the Indian hunter, and the experience made him at least one-part human. His animal reactions are instinctive, not rational, but they are conditioned by a loyalty not less genuine for being based on smell. In the course of the action Mister Jim's life is saved by the Indian and he repays the debt in an unexpected but quite acceptable way.

Rutherford Montgomery is romancer and naturalist in almost equal proportions. Only incidentally is he critic or philosopher. Content to tell a good tale and describe as truly as he can a way of life which he knows intimately, he is not concerned with analysis and interpretation. His books lack the critical quality which distinguish the novel from the romance.

Clearly there are limitations on the animal story which inevitably mean that it can rarely become a novel. Novels are essentially about people in a society. Animals certainly live in societies and some of them have, in human terms, identifiable personalities, but not many humans will know them intimately enough to interpret their lives and passions in terms which give the complexity of the novel's conflict and at the same time are true to zoological fact. The novelist, if he is concerned with animals, is likely to examine them not in isolation but in their relations with humans.

Richard Church is a poet who drew much of his material from the natural world. Like so many cockneys he was highly sensitive to landscape, the seasons' change and the tightly woven tapestry of nature. He loves and knows animals, but he sees them as a part of an interdependent society in which man has a central position. His novel *The White Doe* (1968) is not really about the doe, although she has an important symbolic role to fill; it is about a country estate in the old days and about human and animal relationships.

Tom, the woodman's son, and Billy, whose father is the squire, have been friends from childhood. They have taken the friendship almost for granted, but the arrival of a rich town boy threatens to sour the relationship by destroying its spontaneity and disregard of class. Harold does not consort with 'yokels'. The curious triangle maintained by Billy, who believes in the need to be 'civil', is balanced precariously, and Tom is constantly knocking it awry by his anger and Harold by his contempt. Then a fourth party appears, Harold's half-sister who, while she stands aloof from the main conflict, is not as tolerant as Billy. The story, it will be seen, is one about people, about friendship and hatred and love. The drama is played out against the background of the forest, in which the doe and her white fawn wander, to appear to Tom like a vision of serene beauty at crises in his painful year.

Richard Church, as one would expect, draws his nature pictures beautifully and with conscious craftsmanship. The novel is tightly constructed, so that action, character and setting march together. Ultimately, however, it is character which matters most. Even the objectionable Harold is an interesting study. Margaret, who has suffered from his malice more than most, explains his dilemma in a single sentence: ' "Father is always at a board meeting." '

This, it might be argued, is, apart from the ages of the principals, not specially a novel for young children. An earlier country novel by Richard Church is. *Dog Toby* (1963) is almost, if the phrase does not seem derogatory, tailor-made. The scene is an Iron Curtain country recently subjected to what the author, rather coyly, calls 'a new kind of Government'. It might have been better to take the reader into his confidence and to describe an identified scene and political situation. Politics play a necessarily important part in the plot, not always convincingly. Modern readers are less accustomed

*From* The White Doe (*see opposite page*)

than previous generations to easy solutions, and they do not readily accept that an international incident can be averted by three children and a dog. If the mechanics of the plot belong to a departed and largely discredited tradition however, the rest of the book has firmer foundations. The memorable holiday which Maria, Jan and the pathetic orphan Fritz spend with Dog Toby beyond the barbed-wire of the frontier provides them with experiences which develop their observation and their human understanding. It is not the adventure, the desperate game of hide-and-seek which the children play in the railway tunnel, which one remembers, but keenly observed and eloquently described glimpses of a nature which goes about its business of life and death in total disregard of political manoeuvring. In *Dog Toby* animals are represented by the praying mantis, which ignored the close watching humans in its still battle with a soldier beetle, even though Maria's nose was almost touching it, and by Toby, most of whose life is filled with Fritz. The mantis acts in the same way whether there are human intruders or not; the dog and the boy are each diminished by the absence of the other.

This dependence of man on animal and animal on man is the most interesting feature of that strange literary phenomenon, the pony story. The convention was formulated in the early Thirties and remained almost unchanged. Some writers might do better than others, but all accepted the formula because it was successful and there seemed no alternative. When the pony book was almost dead, killed by sheer exhaustion of possibilities and also, perhaps, by affluence—for children who have a pony hardly need the vicarious experiences offered by pony stories—a talented writer whose reputation had been made in other fields gave the ailing beast a sharp twist of the tail. Kathleen Peyton's *Fly-by-Night* (1968) may prove to be the very last of the pony books. It is certainly one of the best.

Pony stories were from the beginning middle-class. Young riders owned their ponies by unchallenged right; there was no vulgar show of money, and Pony Club subscriptions were paid by some unseen and disembodied daddy. Kathleen Peyton made her pony book into a social novel. The Hollises are middle-class, just about, and their lives are dominated by the need for money to pay the electricity and the mortgage. Ruth buys a pony out of her savings. This is utter folly, especially as she has no reserve for tack and feed. And where in a lower middle-class semi-rural suburban house do you keep a horse? Mrs Peyton faces the problems evoked by this situation with unfailing realism and great good-humour. Ruth has a terrible time, lightened by friendship and by an increasing strength of character. Here is a very ordinary girl, not at first particularly nice or intelligent, who gets through a difficult phase of life by her 'implacable will'. It is an appealing story, to be enjoyed by readers who, far from being conversant with the grim technicalities of riding, cannot with certainty distinguish one end of a horse from the other. There is much satisfaction when Ruth survives her ordeals. It would be an exaggeration to say that she triumphs; at least the white rosette which she gains at the local pony club meeting, while the most that probability would allow her, is the least that justice demands for someone so persistently mulish in pursuit of her ends.

*Fly-by-Night*, although undeniably about a pony, is only marginally a pony-book. Bigger issues, personal and social, keep breaking in. When Mrs Peyton turned again to examine the fortunes of her young heroine, ponies quickly disappeared and she wrote a serious social novel.

The Essex setting of *Fly-by-Night* is neither town nor country, but the country is not far away, offering opportunities for adventure and self-discovery different from those of the city. This is not the country of prepetually holidaying Ransome children, but an environment existing in its own right where people work and love and play because they live there. It can have different meanings, the same coastal levels of Essex being—in Mrs Peyton's *The Plan for Birdsmarsh* (1965)—Paul's 'territory' and Gus's 'nothingness'. It is the country of Elinor Lyon's Scottish adventures, in which children almost as enterprising and resourceful as Ransome's find excitement and satisfaction on their own doorsteps. It is a full, free life even when domestic responsibilities make their demand. Sovra and Ian and their friend Cathie camp and play in delectable surroundings, but they are a part of real life, not detached from it. In *Carver's Journey* (1962) their youth and freedom are the foils to Mr Brown, a drab ugly old man who drifts inexplicably into the Highlands pushing a handcart loaded with his few worldly goods. He may seem the least probable agent of adventure, but Mr Brown is a man with hidden talents. For one thing he is a carver, who engraves enigmatic patterns on stone in the idiom of the Celtic Dark Ages and then hides them behind waterfalls. A trail of these strange works of art marks his journey across Scotland in search of a 'bay far out to the West, where the white beach is ringed round by walls of rock'. The coast which fulfils these conditions is near Lochhead where Cathie lives at Kindrachill House with her guardian the young laird, and here in due course Mr Brown finds a refuge for his retirement and forgets to worry about his ugliness.

Miss Lyon's books have a modest objective but they are marked always by excellent craftsmanship, sincerity and an unsentimental regard for scenery and people. Her children are drawn neatly and with enough subtlety to hold the interest. She is rare among writers for children in her examination of the relationships between adults and children, and rarer still in being fair to both parties. Even the terrible Petts who blunder into this western Eden are not caricatured. Mrs Pett is a broadcaster, and she and her husband make a profession of being keen about things. 'They get excited over birds and seaweed and sheep ticks and practically anything else you can think of.' Sovra optimistically thinks that 'people who are interested in things are usually nicer than people who aren't,' but the Petts's passion does not extend to human relationships. They are fascinated by people as a species but not as individual beings. Their insensitivity brings them into head-on collision with the children who, unlike the grown-ups, have bothered to penetrate Mr Brown's mystery and take up his cause with joyful enthusiasm. To preserve his secret and his integrity they ensure even the dreadful punishment of confinement to quarters; for two long sunny days they clean and darn and chop wood or moon about indoors gazing out at the sunlit hills. These are delightful children, more generous and honest than most perhaps, but it is the writer's perogative to present in acceptable form the values which she believes in. They are certainly not paragons. In *Carver's Journey* Ian makes his first appearance in defence of Mr Brown, who is being hustled by a gang of roughs, and takes on the whole pack of them; his sister helps by hitting the largest of them with a wet, dead mackerel. (By a satisfactory irony the boy lives in the hotel for whose kitchen the fish was destined.) Deeply sunburnt and barefoot, they stride confidently into adventure.

The children in Sheena Porter's novels, too, occupy a part of the everyday world of work and school and grown-ups. Her model was not Ransome but William Mayne; she shares his feeling for landscape and for the byways of human relationships although she lacks both his virtuosity and his indiscipline. Her books are largely novels of character, but her concern with setting is so strong that it seems appropriate to consider some of them here. The scene is nearly always the principal actor in her dramas. Miss Porter's home ground is the remote high country of the Welsh Marches. It is a beautiful country, rich in natural interest and haunted by the memories of a violent past. It is this last which lies at the heart of her finest book, *Nordy Bank*, but this has wider implications which demand examination elsewhere. The past lies across the Long Mynd which is the scene of *The Knockers* (1965). Three memories are built into the fabric of the story. First there is Wild Edric, the Hereward of Shropshire, who waged guerilla warfare for a time after the Conquest and then inexplicably surrendered. The story of the Vicar of Woolstaston, who crossed the Mynd in a blizzard to preach at Ratlinghope is less dramatic but closer to everyday experience. Then there is the memory of the lead-miners who worked the valleys of the Mynd for centuries. These three threads are woven skilfully into the story without detracting from its main theme, which is the reactions of a group of ill-assorted children to one another, their parents and their environment. Miss Porter's skills are workaday, for the most part, and certainly workmanlike. Just once in a while she sounds a deeper note. There is a splendid moment at the end of *The Knockers*. The story has been played out. Wild Edric rides no more over the Mynd in his fancy dress, and the Knockers who haunt the valley are after all only paleontologists researching for the British

Museum. The children watch these amiable and scholarly young men packing up and see them off on their journey back to London. In their last farewell they reveal that they were never in the valley where, in the first moments of the story, the knocking had been heard. A last satisfactory knot ties up the story, but the mystery is open-ended.

> ' "So where does that leave you?" said Stephen Gill.
> "Where we were at the beginning," said Kathy softly.
> "Not knowing." '

There are no supernatural mysteries in *Deerfold* (1966) and no spirits of the past. It is a modern story of border Wales and of a meeting of cultures. The Murrays move from Leicestershire to take over the Youth Hostel at Cwmdella Hall. The silent, empty forest country is strange to them and they shudder at the imagined squalor of the cottages and the Welsh-speaking natives—'little dark people . . . rushing about with huge harps, daffodils in their buttonholes, leeks in their hair, singing arias.' Their neighbour is nothing like this fantasy, for Megan is beautiful, making Hannah Murray feel 'pink and spotty, and as madly freckled as a mistle thrush'. The growing friendship of English and Welsh is jeopardized by a stupid misunderstanding born of Hannah's snobbishness and Megan's defensiveness. For the rest, the action of the story turns on deer-poaching. The plot is well-managed—arguably Miss Porter's best—with the tension controlled throughout. Ultimately however it is not the plot that matters, or even the human story, but Deerfold Forest and its deer. At each stage of the story the writer turns from the greed and the trivialities of men's lives to look again at the deer drifting silently across the shadows between the 'silvered trees'.

In her first books Miss Porter, like most beginners, indulged herself in set pieces of descriptive writing. By the time she came to write *Deerfold* she was a fully mature writer. She still enjoyed description, not for its own beautiful sake but as a structurally essential part of the fabric of the book. At the end of the story, the poachers caught, social justice on the way, friendships cemented by shared anxieties, Miss Porter turns for a last look at the forest in its end-of-summer dress. It would be school next week, hockey and carols, but in Deerfold 'among the level ridgeways of the hills flared the still sunset of a frost.'

Sheena Porter, one might guess, is an amateur country-woman. Her reactions have the fine enthusiasm of the convert. Monica Edwards is the complete professional; one has to look beyond the words of her well-spun tales to uncover a deep satisfaction, so strong and confident that the author no longer feels a need to express it. A prolific writer, Miss Edwards is not always at her best. The time snatched from a busy working life on Punchbowl Farm is not enough to allow each story to be deeply pondered. Many of the plots are contrived. The characters often lack depth. In writing so many books, too, Miss Edwards fails to rise to a peak; all the stories are readable, few are memorable. One may have favourites among them, but one would hesitate to nominate any one as the best. The ultimate impression is a general one, of children leading sensible, useful and happy lives under the shadow of Gibbet Hill or around the Marshland parsonage.

In her historical stories Hester Burton takes the action as quickly as she can into the East Anglian landscape of her own childhood. Her first novel was not historical; at least it dealt with very recent events. *The Great Gale* (1960) was about Norfolk in the floods of 1953. Hester Burton looked at the cataclysm through its effects on a small village community living beside broad and sea.

Reedsmere was flooded in the winter of 1953 because Mark Vaughan, the doctor's son, for a dare, rode a cow. She was so upset by this experience that the normal rhythm of her life was disturbed and she went off for a walk on the Marram Hills. Her sharp hooves cut into the sandbags at the gap and their precious contents blew away along the beach.

Mrs Burton sets the scene beautifully, with scarcely a word of description. Reedsmere is people. She shows us Mark's sister Mary who can spit right over the vicar's garden wall, and her friend Myrtle, a capable little girl whose mother keeps the Post Office. Old Mr Clatworthy cossets his canary. Jim Foulgar, who shot away his hand while out poaching, scavenges for coal on the beach to keep his crippled wife Hepzie warm. Canon Crowfoot prepares his Candlemas sermon. Reedsmere is a real community without false divisions between young and old, rich and poor.

Natural disasters seldom follow the tidy construction of art, and Mrs Burton's narrative, admirably as it deals with each episode, lacks a satisfactory flow of climax and resolution. This need not be blamed entirely on the flood; her later work revealed that structure is not Mrs Burton's strong point. In this context it does not much matter. *The Great Gale* is not a novel so much as a chronicle told in terms of human beings, and it bears throughout the quality of absolute authenticity.

*The Grange at High Force* (1965) is as far from *The Great Gale* as the northern moors are from the Broads. What they have in common is a feeling for community and accuracy in the port-rayal of real people. (It is to be regretted that the illustrating of this charming book went to Papas; he is a brilliant comic artist but essentially a caricaturist, and the characters, although highly amusing, are not the figures of fun whom he draws.)

There are no absolute taboos in children's literature; what-ever subject is made interesting to children will interest them. *The Grange at High Force* is about bikes and boats, gunpowder, Norman architecture, eighteenth-century social history, birds, ballistics. It is an unpromising hotchpotch but it works. As Peter, who is, in Old Charlie the verger's words, 'Rector's youngest devil' and no prig, sums up the situation: ' "There's a church to restore. There's a mystery about a statue to solve. There's a mill-wheel to build. There's a ballista to test. And with a bit of luck, there's a cannon to fire. Smashing." '

*The Grange at High Force* is a very funny story. It is also entirely serious. There is nothing false in its incongruous juxta-position of moments of high seriousness and knockabout clowning; they are all part of a seriously comic philosophy. The author, Philip Turner, is a parson and a lover of God's Little Jester, St Francis. It is not chance which decides that Little St Mary's, a small masterpiece of a 'redundant' church, should become a Franciscan chapel. Turner makes it seem perfectly natural that three high-spirited small boys and a retired admiral and his tough servant should dedicate much time and energy to cleaning and restoring a derelict church and, when the work is done, sing evensong in it with unselfconscious reverence. It is equally natural that they should give the same attention to firing a pair of eighteenth-century naval cannon, rescuing sheep in a blizzard, and saving a half-demented old lady from starvation and freezing. All these things are a part of the absorbing business of living.

Turner's boys go to school in the industrial town of Darnley Mills, and the wide views from High Force Moor look down on the traffic of the Great North Road. The English novelist looks in vain for wild country into which he may put his characters. The best open-air stories have come recently, naturally enough, from the broader acres of Australia, where there is still room to grow. Badge, in Nan Chauncy's stories of the Tasmanian wilds, lives far out of sound of the city and has Tasmanian devils for company, and he acquires by experience and observation the philosophy of tolerance which industrial society has lost. As Badge explains to Bron, the town girl, in *Devils Hill* (1958):

> ' "We was devils to them, Bron. They was here first see? Minding their own business they was when we come along. Aw, I reckon they thought us devils." '

The scene is less wild in Joan Phipson's stories of New South Wales, but her children too learn self-reliance on a poor rabbit-infested farm where existence itself may be jeopardized by disease among the flock or by sickness in the family. *The Family Conspiracy* (1962) deals with lively invention and humour with the realities of poverty which face the Barkers when their mother, without benefit of National Health, has to undergo an operation.

H. F. Brinsmead's view is wider. Her interest and sympathy embrace the whole spectrum of Australia, urban and rural. Her first book, *Pastures of the Blue Crane* (1964), is mostly a country book, however, and one which shows the formative influence of landscape and a free life in the open upon an unhappy, neglected girl.

Ryl has just become an orphan. The idea is not as great a shock as it would be to most, because her father had handed her over to the care of lawyers thirteen years before and of her mother she knew nothing at all. No wonder she had grown armour! 'She seemed never to have been a child.' Then in one day she learns that her father is dead and that she has a grandfather. Grandfather is David Merewether—'Dusty to his friends'—a down-and-out old gentleman. The two are joint beneficiaries of the deceased's will, which brings to them an estate in Murwillumbah. The farm is run down and the house is a 'crazy wreck'. The ill-assorted couple make a success of life together against their own expectations and all the odds. Mrs Brinsmead shows with exquisite sensibility how a girl who has had everything in life except affection grows in contact with real problems. Dusty grows too, and at the same time clings to his old obstinacy and freedom. Both of them characteristically fight the change of their own natures with all their cussedness and strength, and out of the losing battle gain a different kind of strength and wisdom.

No writer today knows more than Mrs Brinsmead about the workings of an adolescent girl's mind; certainly no one expounds her theme with greater affection, but it is an affection free of illusions. Ryl is no saint and she doesn't become one. Her prickles are slowly blunted, but she is slow to lose inbuilt prejudices. That she manages to outgrow her appalling upbringing so well and so quickly is due to Dusty and to the friendly relaxed society of Murwillumbah which takes her without fuss for what she is. A great deal of the credit goes to the farm and its setting among the great hills and to the blue crane which greets her on her first morning. The 'fanciful bird, long-legged, grave and contemplative', returns to her at intervals in the story, and becomes a symbol of her new life and its promise.

# CHAPTER NINE

# School—Home—Family

'We are the Bastables.'

THE SCHOOL STORY PROPER, that is one which does not look beyond the small, enclosed world of school, is dead. It died many years ago of exhaustion and social change. It was necessarily concerned with boarding-school. Directly the little victims escaped home they became different beings. Writers, no longer drawn largely from the ranks of the public schools, were concerned with the everyday scene and with the experience of the majority of their readers. The complex pattern of school, home and the streets and fields offered wider opportunities than those afforded by classroom and dorm. Indeed, even without a social revolution the school story was doomed from within. The possible variations of school, playing-field, bullies, friendship, were arithmetically predictable, and they had been used up.

Though dead, the conventional school story did not readily lie down. An attempt to re-animate the grotesque corpse of Bunter was not altogether successful. It was of sentimental interest to those of middle age whose childhoods, like mine, had been dominated by his gross bulk, but children were not for the most part greatly amused by the hallowed rites of Greyfriars. They liked Jennings better than Bunter; he was less exaggerated and he spoke a language nearer their own. Anthony Buckeridge, surely with his tongue in his cheek, squeezed the last drop of fun out of the prep-school situation, and the results, rather better on radio than on the printed page, were diverting. They were less well adapted to the conventions of television, which is happier with the broad caricature of Bunter than the thinner—in every sense—humour of

Jennings. No writer showed very much enthusiasm for following Buckeridge along his chosen path.

A few looked at the possibilities of the day school. A. Stephen Tring (Laurence Meynell) and Geoffrey Trease were seriously concerned to make something of this. Predictably, Tring was more successful with girls' than boys' schools. His Barry (*Barry's Exciting Year*, 1951) is a nice ordinary boy whose good intentions towards the scholarship exam (Tring had not caught up with the 1944 Act) are at odds with his enthusiasm for cricket and games with the boys. Tring stuck valiantly to the rules, but the very truthfulness of his portrait told against him. Barry is a little too much like the everyday boy to be interesting. Penny is better. In a long series of books Tring followed the fortunes of Penny Andrews, a young woman of personality and character. Mr Andrews's breakfast reading alone is evidence that these are Top People, and the snobbishness in the hearts of most small girls ensured for Penny a sufficiency of readers throughout the long series.

Geoffrey Trease approached the question of the day school from a different position and in a different topographical setting. In a number of 'Black Banner' stories he looked at a group of young people of both sexes in a country community of the North-West (*No Boats on Bannermere*, 1954). These are honestly observed and based on sound principles, although a little dull; the scene, however, quickly moved away from school with its limited canvas. The same is true of Trease's later and slighter books about 'Maythorn'.

By far the most successful presentation of the everyday life of school was made by a distinguished teacher, Mary K. Harris. All her books are marked by complete integrity, although sometimes—in *Emily and the Headmistress* (1958) for example—there was some doubt for what kind of audience the story was intended. Her understanding of young children was profound, but few children of the appropriate age would have the technical skill to read about themselves in such close detail. This reservation does not apply to *The Bus Girls* (1965), a book which has all of Miss Harris's wisdom and insight but which has a direct appeal to young readers. Poor Hetty has been ill. Her impecunious mother—there is no father—cossets

her unbearably. It is humiliating to go to a new school hedged
about with fuss about health, embarrassing to have to endure
the parson's daughter as compulsory escort on the bus. But
Davina is not a conventional 'mother' to the new girl. She is a
terrible child, mannerless, irresponsible, aggressive. She is also,
as Hetty gradually comes to realize, vulnerable and fundamentally pathetic. The drawing of children and staff, and even that
of the awful parents, is brilliantly done.

Mary Harris was an indifferent creator of plots, but no one
was more skilful in evoking the commonplace and making it
fascinating. She was always ruthlessly truthful. In *The Bus
Girls* she was also gay and lively. Children and teachers alike
see the accuracy, as well as the appeal, of Davina's character,
and both would join her proposed Society for the Abolition of
Parents Nosing about in Schools.

Although assembly-line stories of girls at boarding-school
kept alive the tradition of Angela Brazil through and beyond
two world wars, one might have been justified in the belief that
there was no further room for creative writing in this genre.
Happily genius is not predictable. Antonia Forest, using the
old outmoded framework, wrote a school-story of outstanding
and individual brilliance in 1948. She continued the story of
*Autumn Term* in *End of Term* eleven years later. It was an
astonishingly long gap, especially as she picks up the story of
the Marlows at Kingscote School only a year later. If the
characters have matured by only a year in the second book the
writer had made good use of the interval, and there is a greater
depth of understanding and only a small diminution of liveliness in *End of Term*.

The Marlows are among the most convincing of fictional
families (their creator liked them so much that she even
hunted them back to their origins in Shakespeare's England).
The twins Nick and Lawrie—Lawrence really, because a boy
was expected and 'they'd got it all saved up'—are late in going
to school. 'Every time we started we always caught something'.
They are twelve, and the older Marlows are already high in the
councils of the school; Karen indeed is head girl. It is hard on
these lofty personages to have two erratic infants associated
with them, especially when Nicola pulls the communication

cord even before they get to school (she had dropped her knife with sixteen blades out of the corridor window, and she was always a girl of swift reactions).

Fictional twins are notoriously cute, and Nick and Lawrie, admirably contrasted as they are—although physically identical they are temperamentally complementary, making one exceptional human being between them—would have become tedious but for Miss Forest's skill in setting them in their environment. The story is made, indeed, by contrasting them with Tim—Thalia to the teachers—who has the misfortune to be the Head's niece. Tim is a girl of enterprise and character. As Janice, a sixth former says,

> 'I can foresee the most frightful things happening when that Tim child is head girl. Nothing will ever go wrong, exactly, but everything will be hideously unexpected. Ices instead of bread-and-butter and buns for match teas and a box of cigarettes on Keith's table in Hall instead of our decorous little vase of flowers.'

In one glorious term the children had 'set a fashion for Third Removes full of brilliant eccentrics.' Incredibly they won the prize for Form Tidiness.

*Autumn Term* is mainly a happy story. *End of Term* is often sad—Lawrie sheds tears by the bucketfull—and ends seriously. If it has a fault, it repeats rather obviously the formulae of the earlier book. Nick once again gets out of the train on the way to school, this time to capture her pet merlin; and the climax is again a dramatic production. The action moves well, however, and the examination of character is much more profound. The interest is shared over a larger number of girls, including Esther, a child of divorced parents, and Miranda who is a Jewess. Miss Forest has always been concerned with social and moral issues and she tackles the problems of broken homes and anti-semitism sincerely, and always from the point of view of the children. There is a delightful and convincing discussion arising from the Christmas play in which Miranda points out that the original actors were all Jews, to Lawrie's angry bewilderment. She thought they were Christians. After Ironsides (Miss Cromwell of course) had given a long and explicit explanation Lawrie 'saw what she meant, of course. But naturally, it couldn't be true. *Obviously* they'd been Christians. Stands to reason.'

One test of a school story is the treatment of the staff. They are a curious lot at Kingscote. 'Me Auntie', that is Miss Keith the head, has established the odd tradition that parts in school plays and places in school teams are allotted on moral grounds, not on ability. As Tim says, 'Me Auntie's very pertikler what types she lets into her Heavenly Choirs.' On the same principle, Marie Dobson has a place in the netball team because she lacks self-confidence, and Nick, who is the best player, is left out because of a 'rooted conviction that no one can ask anything better of life than to be Nicola Marlow'. What, one might think, a way to run a school!

There is a little of Kingscote in Elfrida Vipont's Heryot. Both are schools where moral values matter. The difference is that Miss Forest is agnostic. She stands back and lets her characters make up their own minds. In the middle of a magnificent and moving description of the Christmas play, Patrick, one of the audience, says to Rowan Marlow

' "D'you mind my asking? Is this something you believe . . ."
"It depends," said Rowan after a pause. "I mean—what I mean is—for quite long stretches I do, and then for quite long stretches I don't. It just depends."
"Which way are you now?"
"Not." '

Miss Vipont might find it difficult to give such words to an admired character. She lacks Antonia Forest's relaxed affection for her creations. She is fiercely partizan, and the reader has to be too. There is no room for half-measures in her work. Fortunately the reader has no difficulty in surrendering totally to Miss Vipont's persuasion. No other modern children's books are so successful in involving the reader's sympathies.

In her first book Miss Vipont managed to combine passion with freshness. *The Lark in the Morn* (1948) is about the emergence of a young girl out of her Ugly Duckling down, and it has a suitably youthful zest to leaven the underlying earnestness. (It was, I think, Geoffrey Trease, who pointed out that here was a new kind of school story with a symbolic title; an earlier writer would not have resisted calling it 'The Lark in the Dorm'.) But this story of Kit Haverard is so inextricably one with its sequel that the two must be considered together later. It was characteristic of Miss Vipont that, not content with deep involvement with Kit, she should pursue the fortunes of the Kitsons and Haverards through another generation. *The Spring of the Year* (1957) has much in common with *The Lark in the Morn*. Both are about a child's self-discovery, and both demanded and got sequels. In nine years Miss Vipont had learnt more about her craft, and the later book, although certainly not 'better', is the more mature and considered work. It is still an emotional book, but it plays more delicately with the reader's sensibilities.

The central character of *The Spring of the Year* is Laura Haverard, youngest daughter of that elder brother of Kit's whose wedding is a high-spot in the earlier book. The Haverards move from Oxford, where father is a don, to the North and they come to the old village of St Marlyon. This place has something in common with the reality of Cartmel, with a great priory church in the centre. It seems to have something to offer all the family, and they embrace their new life with initial enthusiasm. As the Rector says ' "He bringeth them into the haven where they would be." '

Professor Haverard, with a fine democratic gesture, sends his two youngest children to the village school. Miss Vipont is fond of drawing obtuse and imperceptive fathers, and it is largely father's fault that Laura rides for a fall. She crashes her way through the 11-plus examination, scornful of its simplicity. Naturally she fails and is condemned to the limbo of the secondary modern school. Mother is kind about it, but 'Richard Haverard did not know what to say to a daughter who could not pass examinations.' Fortunately the head of the secondary school is a woman of character who, although not without suffering, demolishes Laura's prejudices.

*The Spring of the Year* suffers some of the disabilities of the topical story. The battle for the secondary modern school is over and forgotten now, and a modern child would wonder what all the fuss is about. What still makes the book admirable and wholly readable is not educational theory but human understanding. Miss Vipont explores her not very likeable heroine with tender affection and shows how she gradually comes to terms with reality. As with the story of Kit, there was not room for the whole of Laura in one book and there had to be a sequel in which she ventured into the world beyond school.

Miss Vipont believes profoundly in having life abundantly, and there is much more to her books than school. For something more nearly resembling the traditional school story one turns, ironically, to that arch destroyer of the traditions of children's literature, William Mayne. William Mayne made a tentative début with two stories which gave little indication, other than a wayward brilliance of style, of what was to come. He emerged abruptly as a writer of the first rank with *A Swarm in May* (1955), of all things a boys' school story and a story of boarding-school at that.

As a boy Mayne had been a chorister of Canterbury Cathedral and later he taught in the choir school there. Of all schools choir schools are the strangest. Most schools exist, broadly speaking, to teach the children. The choir school has a different function. As Mr Ardent, that wisest and most unconventional of headmasters, says to the small singing-boy Owen, 'Your first responsibility whilst you are here is to the Cathedral and its services'. Because of this duty the schools have a strange and complicated time-table. They speak their own language, one coming partly from the technicalities of the cathedral, partly from the remote past, for these are among the oldest of all schools with traditions derived from monastic times. The boys are as lively and thoughtless as their contemporaries in more orthodox establishments, but in their cathedral work they are all professionals. This paradox produces some delightful surprises. The head boy of Mayne's school, Trevithic, maintains discipline and discusses music on equal terms with the organist; still, when they go to the seaside for a half-day, he buries Mr Ardent up to the neck in the sand, 'smoothed the mound over and decorated it with pebbles'. The reader is constantly being surprised by the contrasts of dedicated professionalism and childish high spirits. As they have to

leave when their voices break they are all, even Trevithic and
Madington who does extra French and Latin from choice, very
young.

(In a later choir-school story *Words and Music* Mayne has a
boy who takes his teddy-bear to bed with him. It seems an
improbable detail. Shortly after I had read this book, my law-
ful occasions took me to Canterbury Choir School and the
headmaster—not Mr Ardent—kindly showed me round the
ancient building. In one of the dormitories a teddy-bear lay on
the counterpane.)

To the normal pattern of class room and playing-field the
choir school stories add another and an unusual thread, that of
the cathedral. At no stage in their day are the boys unaware of
the great building in which they serve, immeasurably old, full
of deep traditions, controlling the destinies of a complex
society. The viewpoint is always at boy-height. Bishop and
Dean are great figures, but their contacts with the boys are
rarely more than formal. For the children lesser figures in the
hierarchy loom large. Dr Sunderland the organist (Tweedle-
dum) 'mphs' his way through life, 'running out of breath on
words that didn't matter', a 'puffed gorilla' of a man who is
'always glad to see everybody' and who plays the fool in the
organ-loft with immaculate musicianship. Turle the verger
(Tweedledee—he is Dr Sunderland's next-door neighbour in
the Precincts) hides his geniality behind a scowl and a bark and
quotes the psalm of the day to some purpose. The Pargales,
several generations of them, care for the fabric with a proprietory zeal. ' "We've nussed her up from being no more than
a chapel", eldest Pargale would say.' Mayne's view of the
cathedral and its servants is humorous, but one is left in no
doubt about his fundamental seriousness. The portrait is
deeply affectionate and quite free of the grotesque.

Mayne followed the choir school through four books, each of
which examines the school through the fortunes—more often
the misfortunes—of a different boy. The plots are marvellous
as only Mayne's can be. In *A Swarm in May* he invents a
treasure-hunt story so fresh that one might think this an
entirely new genre. This is no reanimation of old bones but a
new creation. The characterization is brilliant, too, down to the

thumbnail sketch of the least figure, singing-boy or cathedral lady. Above all, and as always in Mayne, there is the style. He is incapable of dull or lax writing, but in these early books he was fully master of his medium, not yet tempted to let words and fancies take him down misleading byways. To show Mayne at his best there is the passage in *A Swarm in May* in which Owen unwillingly takes Dr Sunderland's bee-swarm and comforts them with cold water and song. Too long for quotation, it is a beautifully controlled piece of writing and entirely relevant to the story. More in Mayne's typical vein are the many descriptions of music, with Dr Sunderland cooing 'like the soul of a turtle-dove' and inserting 'Baa, baa, black sheep' into Psalm 68, or the superb conclusion of the book when the organ

> 'carried his voyage out of these dangers, into the smooth trade winds, and by the time everyone had come down from the tower into the transept, the music was landlocked on a far coast; and the sailors dancing on shore; and then all the music went but for the single sweeping wind of the Introit, blowing away all thought of sailors and seas, and bringing the music round to itself and quiet.'

Characteristically Mayne breaks with one hallowed tradition of the school story. He shows that children of widely different ages and standing in the school can get on together. In *A Green Rope* (1957)—not itself a school story—the little girl Nan is at first awed by the arrival of Adam, who is head boy of her school, but they are soon on terms of unaffected comradeship. David, in *The Member for the Marsh* (1956), the most under-valued and to me one of the most delightful of his early books, goes to school by bus and is at once elected a member of the Harmonious Mud Stickers. David is only in the second form, but his elders address him with the same elegant formality they accord one another.

Another tradition which dies hard is that teachers are either Olympian or figures of fun. Mayne's choir-school teachers are neither, but then this is no ordinary school. The staff in Kathleen Peyton's *Pennington's Seventeenth Summer* (1970) are nearer everyday reality. They have a hard time with Penn and his contemporaries who kill time until they are old enough to leave and queue for the dole. ' "All we get is useless . . . History and Geography and reading old plays and things, and a load about God".' No wonder Soggy wants to 'cane the living daylights out of him'. Adult readers may sympathize with Soggy more than Mrs Peyton intended. Old Crocker the music master is another matter. In a fine passage Crocker, pushed beyond endurance by Penn's sullen determination not to be interested in anything, explodes:

> ' "We're stuck with it, Pennington . . . Both of us. And we must make the best of it. And let me tell you, Pennington, that this gift God gave you, which you are too thick-headed to acknowledge, is the one and only grace you possess, or are likely to possess, and while I'm stuck with my part in this ill-conceived system, I'm going to make quite sure that you're stuck with yours." '

The scenes in the Beehive Common Room in Mrs Peyton's story are the most convincing in children's fiction. But perhaps she breaks a fundamental rule in letting the reader into this sanctum; the reader should see the action through Penn's eyes throughout. The staff are best kept at a distance, leaving children to speculate, as Nick does in *Autumn Term*, on what they talk about at high table. 'Not ordinary things, she supposed; most likely about examinations and prefects and frightfully difficult Greek and Maths.'

School is a part of a larger society which includes home. Only the most traditional of school stories takes no account of this. There were no clues to Bunter's home background, although he had a suitably gargantuan sister, but even Tom Brown had a home and a family. In the best of school stories, those of Mary Harris and Antonia Forest for example, home and family are of vital importance even when—in some of Miss Harris's stories—they are missing. Mayne drops only a few hints about the home life of Trevithic or Owen, but he made up for this in *Cathedral Wednesday* by making his principal character a day-boy in an essentially resident community with all the conflicts in loyalty that the situation implied.

In books by Antonia Forest and Elfrida Vipont school and home and family are all interdependent parts of the full life.

Some of their books dwell more upon the school situation, but in all of them it is the certainty of home and family which matters. The children are Kitsons and Marlows first, schoolgirls secondly.

Family sagas have long been a part of the children's book scene. Sometimes, as with M. E. Atkinson's Locketts, the fictional family sits on its creator's back more persistently than an Old Man of the Sea. In others, family is so important and so real that the reader eagerly explores more deeply the complex relationships of brothers and sisters and parents.

For many readers, myself among them, the most convincing of fictional families are the Marlows. There is nothing idyllic about their relationships. It would push credibility too far to expect eight brothers and sisters to like one another equally, and Miss Forest, from her detached, tolerant standpoint, shows that antipathies and affections are both parts of the family complex. In the bath—a place for clear thought—Nicola reflects (in *The Ready-Made Family*) that 'of her brothers and sisters she liked Rowan almost equal first with her elder brother Giles. (Lawrie and Peter came next. Then Ginty and Karen. And a long way after, Anne, whom she seldom liked at all.)' And Peter says of his eldest sister ' "Kay is so wet, she's waterlogged".'

So large a family is almost a little world in itself, and it would be tempting for a writer to people it with carefully selected types to produce a symbolic community. Antonia Forest is, however, not an allegorist but a novelist and a highly skilled one. Instead of types she draws people with inbuilt inconsistencies. Of the eight young Marlows only Anne approaches the conventional. She is a touchstone of the ordinary against which to assess the enchanting oddness of the others. Like real families, they form a community by circumstance not of choice. Miss Forest is wise in ensuring that Father, a Naval man, is missing for most of the time. Fathers are notoriously difficult to fit into the family story. Authors more ruthless than Miss Forest prefer to dispose of the bread-winner in a more violent fashion, leaving the family to consolidate in support of the poor widow. There is no nonsense of this kind in the Marlow stories, which prefer sense to sentimentality. Father is on his ship, but his influence helps to keep the Marlows on an even keel in the worst weather.

They are closest together in adversity and, more particularly, in mutual aversion. In *The Ready-Made Family* they are united in dislike of the humourless middle-aged pedant whom Karen marries at eighteen. Miss Forest marshals her forces in some splendid rows in which the wretched Mr Dodd is outmanoeuvred and altogether annihilated by Peter. Peter, a boy of spirit and clearly an admiral in the making, is the most effective of Miss Forest's male characters, but her favourite, and mine, is Nicola, the twin who won the bulk of the initiative when talents were shared out between her and Lawrie. Unlike her twin, who always needs an audience—she is a professional actress in the making—Nick operates well on her own. With so lively and capable a person a writer might well overplay the competence, but Nick is always just a little girl. There is a fine moment in *The Ready-Made Family* when she goes off alone, following a hunch, to Oxford in search of a small and unhappy Dodd child. Hunting through the city she sees a notice outside St Mary the Virgin: *Tower Open—View of the City—Adults 1s, Children under Twelve 6d.*

> ' "Oh yes," she thought, for she liked high places . . . Then she told herself cajolingly "Just this, and then I'll stop. After all, I have been looking for a post office—I've not *just* been rubbernecking." '
> Conscience said *Huh*! but lay down.'

Dear Nicola! Her instincts are admirable. In St Mary's she is disturbed in appreciation of the view by a genuine rubbernecker.

> ' "Oh drop dead!" thought Nicola furiously . . . then remembered that she was in church . . . "Well, not drop dead then— just stuff it" she thought.'

Miss Forest's plots often tremble on the brink of melodrama. She is conscious that in the jungle of the modern world even the most harmless of people are in hazard from wild beasts. Perhaps one might feel that the Marlows have more than their share of perils, and that even without these convincing thrills there would be enough in the ordinary exchanges of a close community to keep the stories going briskly. Ultimately it is not the nightmare of Nicola's Oxford visit that matters, but the reconciliation, partial as it is, with Dodd who turns out to have a scrap of humour after all. There are no miracles. Poor Karen has a difficult time ahead with her husband and ready-made family, but at least she does not, in Nicola's thought, 'look quite as rock-bottomish'.

There is nothing cosy about the home life of the Marlows, as there is sometimes in Noel Streatfeild's recent novels. Often family life is best looked back upon, as Miss Streatfeild showed in her matchless series of autobiographical books in which the Streatfeilds grow up in and then out of their Sussex vicarage. This nostalgia for a past in which home and family had different connotations has produced many books, like E. C. Spykman's *A Lemon and a Star* (English edition 1956) which recalls Nesbit in an American setting.

The acknowledged master in this kind is Gillian Avery. Mrs Avery has studied Victorian social life, especially as it is reflected in contemporary stories, and hers are remarkable reconstructions, almost, one feels, more like Mrs Ewing and Mrs Molesworth than those ladies were themselves. Her stories of the Oxford Smiths and the Greshams are highly professional presentations of a departed world and the comedy springing from a lively and mostly happy family life. Mrs Avery's most individual achievement, however, was her first book, which shows an orphan child discovering the delights of family life from the outside. *The Warden's Niece* (1957) is set in the Oxford of 1875 and, although this is no fantasy, the spirit of a Don of Christ Church broods over the pages. Maria, with no parents and taken from Great-Aunt Lucia and the big Bath house for her own good, has been lodged in Miss Simpson's School where life is a ladylike hell. When she is condemned to wear a label marked 'SLUT' for a week, Maria walks out and goes, almost by chance, to Oxford where Great-Uncle Hadden is Warden of Canterbury College. Maria has neither Latin nor Greek—and little of anything else—but she nurses an ambition to become Professor of Greek at Oxford. The notion appeals to the Warden, who has ideas in advance of his time, and Maria is set to learn with the three Smith boys and their tutor.

It is a pleasant picture of a shy, stubborn girl learning to get on with lively intelligent boys in a relaxed and unfussy household. There are no Victorian repressions here. This is James on the first morning, lying on his stomach on the floor:

> ' "I've got to blow the marble hard enough to knock down that cow before I get up from the floor . . . Joshua, don't tread on the cow or I'll bite your leg. I hope I can blow it down before lessons start or I'll have to stay here—I've vowed to." '

Much of the book turns on the tutor, a very tall clerical gentleman, Mr Copplestone, who appears to be a little deranged. He teaches the children bull-fighting as well as Latin, history and natural science (climbing walls and falling into henhouses). Unfortunately Mr Copplestone, who is intended to be a comic character, is desperately unfunny for most of the time. There is more satisfaction to be had from the kind Warden whose serenity is disturbed only by his housekeeper's ceaseless efforts to protect him from disturbance, and from the Smiths' professional papa, an enlightened man who expects no miracles of good behaviour from the young. As he says to Maria, ' "If you find being good too difficult, you'll have to concentrate on being clever" ', a splendidly un-Victorian maxim. Maria's quest of cleverness turns into a piece of original historical research, conducted in difficult conditions—it was bad enough being a small girl without Mr Copplestone's help—but rising to a satisfactory conclusion. The plot is admirably manipulated and worthy of Mrs Avery's Victorian mentors.

Mrs Avery's stories have a contrived excellence. She is herself clearly in control. The materials of *The Children of the House* (1968) have the untidiness of real life. Brian Fairfax-Lucy's childhood home was Charlecote, that great sprawling Tudor and Victorian mansion beside the Warwickshire Avon. He wrote the story in collaboration with Philippa Pearce out of freely treated memories of Edwardian days. The nature of the partnership has not been precisely revealed. In a prefatory note the writer says that Miss Pearce took a story intended for adults and tilted it in the direction of children, and there are some touches—the masterly conclusion and the exploration of the character of the youngest girl, Margaret—which seem to show her fingerprints.

It is a grim story, relieved only by the affection of the four children for one another and for the friendly servants. Stanford, 'that ancient white elephant', hangs heavily on the shoulders of Papa, a self-made man who lives there by virtue of his marriage to a Stanford heiress. Life is shadowed always by the threat of aristocratic poverty. The children, shabby in their worn and handed-down clothes, are perpetually hungry. They cook moorhen's eggs in the shrubbery and scrounge scraps from dishes on the way to and from the great hall where mama and papa dine in chilly splendour.

The story moves slowly, its tempo dictated by the house with its imperceptible growth. 'Stanford . . . seemed to change only by stealth . . . The clocks ticked and people came and went, mostly the same people in the same clothes.' Hugh joins Tom at public school; their interrupted journey—they got out of the train so that Hugh could get his long curls cut off—makes one of the rare dramatic episodes in the story. Laura broods over her plans to avoid the fate of Stanford ladies—a good marriage. Margaret is only 'ninepence in the shilling', and her life consists only of impulses of fear or momentary happiness. The children seem doomed to follow predetermined courses without hope of change. But the Edwardian age passes and rumours of war creep through the walls of Stanford. Papa sees the war as a chance to further his ambitions and at the same time escape from the house which he loathes. Mama weeps at the prospect of another defeat in her ceaseless war to keep her heritage intact for Tom. Tom and Hugh have been trained at Sandhurst and Dartmouth for just this emergency. For Laura the war offers positive hope of evading marriage and doing something useful. Only Margaret has nothing to hope for.

In a moving epilogue, Victor, the radical schoolmaster's son, who had carried on a furtive friendship with Hugh long ago, returns to Stanford with a coachload of sightseers. The house is empty except for the caretaker and his wife. The children are gone. Victor gets the story, bit by bit, from the old caretaker. Tom and Hugh died in action, Tom with a posthumous V.C.

Laura did her useful job after all and died of 'some hospital fever'. Only Margaret survives, a reluctant heiress. She has refused to marry and can no longer live in Stanford. She won't come back 'because of the others . . . not their ghosts— nothing like that . . . it's that the house remembers', and the memories are too bitter to be borne. The old house echoes 'like a memory of past lives'.

*The Children of the House* is a strong and authentic social document. So recent that Margaret could well be alive today, it shows a way of life infinitely remote. It is a family story, but one in which the parents, for the worst of reasons, are missing. Their contacts with the children are rare and invariably without intimacy or affection. The children had been begotten without love, Laura because she should have been a boy, Tom to be the heir, Hugh in case Tom died, Margaret 'for no particular reason at all'. They get the affection they need from one another and from the butler, a heroic figure who teaches them cricket, the gardener who covers up for them after they raid his fruit trees, and Elsie the between-maid who gives Tom his first innocent lesson in love and comforts Margaret in her loneliness. There is no hero in the book, unless it is the house, and that is more like the villain. The author never describes it, and one sees it physically only through the illustrator's eyes—John Sergeant used a Kentish model. The children of the house never use the front door, which is reserved to Sir Robert and his lady and their guests. But it is this incubus which rules the lives of everyone from Papa to the smallest kitchen-maid.

This idea of the dominant house has prompted some notable books. It is part of the magic of *The Rose Round* (1963), Meriol Trevor's sensitive portrait of a Shropshire house. The book is much more than that. It is, as always with this writer, a story of religious faith. It is also concerned with the plight of disabled children—and adults. It is a love story, and the really important characters are all adult. In the present context the interest of the story lies in its setting. Woodhall is a house without a family. The titular head is Theo, a large, clumsy, disabled man of middle age; his natural diffidence is aggravated by a formidable mama who is embittered by the death of her favourite son and his child, and who lets loose a cruel tongue on Theo. There

is a grand-daughter who usually follows Grandemère's lead in
deriding Theo. On the other side of the servants' door is a
lovely young cook named Caro and, in holiday times, her
brother Matt. On all these the house, with its long history of
goodness and misunderstanding, of faith and denial, works.
The little girl Alix learns a little about tenderness and renuncia-
tion. Caro sees through her shallow and timid lover. (His name
is Jasper and he drives a Jaguar; the reader knows long before
Caro realizes it that he is the villain.) Theo brings crippled
children into the house literally by the back door. The terrible
old grandmother fights them all, and God too, almost to the
end. In the end, however, hatred and bitterness are defeated
and the house, though it almost kills Theo, breaks through the
old lady's barrier of obstinacy. She dies reconciled, and
Woodhall is again filled with children.

This wise, tender story evokes most beautifully the atmosphere of an ancient, neglected and unhappy house. Like
Madame's life, Woodhall has been wasted. By marrying Caro
and bringing the school for handicapped children here Theo
brings back life into it and with life the light which, as the
motto on the old tower in the park reminds us, is the shadow
of God.

Woodhall has decayed graciously. There is no grace in
Flambards. The violent mindlessness of the hunting Russells is
linked inextricably with the house in Kathleen Peyton's remarkable Edwardian novel. When the orphaned Christina is
sent to live there with her uncle, so that in due time she may
come into her inheritance and marry the eldest son of the house,
it seems to her like just another of the transfers from relation
to relation which have made the pattern of her young life.
There is nothing in her past experience to suggest that she too
will become a hard rider to hounds. Is it her blood, or the
influence of Flambards, that makes her, almost against her will,
into a fine horsewoman who delights in the excitement of
hunting and accepts the grotesque rites of blooding without
nausea?

*Flambards* (1967) is a story of turning-points, in history and
in people's lives. Uncle Russell is the past. Crippled in a hunting accident, maddened by pain and frustration, he knows and

cares nothing of any world beyond the house and the hunt. He lives through his son Mark, a hunting Russell of a new generation. Mark is his father made young but not made wise. The future is William, the younger son who hates hunting and is determined to fly. By the chance of a hunting fall he has met a pioneer aeronautical engineer, and his brilliant and, in terms of Flambards, incongruous talents have found an outlet. The future may even belong to Dick, an able and personable young groom whom the older Russells scorn as a mere servant. Between past and future stands Christina who is prepared to enjoy the best of both but is forced to make a choice. There is a nicely symbolic conclusion when Christina and William elope, on impulse, in an early Rolls, pursued vainly by Mark on horseback. 'The car lights veer down the long valley, splintering the dark of her familiar fields'.

The ingredients of *Flambards* come perilously near to those of popular romance. Brutal father, handsome heartless son, betrayed serving-maid, vengeful maiden's brother, clever and misunderstood younger son: we have met them before in not very reputable company. What puts *Flambards* into a different class is, first, the writer's historical integrity. She catches perfectly the atmosphere of decay, of an age ending neither with a bang nor a whimper but in a flurry of meaningless oaths. It is the old Russells who are dying, not the landed gentry. At the Hunt Ball it is not the hard-riding Mark who attracts the attention of Colonel Badstock and the other leaders of rural society, but William who knows how to fly. The house decays with its owners. Towards the end of the book Christina, about her domestic duties, sees Flambards suddenly with perceiving eyes:

> 'the overgrown garden rippling and sighing in the dusk, the great cedar breathing its strange foreign scent to the English spring. The remains of a herb garden, seeding itself, pushed up between the cobbles under her feet; gaunt arms of dried angelica rustled against the walls.
>
> "Flambards," said Christina to the house. "You are dying." '

Mrs Peyton explores this strange world and its inhabitants in depth and with great perception. She wastes no time in psychological speculation, but allows her characters to reveal themselves through their activities and their speech. Splendidly as the story rises to its climax, she had to follow it through two sequels, with a sad decline in creativity. Finally, when she brings a widowed Christina back to Flambards to make a new life, romance takes over.

The home life of the hunting Russells is not a model to follow. How different, one may be tempted to quote, from the home life of our beloved Queen! And from that of the many fictional families who, whatever their inner conflicts, maintain a united front against the outside world! These include the adventuring families of Swallows and Amazons, Tyler Whittle's Spaniards and Elizabethans, Lois Lamplugh's Allens and others, many relaxed and friendly families sponsored by Noel Streatfeild and Kitty Barne, the frivolous Calendars, tossing off gay absurdities in John Verney's amusing stories, and Barbara Willard's lively and enterprising Prydes (in *The House with Roots*, 1959). Readers may find the genealogy of Miss Willard's more recent Towers beyond them, but the Prydes, fighting to keep their deep-rooted house from the developers, are an engaging group.

All these have a common ancestry in the nineteenth century and especially in the stories of Louisa May Alcott. It is appropriate that one of the healthiest strains in the story of family life has come out of America. The best of these were written before the period now under consideration, but by the vagaries of publishing and the intervention of a world war they achieved English editions only since the war. To this group belong those pioneering stories of Laura Ingalls Wilder and Elizabeth Coatsworth, both writers of commanding excellence, and stories of contemporary American life by Elizabeth Enright and Eleanor Estes. Many English children, and adults, must have found these pictures of domestic life of the Melendys and the Moffats a valuable corrective to more sensational and widely publicized views of the New World. Since they reached this country, Elizabeth Enright's *The Saturdays* in 1955, Eleanor Estes's *The Moffats* in 1959, these books have worked powerfully for good among English writers who learnt from them the virtues of clear observation and the accurate rendering of the nuances of character and speech. So a tradition comes

full circle, for these American writers surely, however unconsciously, learnt these skills from the greatest master in this
kind, E. Nesbit.

A similar tradition develops independently in the climate of
Australia, producing an attractive group of novels of family
life in city, farm and bush. Family is an important element in
the writing of Mrs Brinsmead and Mrs Chauncy, and especially
in that of Eleanor Spence, whose *The Year of the Currawong*
(1965) deals effectively with the family stresses produced by a
move from Sydney to a small rural community. This kind of
upheaval, and the personal and material problems involved, is
the theme of Nan Chauncy's autobiographical novel *Half a
World Away* (1962). This is not in the first flight of Mrs
Chauncy's books, but it meant much to her for personal reasons. Like the Lettengars, Nan Chauncy emigrated from Kent
to Tasmania, exchanging a life of genteel poverty for one of
precarious existence in the wild. The former section of *Half a
World Away* is a Nesbitish social comedy, the latter a story of
pioneering adventure. The division does not help artistic unity,
but this is a book to judge not on structural grounds but as a
personal document. It is flooded with nostalgia, but this for
once produces not a sentimental cloud, but a deeper authenticity.

As a generalization, one might say that Europe is not the
natural home of the family story. One obvious exception is *The
Ark*. Margot Benary's moving novel, if not directly autobiographical, must certainly reflect some of her own experiences
after the war. Like Serraillier's *The Silver Sword*, it is about
recovery. Its characters, unlike Serraillier's, belong to the
defeated race who have to rebuild their lives in the shadow of
occupation. The Lechows have a shorter journey to make than
Serraillier's Balickis, first to Parsley Street, 'a little lane like
something out of a picture book' with houses miraculously sur-
viving from the seventeenth century, and then to Rowan Farm
and the disused railway carriage which becomes their Ark.

The charm of *The Ark* springs from its concern with the
realities of love and hunger. Food was a constant preoccupation of the families who clung to life in the harsh years of
recovery, and the book is full of the bitterness of hunger and

*From* Beat of the City (*see page 227*)

the glorious smell of food. When the children go into the country from the starving town, 'the whole village smelled of food', and Lenchen, a nice little girl whose father is the butcher, 'smelt so nicely of smoked meat'. Children's literature is full of feasts, but few are described with such loving concern over each mouthful than the Lechows' Advent party with its four miraculous cakes.

The wonder of *The Ark* is not that it is a good book, for in many ways it falls short of excellence, but that it should have been written at all. It came out of war and defeat and out of the chaos that preceded reconstruction. Of the war there is little in the book; the author and the characters avoid direct reference to it when they can. Dieter, the young musician, recalls briefly his work on the West Wall and remembers: 'At home we never cared much for all the heiling and hurrahing'. After the war there is extreme hardship, humiliation as well as hunger, and the boredom of queueing. Mrs Benary and the Lechows rise above it, largely through a strong sense of family which extends to their motley collection of friends, partly because deprivation and suffering help them to comprehend fundamental truths. Christmas in Parsley Street means more to the children than it had done in happier days. 'The Christmas story was dearer and more familiar to them, perhaps, than it had ever been before to children in all the world's past.'

In its warmth and tenderness *The Ark* comes often to the brink of sentimentality. It never quite topples over. Mrs Benary always harnesses sentiment to reality. Her finest achievement is the character of Margret, who more than the others carries into peacetime the scars of war. There is a remarkable episode in which she fights for the life of the puppies in her charge at Rowan Farm. Somehow the animals become associated in her mind with the dead children she had seen on the refugees' marches. It might be an incongruous and embarrassing moment were the writer's touch less sure. But the reader accepts that 'all the world's suffering had come down at once upon her.'

For the richest and most heart-warming of family stories one turns not to England, Europe, America or Australia but to the friendly poverty-haunted villages of Southern Ireland and to Patricia Lynch. It is the inevitable fate of a writer as prolific and compulsive as Patricia Lynch that she should have written her best books too soon. She has never bettered *The Grey Goose of Kilnevin* in fantasy and *Fiddler's Quest* in homely adventure, but her restless demon has driven her on to write many books in similar veins. As a result the aggregate of her achievement has tended to be undervalued. Despite the conventional expressions of delight which greet each new book, less than critical justice has been done to one of the outstanding creative artists of the century.

Like E. Nesbit and many others, Miss Lynch writes out of the experience of her own childhood. This leads inevitably to repetitiveness. Nearly all her families seem to be the same family: hard-working mother, cheerful—sometimes feckless—father, serious and practical brother, dreamy sister. This last is surely the author herself, greedy for stories. Delia Daly, at the end of her real-life adventure in *Delia Daly of Galloping Green* (1953), looks across at her Uncle Garry relaxing from his travels. ' "I expect he knows more stories than anyone in Dunooka", she thought happily. "When he's told them all to me, I'll write them the way I want them and no one will mind." ' Miss Lynch has done just this throughout a long life, and countless children don't mind.

We know from her autobiography that Miss Lynch learnt her craft from one of the old Shanachies who keep alive the oral traditions of Ireland. It is as a story-teller that she excels, hiding the essential sameness of her tales behind a screen of verbal eloquence and brilliant timing.

Patricia Lynch is a master of the commonplace. She is excited, and she excites the reader, with the wonder of ordinary things. Her families are always poor but they are never bored. There is always some marvel to be enjoyed, a beach of coloured pebbles or pancakes for tea with rhubarb jam and ginger. Grandfather Burke, in *Delia Daly*, sums up their contentment: ' "We've a roof over our heads, enough to eat, decent clothes, and a book to read. What more could we want?" ' In lesser hands this could become complacency or cloying sentimentality but not in Miss Lynch's. For her, love is as natural, and as necessary, as breathing.

Among Patricia Lynch's post-war books *Delia Daly* is the most characteristic. *The Bookshop on the Quay* (1956) is unusual in its city setting. The O'Clerys live in Dublin with Dean Swift —whose spirit walks at night, not quite convincingly—for neighbour, and the quality of the city comes out clearly with scarcely a word of description. The story is exceptional too in having a stranger for hero. Against the secure home-life of the O'Clerys is set the insecurity of Shane, an orphan on the run. Happily for Shane, the O'Clerys are 'terribly good' and he finds a home with them while he continues his quest of his lively Uncle Tim.

*The Old Black Sea Chest* (1958) is more typical. Here Miss Lynch is back in her Southern country. The Driscolls live in Bantry and their farthest horizon is Cork. The Driscolls live on memories of their father and hopes that Mick Rafferty the postman will bring a letter from him. Mother privately hopes that there will be a money order too, but 'Sally thought a letter from her father worth all the money orders in the world'. This time, however, the letter contains more than money—the promise of the prodigal's early return. Then Timothy Driscoll comes home with his black sea chest full of impractical treasures, but he has somehow managed to mislay five thousand pounds. Timothy is a splendid Lynch father, volatile, feckless, a grand story-teller, and as affectionate as he is unreliable. The story, however, belongs not to him but to Sally, who will 'go climbing after the stars, like her da', but who has a strain of obstinacy to strengthen her dreams. When Timothy goes on his travels again, chauffeur-driven, at the end of the book she alone does not stay to see the gleaming car into the distance, but goes in to sit on the old black sea chest and listen to its silent tales.

These are stories of family and of community too. The people of Bantry and Dunooka are united in poverty and generosity. They share their goods communally: food and news, happiness and grief. For Miss Lynch the Irish village is itself a family.

# CHAPTER TEN

# *Work*

'Natural and right ways of earning your living . . . sowing and reaping, and doing things with animals.'

'"Me, I don't understand bothering with anything unless you mean to work at it." ' Ted, in Noel Streatfeild's *The Circus is Coming*, stated long ago the principle on which all stories about careers should be based.

The seeds of the career novel were sown when Miss Streatfeild, in her brief acting career, watched a troupe of child performers at work and observed how absolute was their dedication of their skills. Out of that experience came the first, and still one of the most truthful as well as the most charming, of books about young people discovering and fostering their potential skills, *Ballet Shoes*. Miss Streatfeild was a pioneer of the modern children's novel with its inner integrity and its carefully researched background. She believed in research among primary sources, and these included going tenting with Bertram Mills's Circus. When she returned to her favourite sphere of writing after the war she wisely contented herself with vicarious experience, and it was, I believe, not she but her secretary who endured the bumps and falls which were a necessary part of the research for her story of the making of a skating champion, *White Boots* (1951).

Noel Streatfeild had a few companions in writing about the realities of a working life in the pre-war years. Kitty Barne showed what effort and drudgery went to the making of a musician in *She Shall Have Music*, and her stories of Sussex country life, although primarily about family affairs, gave an authentic glimpse into the working of a farm. Perhaps the nearest to the modern concept of a career novel was a now-forgotten book which had in it the seeds of many of the most admired features of the children's novel today, Monica Redlich's *Five Farthings*. This showed, *inter alia*, a young girl taking her first tentative steps into the world of publishing.

The career-book proper, that is a novel designed deliberately to convey in story form reliable information about specific fields of work and at the same time to give authentic impressions of the nature of the work, was an invention of the post-war period. It came not from the spirit of the times—although this no doubt played a part in the enterprise—but from a deliberately adopted policy of certain publishing houses. I must accept a very small part of the blame personally. I was one of those who, soon after the war, pointed out the need for books which would give the growing child some idea of what it was like to work. I had not expected that my wish would be granted, as if by some malignant Psammead, in such embarrassing profusion.

It is not often that work of really creative quality is produced in order to fill a need. At best one can hope for careful competence, and that is what, at best, we got in the Fifties. The career novel was usually the work of professional writers, extremely responsible and capable authors like Laurence Meynell who brought their technical skills to this as to any other job. Meynell was equally at home with stories about boys' and girls' careers, although for reasons of publishing policy the latter appeared under the pseudonym of Valerie Baxter. In general these books which, if they were inspired by no sense of vocation, had the benefit of literary professionalism, were to be preferred to stories written, with much less skill, by amateur writers whose eminence in their chosen spheres by no means compensated for their floundering in the seas of fiction. The experts were a great deal more at ease in purely factual career books.

The most considerable body of work in this form came from the Bodley Head and Chatto and Windus. The Oxford University Press, however, had been earlier in the field, even before the clamour for career books began. J. S. Arey's *Student at Queens*, a serious look at the realities of medical training, appeared in 1945 and might reasonably claim to be the true parent of all the formal career novels which followed. If one

may risk a generalization, the Oxford series was more successful than the Bodley Head group. It was a shorter list, and the
writers were concerned with broad impressions and personal
reactions rather than the minutiae of training and qualification. They included Peter Dawlish on the Merchant Navy and
Roland Pertwee on the stage, both, it will be noted, from a
male standpoint. In many of the girls' career books the chosen
career turned out, inevitably and not reprehensibly, to be
domesticity. The heroine's aim was to marry the boss or, better
still, the boss's handsome and well-heeled son.

While these pleasant, worthy and mainly unimportant
books were appearing, another and a very different force was
at work. Richard Armstrong, who had made a tentative start
to a literary career with two slight stories about industry on
Tyneside, published *Sea Change* in 1948. In its unobtrusive
way this was a revolutionary book. Although it belonged to an
old tradition of sea stories it broke drastically with the tradition in showing the essentially unromantic nature of life at sea.
It substituted for romance a robust facing of reality.

Richard Armstrong knew precisely what he was talking
about. He has written about the crisis in his own life when he
'lived between two worlds—one, the real world with which I
had to come to grips, and the other a dream world, the world I
wanted to be, into which I retreated with all those things that
were incomprehensible and made them tolerable by turning
them into fantasy.' He finally made his agonizing choice, but it
came as the end of a long and difficult struggle. His decision to
write was a conscious attempt to make reparation for wasted
years by helping boys to make their own choice with clear eyes.
This had nothing to do with the choice of a specific career.
Armstrong wrote about the sea, because this was the world he
knew, but his premises and his conclusions apply to all careers
because they are concerned with the basic realities of life, not
with its techniques and details. Ultimately what matters in
*Sea Change*—and the same is true of all Armstrong's books—is
that a boy should become aware through his reading of 'his
own power, his value as a human being; to give him confidence
in himself, in the richness of life in the real world and his
capacity for living it.'

*Sea Change* is a story of the Merchant Navy. The sea change of the subtle title is suffered by Cam Renton, a lad who has become an apprentice with high hopes of a swift training and a second-mate's certificate in record time. This is his fantasy. Reality is quite different. On the S.S. *Langdale* there is a promise of grim hard work under the booming voice of the bosun but no sign of professional training. Cam is tempted to rebel, but common sense tells him to get on with the job. After an hour or so he looks at what has been done 'with a little thrill of pride'. Without knowing it he has learnt a first lesson. The others follow quickly. He discovers the satisfaction of doing a job well and with economy of effort, and he learns how to become part of a team, taking his just share and enjoying the discovery of comradeship. Even the melancholy able seaman Calamity Calshot, who sees disaster around every corner, has something to teach him.

If the book went on in this vein we would have a Samuel Smiles success story but not a novel and a Carnegie Medal winner. Life is not simple. Cam finds himself at odds with old Andy the mate and gets into trouble by breaking out of the strait-jacket of ship's discipline. The story now seems set upon a different kind of collision course. The old-style sea-story would have let Cam sink deeper into trouble, to redeem himself at last by some dramatic act of heroism. Armstrong is not that kind of writer or S.S. *Langdale* that kind of ship. Cam has an interview with the Captain who blows him up in a friendly fashion and then sorts out his grievances. Cam discovers with surprise that all the menial chores which have come his way have been a part of his training.

> 'He saw how every little niggling thing old Andy had given him to do counted—how one developed his muscle, another his eye, a third his judgement of line and distance; how each hour he spent working with the foremast hands taught him to know and understand them better against the day when such men as they were would look to him for guidance.'

All this, it will be seen, makes an admirable textbook for life. Is it also a novel? There is no simple answer, but on balance the judgement goes in Armstrong's favour. He is no great stylist. He has a straight man-to-man attitude towards words,

*From* Sea Change (*see page 187*)

which he expects to do their job without fuss. There is nothing evocative in his writing. The sea is without wonder or mystery —just a necessary part of the seaman's equipment. His style has chosen limits and within them it is adequate to its task. In dialogue he is, if anything, too truthful. The conversation of ordinary lads serves for communication, but rendered exactly in print it is extremely dull.

It is in the exposition and analysis of character that Armstrong excels. He understands with remarkable clarity the workings of a young mind. Cam is not an exceptionally able or admirable person. It is his essential ordinariness which comes out of the story, and this is part of Armstrong's anti-romantic message. Cam is not, and is unlikely to become, a hero. It is upon the unspectacular reliability and honesty of such that society is based. With a mass of quiet telling details Armstrong shows Cam in all his common decency, a fundamentally simple person struggling to come to terms with a complex world.

Cam's world is that of the ship. It is an important part of Armstrong's qualification as a novelist that he can present and expound a shipboard society. He shows the relationship between all grades of this ordered hierarchy and the vital part that each cog in this complicated machine plays.

Style, characterization and setting are all at the service of an admirable plot. Armstrong tells a story very well. He knows how to lay his foundations and how to build up to a climax and pass to a resolution. There is plenty of excitement in *Sea Change*, but it is not a contrived excitement, coming not from the narrator's inventiveness but from his skilled and selective presentation of reality.

Armstrong has written many sea stories since 1948. They are all concerned with young men coming to terms with themselves and with life, and they all, it must be confessed, have a certain sameness in their handling of this central theme. Armstrong's message was important enough to be repeated many times. In only one other book, I think, does he strike the original note of *Sea Change* again. This is *The Whinstone Drift* (1951).

The scene is the author's own Northumbrian industrial country where mines and wild moorland exist side by side.

Dewley is a village given over to coal-mining. Even the young men of the place are dedicated to coal and get genuine if inarticulate satisfaction from their job. Only Peter is unhappy. While he has been away at school in the soft south country his old friends have grown up and away from him. He hates the idea of the pit but can think of no other career. Besides, he fears that the Whindyke Pit on which Dewley depends is almost worked out. There is plenty of coal, but a great geological fault blocks the way to it. If only the legendary Whinstone Drift could be found the future might open up again for Dewley.

Here melodrama enters the story. There are rum goings-on in Folly Wood where a stone column—Blenkinsop's Folly—towers above the trees. The wood is guarded by tall stone walls. There seems nothing much worth protecting, only the ruins of the old house of the Blenkinsops who once owned the valley, yet guard-dogs keep out intruders and a strange old lady drives in and out in her big chauffeur-driven car. The boys naturally investigate and are of course caught. It is a contrived situation and the resolution is no more convincing.

If this were all there would be no place for comment on *The Whinstone Drift* in a survey, however comprehensive, of modern books for children; but the absurd plot is not all. There is great interest in the character of Peter who, when not chasing or being chased by villains, puzzles out his future. Coal is in his blood and only reason keeps him out of the pit. When, after the resolution of the complicated narrative, the future of Dewley becomes clear, reason joins instinct and he takes his place at the coal face.

Like the sea in *Sea Change*, coal is something which claims the allegiance of men, not for romantic reasons but because it offers the opportunity for satisfaction in a job of work well done. 'There was a right way and a wrong way to do everything . . . and Ginger Henderson . . . made sure the purpose behind every little rule they had learned was clear.' There are no heroics in the pit. It is a tough life but one where intelligence and knowledge count. There is room in it for a bright young man like Peter who has as much to offer to coal—and to gain from it—as he has to village society and to sport.

Richard Armstrong writes of the coal industry after nationalization (although one feels that the National Coal Board in reality would have dealt with barmy Miss Dorothy May Blenkinsop's plot to sabotage Whinstone coal without help from Peter and his young friends). His book makes an interesting contrast to Frederick Grice's *The Bonny Pit Laddie* (1960) which takes a similar situation in the early days of coal and presents it with uncompromising realism.

Most writers found the anti-romantic career story too arid to be followed. In a story about a young girl in farming, however, M. E. Allen brought some of Armstrong's aggressive honesty to a different situation. *Room for the Cuckoo* (1953) conveys with almost physical intensity the feeling of exhaustion which comes from a concentrated spell of hard manual work. The 'cuckoo' is a girl in a man's world, and she expects and accepts no concessions. Romance enters the story at the end, and rightly; the poor girl had earned some relief.

The career story is geared mostly to the 'glamour' professions. It would be possible for a good writer to make a creative story around the routine of office life, showing young people getting satisfaction and a sense of achievement from it, but so far as I know no one has succeeded in doing this. It takes an Armstrong to write about industry with neither glamour nor boredom, and he writes about and for boys with their, at present, greater opportunities for action. Girl readers, unless they are to be content with the production-line formulae of the career book, must read about ballet, music and the stage and about heroines who are heading for the stars.

Pamela Brown was first in this field after the war. Her series of stage stories (*Maddy Alone*, 1946, and others) were in a sense autobiographical, for the author—she was extremely young at the time of writing these first books—was writing about a world and about career struggles which she knew at intimate first-hand. At times her knowledge and her wish to write exciting and romantic stories were at odds, and romance usually won the battle. There is, however, a freshness in her early novels which is directly appealing.

The long novel by a Yugoslav writer—*Ballerina* (1961)—is much more impressive. Nadia Curcija-Prodanovic, among many other activities, holds a high position in the State Ballet, and her account of the training of a dancer is absolutely authentic. Since this is the most truly international of the arts, the book is relevant to readers in all countries. Ballet may be among the most glamorous of the arts, but Mme Prodanovic keeps her story firmly tied to the realities of weariness and frustration and the harsh disciplines which are the price of achievement.

Discipline has a place in Pamela Harris's story of musical life, *Star in the Family* (1965), and, with fine incongruity, in Kathleen Peyton's further exploration of the character and career of her reluctant adolescent, Pennington. In *The Beethoven Medal* (1971) Penn is torn by his opposing wishes to be a great pianist and a normal human being, and he is not helped by the interested parties who pull him in different directions. This is in no real sense a career story but a book about a boy in society, but it speaks clearly to young people about one of the major dilemmas faced by those who want both success and normality. It is not part of Mrs Peyton's scheme to show in detail the drudgery which is a large part of the executant musician's life. One sees Penn hammering away at Rachmaninoff on the Village Hall piano, all among the expectant and nursing mothers on Clinic Day. This is the careerist at work, but Penn seems most himself when playing for a Saturday night sing-song in the pub. Happiness, Mrs Peyton is saying, but not so crudely, is not enough.

In Elfrida Vipont's simpler but not necessarily less accurate view, happiness and fulfilment in work are parts of the same thing. Any career can offer fulfilment. To Penn, in *Flowering Spring* (1960), dress-designing is ' "more than fun—it's—well, I suppose you could call it a mission." ' There is no simple profit-and-loss account in a career. Laura in this book, like her Aunt Kit, knows about 'the price you had to pay to be in the job on which you had set your heart; perhaps part of the price was being prepared to do the job for its own sake, without hoping to get anything out of it for yourself at all.'

In Miss Vipont's stories, and perhaps in her experience, parents are hopeless about careers. Laura's send her to school at Heryot to make her forget her fancies about acting, and they tell the head that she wants to teach. Miss Vipont's heads are invariably wise. Laura's tells her: ' "The best thing to do for people who want to go on the stage is to discourage them, because if they're really serious about it, they'll go ahead, and if they're not, they'll be saved a lot of worry and disappointment." '

Elfrida Vipont's opposite poles are represented by Milly and Kit. Milly is an actress. The one pure gold thread in her life was her love for a missionary who went East and got himself killed by tribesmen. Now she is a bright star of the London stage, but her greatest part is the brittle brilliance of Millamant. Kit sings 'The Hill of the Lord', and in its elegiac splendour transmutes her own grief at the death of Laurence Cray. Milly, the sweetness of whose garden 'had been laid waste by the frost' of his death, gets from her grief only the surface hardness which makes her a mistress of high comedy.

Kit Haverard, one feels, is Miss Vipont's own favourite creation as she is the favourite of most readers. The Ugly Duckling is one of the basic themes of literature, fulfilling a deep need in humanity. Kit is never ugly, but she is a scruffy, awkward and undirected child when she first appears in *The Lark in the Morn*. Wise and stupid influences fight for possession of her through this first book, but at the end she discovers herself and her purpose. She will sing. In the following book, *The Lark on the Wing* (1950), insensitive reality, in the form of her father's earnest committee-member housekeeper, attempts to break her resolution but without success. A weakness of Cousin Laura's technique of government by discouragement is that an intelligent sufferer from it may develop a countertechnique of resistance by inertia. Kit seems to go along with Laura's wish, but she keeps her resolution intact so that when her moment comes she will be ready for it.

In summary Kit may seem to be a prig. In fact she is nothing of the sort. Like other dedicated professionals, she combines a capacity for hard work with an ability to enjoy life fully. When she promises the old composer that she will work —' "Oh, how I'll work!" '—he adds gently ' "And live, my child" '; and so she does. She makes mistakes too. Bored by her teacher's insistence on endless technique, she escapes to the seaside and sings in a restaurant with Kitsons' Blue Girls, sugaring her songs in an attempt to please reluctant listeners. Papa Andreas, her wise old teacher, understands. ' "They do not want to listen, and you find you have nothing to say to them, so you give them what you think they will like. But one day . . . they will take what you have to give." '

One of the delights of *The Lark on the Wing* is that it is not all careers. Kit goes to London to work in an office and shares a flat with her friends. The intensity of study is lightened by house-cleaning and fish-and-chip teas eaten out of the newspaper. And when Kit has had her triumph, and had the joy of it tarnished by Cousin Laura's casual malice, she runs away and spring-cleans the flat. Music is Kit's life but not quite all of it.

*The Lark on the Wing* is about work, but it is not, of course, a Career Book. It is a book about music and God, and self-discovery and love. It is in fact a novel and cannot be slotted into one convenient category.

Children may gain from books like this an idea about the adult world of work and the training and study which go towards achievement. Equally they will find out much from many books which never attempt to expound the idea of a career. They will learn about work from the drunken Irish labourer in Alan Garner's *Elidor* and from Helen Cresswell's fantastic craftsmen. Work is one aspect of life, and the good novelist takes all life as his province.

# CHAPTER ELEVEN

# *Self and Society*

'The author does think of so many things besides the story, and sometimes he puts them in.'

ALL WORK IS A FORM of self-discovery. Almost every kind of work involves the worker in society. It is a logical progression from the career novel to the novel proper, that is the story which is concerned with a man's relationship with his fellow beings and with himself.

Some of the most powerful of children's novels are about identity, about children exploring—in William Penn's phrase —'the houses of their mind'. These too are books in which the distinction between adult and child is at its most indistinct. Some of Mary Harris's stories of very small children discovering their own personalities appeal to an essentially adult interest in the analysis of character. In others, however, the close examination of personality goes in harness with a tense and powerful narrative which speaks directly to children. This may be true of *I am David* (1965; published originally in Denmark as *David* in 1963.) Anne Holm wrote here one of the most profoundly disturbing of contemporary novels. The theme is both contemporary and timeless. David is a boy in a Balkan labour camp. He has been there so long that the memory of a free life has almost faded, and it seems likely that he will stay in captivity until premature death releases him as it released his friend Johannes. The thought of death is not repulsive to him until he escapes and discovers with surprise that the world is beautiful. The sight of 'a sea bluer than any sky' makes the boy weep, and the tears anger him because they blur the beauty. 'Now that he had learned about beauty he wanted to live.'

David—the name is all that he knows about himself—

escapes with the help of the man whom he hates, who was responsible for destroying his father and for his own captivity. It is an enigma which occupies some of his mind as he makes his way to the coast, across the sea and up Italy and through the heart of Europe to a home in Denmark. Throughout this journey he is essentially alone. He meets people, brutal, kind, possessive, interfering, but he avoids personal involvement because of the distrust built into him by past experience and because he knows that kindness and cruelty alike will delay his journey.

What a hero for a children's novel! A boy who rejects love, a boy with 'the eyes of an old man, an old man who's seen so much in life that he no longer cares to go on living'. What sustains him through his appalling ordeals is his sense of identity; he has no hope, but he is himself. ' "I am David. Amen" ' marks the conclusion of his prayers, and it stands for the only certain article in his creed.

Necessarily the happy ending is contrived, but it is essential. David has gone on discovering fresh resources within himself at every crisis of the journey. The dog which, of all those whom he has encountered, is the only creature with which he has risked a personal relationship, has died for him. It is time that he cast this intolerable burden on someone else. The end comes swiftly. It is quite unsentimental and the reader accepts it gratefully.

The greatest problem in Anne Holm's novel is how to develop a story in which there is really only one single character. David, in a crowded Europe, is as lonely as Crusoe, and like Defoe she keeps her hero going with fine circumstantial detail and with exquisite timing. Despite the tension and the occasional violence of the action, *I am David* is a quiet book, a story whose real action takes place inside the principal character. It may be a better book in conception than in performance; there is a flatness in the telling (it may come from translation) which underlines the monotone of David's thoughts. It is nevertheless a book of the greatest significance, not perhaps to the majority but to the susceptible reader who finds that its anguish and melancholy lodge in the mind until they become part of his own personality.

David discovers himself in isolation and through suffering, and so, in a very different way, does David the deaf boy in Veronica Robinson's remarkable *David in Silence* (1965). Others, more happily, find their way to self-knowledge through society and affection, like 'Binnie Bijou', the enchanting heroine of H. F. Brinsmead's *A Sapphire for September* (1967) and Perdita, *The Witch's Daughter* of Nina Bawden's novel published in 1966. When Perdita forces herself to run down to the jetty, 'her legs . . . queer as if they might easily bend backwards as well as forwards and her head . . . singing', to give a bunch of wild flowers to her departing friend Janey, she gets rid once for all of the witch's daughter's bitterness. She is no longer 'Perdita, which means lost.'

Like Perdita, Tom Long is lonely and, like her, he finds a friend who helps him towards understanding of self. *Tom's Midnight Garden* (1958) is one of those rare, miraculously individual books which belong to no category and demand absolute acceptance from the reader. Philippa Pearce wrote here a kind of ghost story, except that the ghost was still alive, and a kind of historical novel, its period carefully concealed from the reader.

Tom goes to stay with his uncle and aunt because his brother Peter has caught measles. The Kitsons live in a big old house which has been broken up into flats. Even if Tom had not been feeling resentful the house would have restricted him. It is hedged in with new estates. There is no garden. Mrs Bartholomew, who owns the house and lives in the top flat, is an unseen disapproving presence. Besides, Aunt Gwen, although well-meaning, feeds him so well that he becomes sluggish and sleepless. It is this that makes Tom get up when Mrs Bartholomew's grandfather clock strikes thirteen and go out into the moonlit garden which is not there by day. While the Kitsons toss in bed, disturbed by the clock's noise, and old Mrs Bartholomew, her false teeth grinning in the bedside glass, dreams of her childhood, Tom explores the garden and plays with Hatty, a 'Princess in disguise' whose own loneliness leads her into fantasy until the greater fantasy of a boy from the future transforms her. Tom realizes that she is no princess, 'yet it was true that she had made this garden a kind of kingdom'.

The time-scales of Hatty's and Tom's worlds are different. She grows nightly while Tom remains his own age. As she approaches maturity and the date of her wedding and Tom's period of quarantine runs out, his vision grows dim and the garden vanishes by night as well as day. The bitterness of his loss makes Tom cry aloud for Hatty, and she hears him. The concluding passages have a perfection unmatched in children's literature.

Part of the wonder of *Tom's Midnight Garden* lies in purely literary qualities. Philippa Pearce is a master of style. Unlike William Mayne, a greater virtuoso performer who is often carried away by the enchantment of his own skill, she is always in control. She uses words as if she had just discovered them. With them she discloses the mystery of the garden and explores in depth the complex personalities of Tom and Hatty. No one, not even E. Nesbit in the 'Arden' books, has managed better the transition from present to past. The moonlight in Mrs Bartholomew's hall has a hypnotic effect. ' "Hurry! hurry! the house seemed to whisper . . . The hour is passing— passing . . ." ' And at the close of each adventure into the past Tom sees the impedimenta of the Victorian age fading away or 'rather beginning to fail to be there'. Similarly, as Hatty grows towards adulthood Tom becomes 'thinner' to her, and the Angel of Revelation's warning 'Time No Longer' engraved on the clock-face begins 'to seem full of enormous possibilities'.

*Tom's Midnight Garden* was Philippa Pearce's second book. Her first—*Minnow on the Say* (1955)—is an enchanting story of a treasure-hunt and of little boys messing about on the river, as fresh and fragile as a spring day. It is structurally disastrous. In three years Miss Pearce learnt all about her craft. The construction of *Tom's Midnight Garden*, its firm development, the subtle variation from episode to episode, is beyond criticism.

Miss Pearce's third book—*A Dog So Small* (1962)—is also in part about self-discovery. Ben wanted a dog of his own. He lived in London and there was no room for one, even a small dog. Grandpa lives in the country and so does his dog Tilly, but Ben, like his father, 'could no more live out of London than a fish could live out of water'. It seems impossible to reconcile

London with owning a dog, except perhaps 'a dog so small you can see it only with your eyes shut'. Much of the action of this story exists, like the dog, only in Ben's head. It is a difficult book, its subtle interior action and its deep understanding not fully tuned to the reader's wavelength.

Ben's is a happy family and his loneliness is largely self-imposed. He is that kind of boy. Marianne is reluctantly lonely. *Marianne Dreams* (1958) is the story of how she breaks out of her isolation by the power of imagination. Catherine Storr shows a little girl distressed by illness which keeps her from the pleasant normality of school and friends. She escapes into dreams whose pattern is determined by the pictures she draws in her waking hours. In time these dreams become confused with the reality of Mark who is paralysed and who is linked with Marianne by their sharing a peripatetic teacher. Together they share dream adventures of a terrifying realism which move gradually towards the recovery of both children. They escape from the perils that surround Marianne's scribble-house, and take refuge in a dream tower cluttered with all the useful and interesting things that Marianne's imagination has suggested to her. She is happy in this refuge, but Mark's ambition makes him restless. It is he who devises the mechanism by which he can descend from the tower.

This strange book is about the power of imagination to defeat sickness and depression. It is also about companionship. Marianne and Mark are more interesting and likeable people as a result of their dream friendship than either was alone. Each finds himself with the other's help. Well at last, Marianne goes to the seaside for convalescence and here, she knows, she will find Mark in the real world.

It is possible for identity to be achieved in isolation. Richard Church, however, shows, in *The Cave* (1950), how people find their true selves in moments of crisis. A party of boys explore a cave. (It was a foolhardy and ill-planned operation; the Swallows and Amazons would have managed it better.) In the face of danger the self-appointed leader, Alan, breaks and other, apparently less able, members of the party show their individual qualities.

Sheena Porter's *Nordy Bank* (1964) is also concerned with

the discovery of personality. Bron, a half-Welsh girl of the border country, has plenty of friends and yet she is not quite of them, being completely at ease only with animals. She goes camping with her friends on the Brown Clee which is 'full of quietness and dreams'. The words are her own, but she has not anticipated that some of the dreams can be unquiet. For the camp site is on Nordy Bank, a hill-fort, and Bron is more in tune with the bitter struggles of the past than her practical Anglo-Saxon companions. She feels 'the sleeping war'. She knows too by some unsuspected instinct just where the Iron Age warriors made their cache of sling-shot. There are strange forces in this quiet little girl, and the ancient fortress has released them.

The camping scenes in *Nordy Bank* are beautifully done. They convey the sense of adventure and the fresh winds of these Marchland heights, as well as the good companionship of the campers. It was a pity that Bron's story had to be followed back home and traced through the domestic scenes with her rather dreary parents. The last pages are admirably written. Bron faces her destiny and makes the hardest choice, but her parents—a little out of character—have made their own choice, and it is for her benefit. Bron is free to follow her new life in the company of her friends. 'Nordy Bank was there, but it belonged to the hill's past now and she belonged to herself.' It is a marvellous discovery for Bron to have made unaided, but then she is rather a marvellous girl. Earlier in the story she reflects that 'she never minded being alone, and in fact liked it more than being with other people'. By the story's close she is no less independent, but without losing any of her personal integrity she has begun to value other people.

In *Nordy Bank* Sheena Porter shows how self-discovery can go hand-in-hand with the discovery of society. It is an effective lesson, the more so because the lesson is contained in an absorbing and dramatic story and the inner and outer themes are inseparable.

The fulfilment of self which Bron achieved in just one Easter holiday may be spread over more than one generation. This is the essence of Ruth Arthur's most moving and tragic story, *A Candle in Her Room* (1966). The story begins in Edwardian days when a doctor and his young family move into an old house on the Pembrokeshire coast. Two of the three girls are already showing signs of developed personalities. Melissa, the eldest, is wise beyond her years and warmly sympathetic too. Judith is elegant, strong and aggressive. Briony, the youngest, is gentle and conventional. They share the rambling house with Emmy Lee, the little orphan who helps around the house and protects Melissa with a fiercely proprietory zeal.

The weather seems to be set fair for a pleasant story of family life in a lovely country setting, and so it might have been—I am not sure; there was a devil in Judith from the outset—but for Dido. Briony finds Dido, the old wooden doll, but Judith steals her and hides her away. Dido does not belong in this well-ordered, civilized household. 'She was like a flaming wild poppy in a well-tended rose garden'. She inspires Judith to a brilliant career in painting and then destroys her, but not before Judith has herself destroyed her sister's happiness. For Liss expects to marry Carew, who loves her, but she has an accident which leaves her paralysed, and while she lies helpless Carew and Judith elope.

If so complex a novel can be said to have one theme, it is that of Liss's fulfilment. Carew dies in the first world war and Judith comes home with her baby Dilys. The child grows up, hated by her mother and living on the affection of Aunt Liss. She meets a young Polish student who works on a neighbouring farm, falls in love with him and goes to Poland with him on the eve of war. Judith dies of pneumonia, brought on by crazy nights on the hills. The second war ends without news of Dilly. Liss, still in her invalid chair, is sustained only by the certainty that Dilly will come home again. In her loneliness she becomes haunted by the vision of a child, a little girl whose eyes are those of the lost Dilly. This, she is convinced, is Dilly's child, adrift somewhere among the refugee millions of Europe. In setting herself the task of finding the child Liss conquers her paralysis and recovers herself after a long empty life.

In a masterly concluding section Nina, a child of the refugee camps, comes to live in the Old Court and falls under the influence of Dido. But Nina has been through hell herself and is stronger than her grandmother. She resists the malignant power of the doll and destroys Dido. Hurt, but for the first time in her brief life hopeful, she goes home to a house which has lost its shadows.

*A Candle in Her Room* is a true novel in that it presents a story of people living in a clearly defined setting, influencing one another for good and ill, and interpreting in their lives the spirit of their age. It is a passionate story, deeply disturbing in its tragedy; a book which the reader cannot share without personal involvement. A complicated narrative technique—the four sections of the book are shared between three narrators—is remarkably successful in avoiding monotony and presenting different facets of the same theme.

The book is, among other things, a story about growing up in wartime. Margot Benary approaches this theme from the other side in her *Dangerous Spring* (1961). Karin, the adolescent daughter of a German liberal doctor, falls in love with a saintly pastor. Helmut is 'the sort of man for whom girls sew on buttons'. Karin is perhaps in love with him, or with life, or with the spring; in the last weeks of war she is wide open to influences, from art and nature and religion, and the lame and half-blind pastor provides the catalyst for her teeming emotions. It is a tender, pathetic, very slightly comic, picture of young love. But growth is accelerated in wartime, and during the terrors of bombing and greater perils from the liberating Russians, Karin grows up and gains the strength to lose her pastor.

This is a wise story, authentic in its details, which are based on the author's own experiences, yet surprisingly detached; the reader remains an observer instead of becoming, as in Ruth Arthur's books, a partisan. The same is true, to some extent, of Grace Hogarth's *As a May Morning* (1958), another wise and understanding story of young love in which the writer is almost too skilful in dissecting the emotions of her heroine.

For me Patricia Wrightson's *The Feather Star* (1962) is a more satisfactory analysis of the pains of growing up. The canvas is smaller, and Patricia Wrightson refrains from explicit comment, but hers is an exquisite sketch of a young girl who moves slowly and awkwardly towards adult life. Lindy is still at least half a child when she goes on holiday. She is fifteen, acutely conscious of herself and her sex. The sight of pelicans sends her racing childlike to the beach, from which she returns 'very pink and dignified' after an encounter with a flippant young man. She gets into scrapes from which this and other boys rescue her, leaving her with the feeling that 'after this she would never be able to look Bill Grant in the face.' A dear girl! On the beach she collects shells and pebbles, exquisite, useless things, as she has done on every holiday of her short life. This year they are as lovely as ever but she has changed.

> 'What would she do with these things if she took them home? Shut them up in a cupboard in memory of the wind and the noisy cabbage-green water? And yet the shells were so small and perfect, the driftwood so like a snake. She put them all down on a stone so that she could forget them without actually throwing them away . . .'

Lindy gathers experiences like seashells, reacting to the loveliness of the feather-star which glows in a cave pool and to the friendship of Bill and the other relaxed boys who play on the beach, and shocked to the heart by contact with Abel, a bitter loveless old man with 'eyes on the ground refusing life, wasting all the adventure and beauty of a whirling planet in space'.

The holiday ends. Lindy goes home, promising to remember Bill.

> 'She did remember him, too. For six months she remembered him very well, and for twelve months a little. After that life became very busy, and the memory of Bill lay among the shells and driftwood and cuttle-fish of childhood holidays. Still, she remembered him; because all her life she never forgot the feather-star. From time to time she would think of a living light that glowed and faded in the darkness of a wall, and by that light she remembered Bill.'

Even these stories of young love are essentially stories of one person. It is the self-discovery of Lindy and Karin and Jenny which matters, and Bill and Helmut and Arthur are important only because they contribute to this discovery.

The problem of deprived children was a favourite theme of Victorian novelists and it has had a profitable revival in recent years. Orphans, adopted children, reluctant step-children:

these have become a staple of novelists seeking to explore human relationships, or to harrow the reader's heart, or perhaps just to tell an effective story.

I am not sure to what extent adoption was a problem before the novelists made it one. Children eager for love may reasonably find a greater assurance from adoptive than from natural parents. As Josephine Kamm's Mrs Stevens (in *No Strangers Here*, 1968) says: ' "Our own children were born to us: we just had to take what was coming. But you we chose because we wanted you." ' Mrs Kamm's theory is always beyond reproach. We can admire it without reservation even if we think less well of her art. *No Strangers Here* is a typical example. She is utterly sincere, but she lacks selectivity. In order to bring the story home to ordinary readers, she fills it with a mass of homely detail under which the theme is often submerged.

An identical situation produces a profoundly different book from Ruth Arthur. *Requiem for a Princess* (1967) has a typical heroine in Willow Penelope Forester (even the name is typical; did Miss Arthur ever write about a Jane or a Pat?).

'It happened to *me*, and I . . . am quite ordinary,' says Willow. It is obviously untrue. Ruth Arthur—it is both her strength and her weakness—has never gone in for ordinary people. Her very modern and unconventional tales belong in one respect to an old tradition of children's literature: they are uncompromisingly middle-class. The families may not always be affluent but they are always highly respectable. This has sometimes been held against them, as if to concern oneself with anything but working-class or classless situations is anti-social if not immoral. But fiction is a matter of people, not classes, and Ruth Arthur's books, sponsored by a prominent left-wing publisher, are outstandingly interesting as studies of unusual, sensitive and cultured people.

Unlike *No Strangers Here*, *Requiem for a Princess* is not 'about' adoption; it is about people. In it Miss Arthur deals discreetly with a human situation, which she presents through the medium of a most subtle and complex story, sensitively told. She is one of the past-masters of first-person narrative, and she treads delicately over the quicksands of this perilous device. The method is indeed essential to her story, enabling the reader to accept identification with the heroine-narrator.

*Requiem for a Princess* is a 'mirror' story. Willow is able to examine her own problem closely because she encounters its mirrored image in another life. She has been deeply shocked by the discovery that she is an adopted child, and the shock is accentuated by illness. In this sensitive condition she becomes involved with a long-dead girl, a Spanish Infanta who also lost her family and was adopted. In dreams Willow finds that she *is* the Spanish Isabel, experiencing love and danger as the exile did in Elizabethan Cornwall. Out of these dreams and psychic experiences Willow pieces together the story of the dead Infanta. It is an absorbing exercise in historical research, and by her involvement in it Willow learns at last to face and solve her personal problem. She no longer needs a refuge, either in the past or in a holiday house, for she has discovered that her adoption does not matter any more.

Stories like this come perilously near to sentimental romance. But Ruth Arthur is as intelligent as she is sensitive, and there is never any real danger. She explores the dilemma of her attractive heroine tenderly and with wisdom, and enriches the story by giving it a richly coloured and relevant setting.

Willow finds a satisfactory solution to her problem. Arnold, in John Rowe Townsend's brilliant novel *The Intruder* (1969), finds that there is no real solution; identity is something he has to learn to live with or without.

*The Intruder* is about Arnold Haithwaite, acting Sand Pilot of Skirlston; the co-hero is Skirlston itself, a little decayed port of the North-West. (Mr Townsend is an artist, not a photographer, and the setting is imagined, but it owes something to Ravenglass and to Morecambe Bay.) The sea has left Skirlston behind, except when the spring tides sweep over the sands. It is a sad, grey, harsh place, 'sea, sand, stone, slate, sky'. Not many people can make a living here, but Arnold picks up a few small earnings by guiding visitors across the treacherous sands when the Admiral is too busy or tired. It is not a bad life for a lad who is not over-fond of company, and he has his home and his 'Dad'. Then two things destroy his delicately balanced contentment. The lesser is Jane Ellison who is living briefly in Skirlston while her father builds a power-station. Jane is lovely and serene, even when trying to master Latin; she belongs to a world which Arnold had scarcely dreamed of. The greater disturbance comes from the intruder. He is not physically impressive; thin, shabby, boss-eyed, he seems to lack distinction as well as manners. Besides, he is more than a little mad, with his ridiculous plans for modernizing Skirlston and his claim to be Arnold Haithwaite. Arnold's natural reaction—'You're daft'—is no more than the situation demands; the stranger is daft but not dangerous. Yet the stranger tries to drown Arnold in the flood-tide, and before long he seems likely to supplant the boy in his father's affections. The old man, who is feeble and approaching senility, accepts the stranger's claim of kinship and installs him in the old house with the cotton-tree which is a landmark of Skirlston.

Perhaps the stranger—his nickname, incongruously, is Sonny—is a little sinister. He certainly dominates Miss Binns, the wretched woman whom he describes as his fiancée, and he strikes the Admiral when the old man makes fun of him. Sonny is undeniably unpleasant, but for Arnold he is something more —a grotesque symbol of a world in which Arnold has no real part. Arnold's fundamental trouble is that he doesn't know who he is. The old man cannot be his father, yet no one—not even Miss Hendry who knows everything about the history of Skirlston—will enlighten him. The one certainty in Arnold's life is his hatred of Sonny, who plans to drive him out of Skirlston or kill him.

In the moment of his greatest despair Arnold learns the truth about himself, or as much of the truth as can be known. He is the bastard son of a girl from Irontown and—maybe—a Haithwaite. Or perhaps the father was a sailor from Cardiff. ' "Nobody knows for sure, or ever will." '

The end is dramatic, or melodramatic. Sonny's plans to improve Skirlston bring him into conflict with 'power and tradition and authority' in the shape of the Duchy agent who is virtually the ruler of the little town. Sonny may be a strong man when dominating old men, women and boys, but he is afraid of the agent. Frustrated in his ambitions, he turns on Arnold and tries to murder him, but is himself drowned in the tide. The fact distresses Arnold, despite his hatred of the man, because 'everyone was on the same side against the sea'. Arnold survives to become Sand Pilot and in time Admiral, and to marry not the remote and lovely Jane but Norma Benson after she gets tired of hanging around the cinema in Irontown. 'Arnold reckons it will be safest to marry one who is used to Skirlston, for an incomer might not stay.'

In setting, characterization and narrative power *The Intruder* is one of the outstanding books of its decade. It commands admiration but not, for me, affection. There is a coldness in it which is repellant. A convincing case-history, it lacks the quality of involvement. One does not identify with Arnold, still less with Sonny—he was the real Arnold Haithwaite after all, by the way. *The Intruder* is a masterly novel, but its message is arid. Arnold gets a chilly satisfaction from his job, which 'will live as long as he does, and that is enough'. It is not, one hopes, enough to satisfy the young reader.

Arnold is technically adopted, although not yet an orphan; his mother is probably alive in Liverpool, but no one will know for certain until she needs money again; his father, if a Haithwaite, is dead, if the sailor 'anywhere in the world or out of it'. Anna is 'sort of adopted'. The pathetic, prickly little girl whom the reader meets at the opening of *When Marnie Was There* (1967) is looked after by 'auntie'. Through experience she has learnt to wear her 'ordinary' face, shutting the rest of humanity out of her vulnerable heart. 'Things like parties and best friends . . . were fine for everyone else'. Anna herself is outside the circle and almost outside life.

Joan Robinson's tender and sensitive story explores the world of a child who has no family but who is denied the comfort which might follow acceptance of her lot by the memory, mostly submerged, of a past in which she had once been loved.

After an illness Anna goes away to stay with Mr and Mrs Pegg in their cottage on the Norfolk coast. The house 'smells different from home'. At this safe distance from her foster-mother Anna feels able to send her a message that 'of course she loved her, without committing herself'. On the staithe at Little Overton she sees a house standing alone, 'as if it had been there so long . . . that it had forgotten the busyness of life going on ashore behind it, and had sunk into a quiet dream'.

The house brings to Anna 'a dream of summer holidays' which she had never known. It looks 'safe and everlasting'. The whole scene seems to speak to her, just like the bird which flies overhead crying 'Pity me! oh, pity me!' So, strangely enough, does Wuntermanny, the silent fisherman. (Anna has no family, Wuntermanny too many—hence his name.)

Even in this delectable place Anna still keeps her defences up, that is until Mrs Pegg's Bingo Night, when she can venture out into the dusk and row and drift through the marshy creeks until her boat bumps against the jetty of Marsh House. Here she finds Marnie, a girl who looks unearthly in her light filmy dress which turns out to be her nightdress, but who is 'warm and firm' to the touch. In the next nights the two little girls play together while the Peggs are sitting 'like two ancient monuments' watching telly, and Anna has a glimpse of Marnie's home-life, her gay father and her lovely heedless mother. For Marnie, with all her gaiety, is unhappy too, neglected by frivolous parents and tormented by the servants. The children, alike in their loneliness, are happy together until, one terrifying night when they are trapped together in the old windmill, Marnie inexplicably abandons Anna. This is their last meeting. Anna has one last glimpse of Marnie at an upstairs window of Marsh House, apparently a prisoner. The strange story unwinds slowly and convincingly into the revelation that Anna's mother had been Marnie's unhappy daughter. Had Marnie been a ghost? It is not made clear whether Anna's experience had been psychic or psychological. Everything she does with the ghostly little girl she might have heard in earliest childhood from the grandmother who brought her up, and in her loneliness she may have drawn upon these memories for comfort. Whichever explanation is correct, Marnie rescues Anna from the emptiness of a loveless childhood which she had herself suffered and opens the bitter child's heart to love.

Before writing *When Marnie Was There* Joan Robinson was known only as the writer of some charming slight stories for small children. The book marks a change of direction almost without parallel in children's literature. It is a most beautiful and sensitive examination of a little girl and of the landscape which works so powerfully upon her. The conclusion is deeply satisfying and the processes which lead to it are completely convincing. If coincidence plays a part in the denouement, it is no more than probability will allow. The wisdom is always dressed in relevant terms. Gillie, who had known Marnie in her own time, tells Anna and her newly acquired friends the sad story of the loveless relationship between Marnie and her daughter. Jane, one of the children, realizes that 'because Marnie wasn't loved when she was little, she wasn't able to be a loving mother herself, when her turn came', and Gillie agrees with this elementary psychology, saying ' "Being loved, oddly enough, is one of the things that helps us to grow up." '

Invisible companions can be powerful agents for growth. Marnie helped Anna to discover herself, rather as another and a more exotic companion helps Mark to self-realization in Anne Barrett's *Midway* (1967).

Charity, in Barbara Willard's *Charity at Home* (1965), does not lack love; she is looked after well and with genuine affection by Auntie Joycie and Uncle Steve and she has plenty of friends. Nagging thoughts about her dead parents make her prickly; moreover there is the mystery of her unexpected and recently discovered artistic skill. At school she models a head which is like her aunt's but not quite. How had she inherited this talent? Charity slips easily into a fantasy world which involves Mr Tressider, the rich, lonely owner of the big house. It is a dangerous game of make-believe that she plays and she is lucky to come out of it with few scars.

Charity's search is for identity. This, too, is the objective before Kate (in *Kate and the Family Tree*, 1965). Margaret Storey draws a pathetic picture of a little girl who has never known her parents and has grown up in the care of reluctant relatives whom she 'never much liked'. After a row with Aunt Millicent she is packed off abruptly to Cousin Lawrence, a recluse who lives alone in a large country house. Cousin Lawrence is not unkind, but his capacity for love has grown rusty from long disuse and he has no idea what to do with a small cousin. Thrown on her own resources, Kate explores the house and with it the story of her unknown family. In the attic lie the unheeded Chatteris archives, and she puts together the tiny interlocking fragments of the family jigsaw. It is an absorbing task, and Kate might have forgotten her loneliness, even without the company of Dirk, the boy who very nearly was one of the family. In reconstructing her family tree Kate finds herself. Still more remarkable is the effect on Cousin Lawrence. He remains taciturn because not even a charming little cousin can alter a lifetime's habits, but the wall which he had built to protect him from the pain of past unhappiness is pulled down brick by brick as Kate explores the house and releases its ghosts. The cold old man acknowledges that Kate 'could make the streams run in their courses' for him.

In the same year Margaret Storey published another novel about an orphan. *Pauline* is a more painful book than *Kate and the Family Tree*, and a more complex one. Kate lost her parents long ago and is barely aware that she has missed them; moreover she lives with a man who, in his odd way, loves her. The death of Pauline's father precipitates a financial crisis, and she has to leave her kind and familiar Aunt Terry and go to live with the Scarleighs. (A realistic observer might remark that Aunt Terry could have cut her expenses by taking Pauline away from her snob school and sending her to the local Secondary Modern, but then there would have been no story!)

Miss Storey draws the Scarleigh family from the life. They are a nice, ordinary middle-class family, and they are awful. Uncle Harry and Aunt Madge take Pauline in without thought to their own inconvenience and they are prepared to give her love as well as security. It is not really their fault that they cannot understand her, or indeed any idea contrary to their own. Uncle Harry wants to build her up by feeding her milk, which she cannot assimilate. Aunt Madge makes her feel at home by talking platitudes when she is trying to read. Mostly the inconveniences are trivial, but the cumulative effect is formidable.

Pauline's escape-route leads to the Blacketts. Uncle Harry could not be expected to approve of the Blacketts, whose parents have taught them to think for themselves and to say what they think. In their company Pauline can relax and discover herself. As Cousin Paul says ' "Nobody else seems as alive as they are" '. In order to see them Pauline and Paul are forced into deception.

There is no real escape for Pauline. All she can hope for at best is a measure of freedom to choose her own friends and think her own thoughts, and she in turn learns to live with Uncle Harry. It is not a happy ending, but it is painfully convincing.

*Pauline* is an astonishingly mature novel for a new writer. The narrative, and especially the dialogue, is brilliantly done. Miss Storey keeps a large number of characters in movement and defines each precisely, and she puts them into an identifiable social setting without recourse to elaborate description. Her masterpiece is not Pauline, or Blackie the lively Blackett girl, but Uncle Harry himself. His good intentions defeated by his insensitivity, his abundant self-confidence shattered by contact with the inexplicable reactions of a different generation but built anew each time by his obtuse conceit, he is neither a figure of fun nor the unchangeable egotist whom a lesser artist might have drawn. Almost imperceptibly Uncle Harry changes under the pressure of experience, yet there are no miracles. He is more bearable at the end of the story, a degree more flexible, but he is still kind, thick-headed Uncle Harry. At least he can bear to face with good humour the fact that his own daughter thinks he is a donkey.

Miss Storey draws Uncle Harry with a host of small, apparently casual lines. There is a nice example one evening when Betty, the youngest Scarleigh, goes off to her bath singing 'Fifteen men on a dead man's chest.' Uncle Harry explains to her that the fifteen 'men' were bottles and the chest was a sea-chest. It is a good lesson in general knowledge but 'Betty stopped singing'.

Stepmothers have always been a staple ingredient of children's stories. One wonders whether the wicked stepmother was invented by the folk-tale or by reality. In recent fiction the stepmother is more sinned against than sinning. There are no Murdstone situations. Instead, step-parents struggle towards a *modus vivendi* with the 'ready-made' families they have inherited. For the most part the difficulty lies with stepdaughters. Carys, in Sheena Porter's *The Scapegoat* (1968), is driven into rebellion and ultimately into delinquency by jealousy of her pretty young stepmother Janet. She is cured

not by any marvellous change of heart but by the absorbing
interest of an archaeological adventure which puts her home
problems into perspective. Not an entirely convincing solution, but a fascinating story.

There is greater depth and subtlety in the examination of
personal relationships in Ruth Arthur's *The Whistling Boy*
(1969). This, like others of this remarkable writer's work, is a
kind of ghost story, but the supernatural is used as a means
towards coming to terms with the natural. Kirsty cannot, as
her twin brothers have done, accept the stepmother who has so
soon taken the place of her dead mother. Her feeling of hatred
frightens even herself and threatens to make her physically ill.
She escapes for a working holiday, fruit-picking on the Norfolk
coast and staying in an ancient farmhouse. Here she finds peace
and the unforced affection of ordinary people; here too she
meets Jake, a boy with a 'bruised look', and the ghost of the
whistling boy whose fate is strangely entangled with his. In
loving Jake, and protecting him from the whistling boy's
incitement to suicide, Kirsty forgets her own personal dilemma.

Kirsty sees herself more clearly by contrast with her friend
Dinah. Dinah has an alcoholic mother and a drug-taking boy-
friend. In her despair she goes shop-lifting and is arrested. Her
appalling home-life is exposed to the light and so, in a violent
way, she finds a solution to her problem. Now she 'can be just a
schoolgirl'.

This is another of Miss Arthur's 'mirror' stories. Kirsty sees
her own problem reflected in others. The whistling boy is the
unquiet spirit of a Huguenot who was taken away from home
and love and forced into an alien setting; his vision of a refuge
under the sea tempts others, including Jake, to follow him
along the path of the sea. The whistling boy died for lack of
love. In loving Jake, Kirsty saves both herself and him.

This simple theme is decked out with all Miss Arthur's art,
with a lovingly drawn Norfolk landscape and a gallery of
sensitive portraits of complex, vulnerable people. She is a
master of inference, rarely using formal description but building up a picture by indirect detail conveyed in action and
dialogue.

Both Ruth Arthur and Sheena Porter make much of the

stepmother situation. William Mayne plays it down in *Underground Alley* (1958). Patty has been used to looking after her father. When he marries again, she competes with Gwen over her former duties. When father calls her 'mother' Patty corrects it to 'stepmother' not out of resentment but for accuracy. Their good-natured antagonism is a pleasant contrast to the agonized conflicts favoured by other writers. Gwen may be 'not energetic enough even to fill the kettle after it had been emptied', but she is no intruder. Even when, for once, she sends Patty to bed early for a punishment, no one makes a fuss about it, and their casual relationship remains undisturbed. Mayne excels in these informal partnerships, like that of Marlene and her mother in *The Twelve Dancers* (1962) and the curious love–hate between Harriet and her father in that very strange story—even by Mayne standards—*Royal Harry* (1971). There is also a penetrating study of the antagonism between brother and sister in *Sand* (1964).

Mayne is not interested in social problems as such; he is interested in people and places. He does not labour the questionable marital status of Marlene's mother in *The Twelve Dancers*. Certainly he would not choose to write about an unmarried mother as his principal theme. This is precisely Josephine Kamm's kind of theme, and it was no occasion for surprise when that tireless seeker-out of causes turned to the subject in 1965. *Young Mother* is an entirely serious and responsible book, approaching sincerely a growing problem of the day. It is unfortunately, unlike young Pat, sterile. Mrs Kamm makes each point with meticulous care, showing breadth of understanding and a strong sense of purpose. She lacks, however, a creative touch. Her characters remain lay figures in a static display, illustrating a social disease but not bringing it home to the reader, because characters and action alike are manipulated by the author. They lack the independence of characters in a creative novel, who are apt to take charge and go their own way regardless of the author's original intentions.

Honor Arundel makes more effective use of the same theme in *The Longest Weekend* (1969). Eileen, in this story, has already had her baby. Eileen is a mixed-up kid, overshadowed by talented, earnest, liberal parents. In a vague, indefinite way she has been fumbling her way towards identification; 'it was time, she thought, that she made up her mind who she was'. Pregnancy comes as a shock, but the shock brings with it relief. This is something she could do without her parents' help, 'not requiring any special talent. Not like a bungled school essay, a badly furnished room, a botched career.' So she has Gay. But Gay does not belong to her. Mother takes over, managing the baby with the same easy competence which has made her life so irritating a success.

With rare initiative Eileen takes the baby away for a long weekend in the country, where she can get to know her own child. It is nearly a disaster. Under the strain of coping with unfamiliar tasks her nerve gives way, her liberal principles disappear, and she spanks Gay. 'All her mother's precepts pounced on her like jackdaws on a grain of corn'. But Gay, against the rules, accepts her punishment and goes to sleep. For the first time Eileen feels a sense of achievement. 'She felt content and serene and the only flaw in her serenity was that there was nobody there to admire it.' In time somebody comes, Joel who is Gay's father, and they work out a solution to Eileen's problem.

I am not sure that Honor Arundel has proved her own thesis in this story. The conclusion is conventional, which is in itself no criticism, but the denouement is just a little too easy. Life is never as simple as the story suggests.

Where the book excels is in characterization, especially in the portraits of the parents. Intellectual and enlightened grown-ups are always fair game. (The most brilliant of John Rowe Townsend's portraits in *The Intruder* is that of Helen Ellison, who is not inquisitive about her son's actions but who does 'wonder'.) Eileen's parents discuss endlessly the theory of family upbringing while Eileen awaits permission to start living. 'Sometimes she wondered if life would not be simpler if she were forbidden to do things so that she could respond with open defiance.' The parents' confusion when they discover that their child is not made in their own image is beautifully conveyed.

Books of this kind may come from a genuine creative impulse; they may be written 'to fill a need', which is not the same thing at all. There has been a spate of books in recent years which 'fill a need'. They show in contrived situations the major and minor problems of the day and the theoretical solutions. One need not question the sincere good intention of the writers, but this is no way to write a good novel. The novel is about people in society, not about social problems. The problems may be aired, or even solved, but the solution comes from the inter-action of human beings. There is, it seems to me, more to be learnt about race relations from Mrs Brinsmead's books, which are not about race, than from Mrs Kamm's and Mrs Sterling's, which are.

This may be unfair, as well as unkind, to two very sincere writers. Josephine Kamm is clearly deeply concerned about the problem of mixed marriages, and she presents this in terms of ordinary people in *Out of Step* (1962). This has a Notting Hill kind of situation. It is partly the romance of her meeting with Bob which impresses Betty, for she plays a small part in rescuing him when he is attacked by a gang of thugs. She con-vinces herself that she loves him, and she holds to this con-viction in the face of opposition from her conventional mother and broad-minded father; but she may not be right. In the inconclusive ending there is an element of doubt, and this is the saving grace of the story. Mrs Kamm is scrupulously fair. If only she were a better writer! It is admirable to present the dilemma of ordinary people if they can be made interesting, but Betty and Bob are ordinary and dull. The style is flat, too. This is an author who cannot bear to leave anything out, and she describes every trivial incident in remorseless detail.

*Mary Jane* (1959; English edition 1960) is another matter. Like Josephine Kamm, Dorothy Sterling was commenting on a contemporary situation, in this instance the 'integration' riots in Little Rock, Arkansas. Mrs Sterling, however, does not attempt to show the problem dispassionately. She is out in front fighting for Mary Jane, who wants to go to Wilson High not because it is a white school but because it will give her the kind of education she needs. Mary Jane faces screaming crowds outside the school and crude violence and insults from her school-fellows, and this open hatred is no harder to bear than the ignorant kindness of those who expect her to behave like a Stephen Foster darkie. She is neither the sinister figure conjured up by the Mothers' League nor a cute piccaninny but a complete and rounded personality. By the end of the story a few of the children and staff at Wilson High have come to recognize her quality, and Randall, president of the Science Club, can make a joke about integration with no trace of malice in it. It is, in a way, a happy ending.

Race comes into H. F. Brinsmead's first book, *Pastures of the Blue Crane*, where the race-proud girl Ryl turns out to be of mixed blood. It is an important element in *Listen to the Wind* (1970). However deeply Mrs Brinsmead may feel about race she keeps her touch light, and *Listen to the Wind*, which has serious, indeed tragic, implications, is essentially a gay story. Bella Greenrush, who claims to be of royal blood—and who could doubt it?—is a person of heroic stature. 'Her brow is wide . . . and gleaming like the cedar-wood from the old times, from the mountains of the old days, beneath her red scarf. It is the brow of a princess.' The princess rules her tribe with benign authority in the house with the notice outside:

MEETING-PLACE OF THE CHURCH OF THE NAZARENE
*Seek ye first the kingdom of God*
No Smoking or Drinking. By Favour.
Worms for Sale

One of her tribe is Tam who works for, and loves, Loveday Smith, a girl with golden skin and hair as fair as a Viking's. Loveday is the meeting-point of black and white, and the working out of her relationship with Tam, inconclusive but quite satisfactory, makes the core of a rich and varied story. There is a charming penultimate chapter in which Tam points out the disadvantage of involvement with someone who is 'related to practically every coloured person in Australia—*and* the Pacific Islands. Maybe in the world.' Loveday's response is favourable, but Tam continues to 'play it cool.'

There is drama and exciting action in this story, more than is common in Mrs Brinsmead's books, but it is the tenderness and the gaiety which remains longest in the mind. Best of all is the joint action of God and Uncle Zac in providing a church for Bella's tribe. Zac was invited home to launch the fund for the new church, and it took the old prize-fighter a long time, and many drinks, to get from Brisbane to O'Brian's Point, and on the way chance and God produced a church, or at least a packing-shed of just the right size.

There is bitterness alongside the fun in the story. Bella may be essentially a comic character, but she is serious about the integrity of her race. She does not want to be like the 'white-fellers' who took her people's land and now give them 'money and free food and send us the odd social worker.' The bitterness comes from the memories of the old.

Racial prejudice finds infertile soil among the young. There is an enchanting illustration of this in *The Winter Princess* (1962), perhaps the most delightful book by a most talented writer, Mary Treadgold. Miss Treadgold won a Carnegie Medal during the thin war years. The recognition came prematurely and she wrote nothing of any great moment in the next fifteen years. *The Winter Princess* seems to me to come as near per-fection within its self-imposed range as any post-war book. The touch is light and certain, the writing crisp yet sensitive, the pitch just high enough to make the young reader reach upwards.

The story is about Hampton Court. Four children, three girls and a boy 'so slight he looked like a tiny stick-insect' won an essay competition on Africa, because they had 'ideas, not information'. Part of the prize was tea with Lady Carron, widow of a colonial administrator and tenant of a grace-and-favour appartment in the Palace. The children are such a success that the Friday tea-party becomes a regular occasion when Sara puts on her Friday petticoat and they go through the darkened courts of the Palace, and Ford brings in the tray with its 'shining silver teapot, and the beautiful little deep blue cups, and the cucumber sandwiches, and the tiny iced cakes', and hear about Lady Carron's Glory Days. One thing alone is lacking: there should be kings and queens in Hampton Court.

Lady Carron's husband had been Governor of Kalinde. One of the paramount chiefs of Kalinde comes to England on a state visit and his daughter Ola is at boarding-school here. Princess Ola is coming to stay in Hampton Court and the children's wish will come true. The Winter Princess is a real

*From* The Winter Princess (*see opposite page*)

princess, even if she does dash away with the smoothing iron in Sara's mother's kitchen. Her face is 'black as the blackest of shining summer cherries', and there is such a natural dignity in her gaiety that Sara 'gravely went down nearly to the ground in her best school curtsey, with hardly a wobble.' Princess Ola teaches the children to dance the Highlife and to sing 'everybody — everybody — everybody — everybody — everybody love Saturday night'. Ola and her father bring back the great days briefly to the cold winter rooms of Hampton Court.

Drama enters the story with Tommy Bly the newsman who hopes to climb into Fleet Street by way of the sewers. His reaction to the story of Sir Alfred Carron's heroism is to disbelieve it. Miss Treadgold makes Tommy horribly real; with a character already half-way to caricature a singly clumsy move would send him toppling over, but she captures every nuance of his nastiness as well as his face which, 'thought Sara, was like the face of the pike in the school museum—crafty, and yet stupid.'

In spite of Tommy Bly, this is essentially a happy story. There are genuinely relaxed and satisfactory relationships between the children and with the adults. Even Sara and Marilla, who are always fighting, are only antagonists on the surface. The whole community—except the Blys—are bound together in spontaneous affection for the little Winter Princess.

The discreet touches which conjure up a setting are here at their most masterly. There is a memorable passage in which Sara, on the eve of Guy Fawkes Day, goes out to get ice-cream from the van. She runs tentatively in the direction of the elusive chimes. The darkness, and the sounds of the dim streets, and the splashes of light come together to create a vivid fleeting experience. Mary Treadgold is equally good with portraits. One of her most subtle creations is that of Sara's older sister Marilla who is a musical genius. Thinking of Hampton Court—from the outside, because she has no part in the Friday tea-parties—has given her a fixation on Henry VIII, and she has his picture—'the one with piggy eyes'—over her bed. She too goes to the Palace for Lady Carron's Glory Day in honour of Princess Ola and her father. The Paramount chief is 'huge, magnificent, and laughing'. 'Marilla's gaze was fixed admiringly upon the Paramount chief. Sara caught Mother's eye. Sara and Mother knew, in the same instant, that King Henry VIII had had it.'

*The Winter Princess* makes an effective contribution to the race question because there is no mention of it. Even Tommy Bly does not think of sneering at Princess Ola and her father. Everyone, large and small, takes it for granted that these are splendid and admirable people, and colour is mentioned only with warm approval. We are far away from the world of *Out of Step* and *Mary Jane*, and in the child's world where behaviour counts, but not colour or race.

*A Castle for the Kopcheks* (1963) is about race, not colour. James Stagg shows a family of refugees from behind the Iron Curtain who settle in England. They come prepared to work and to pay their way, but they meet prejudice in varying degrees as well as some flat hostility. It is only after much discomfort and real suffering that the Kopcheks enjoy their castle by right of conquest and put their roots deep 'in happy soil'.

*A Castle for the Kopcheks* won the E. Nesbit Award, and rightly, for it has some of the real Nesbit qualities: concern for people, especially the underdog, a feeling for places and for the cadences of speech. The characteristic Nesbit humour alone is missing. Like E. Nesbit too, Stagg is not afraid of a few improbabilities in the course of his narrative. His hostile schoolmistress is hard to swallow. For the most part, however, friendliness and hostility alike spring from acceptable sources. The happiest of the Kopcheks is the youngest, Sandor, who is lame and independent. He makes friends naturally, even within the enemy camp. When the other boys call him Gimpy his family smell an insult, but Sandor calls his best friend Chunkhead and honour is satisfied.

The Kopcheks are, in European terms, intellectuals whose dead father had been a writer, and in England they settle into a middle-class niche even if mother works as caretaker of the public hall. Their friends range across the social spectrum. The children's novel is slowly shedding its middle-class skin. Some writers have tried to hasten the process artificially, but E. W. Hildick's school stories and Reginald Taylor's of slum life are a little too self-conscious to be fully effective. This may even be true of a more individual writer, Elizabeth Stucley. *Magnolia Buildings* caused a small stir when it first appeared in 1960. Here at last was the true proletarian novel. In time the book slipped into its place as an up-dated One-End Street, sincere, humorous, lively, but essentially a peep into the working-class world from outside. Ally—her name was Gloria, hence Glory Alleluia, shortened to Ally—and Doreen, the clever member of the family, Val who was always fighting, Len, a snivelly child; they are all neatly drawn, but they seem to be specimens rather than people. Prudence Andrew and Nina Bawden are closer to the realities of ordinary life.

So too is Janet McNeill. After a number of fantasies and humorous sketches this gifted writer found her true style in two brilliant stories of town life, *The Battle of St George Without* (1966) and its sequel *Goodbye Dove Square* (1969). In the former she caught accurately the atmosphere of decay among fine buildings falling through neglect, in the latter the more deadly spiritual decay of flat-life. As the children grow their environment shrinks. 'If he stretched out his arms he could reach across this kitchen, touching with his finger-tips the border of washable flowers of which his mother was so proud. No room here to prance or rampage . . . Hardly room to whistle or yawn.' In the New Jerusalem of the tower-blocks only grown-ups are happy 'with Green Stamps and Pink Stamps and Tuppence Off and Bargain Offers.'

Both stories, although they are told with great vigour, are conventional in outline. Boys and girls bicker and fight, join sides and enjoy the thrills of gang warfare. The books are stories of strong action, but essentially they present critical portraits of society. The McGinleys and the Flints alike are propelled out of the homely squalor of their tenements into the chilly convenience of modern city dwellings, and they adjust with differing degrees of success to new circumstances. There may be a social message in the books; there certainly is relevant social comment conveyed through the medium of clearly defined characters. The dialogue is excellent. Miss McNeill has been among these people, not with a tape-recorder —for the speech is a re-creation not a transcript—but with her ears sharp for the off-beat musical cadence of real voices. She seems to do this better than John Rowe Townsend whose stories of West Riding industrial towns are rather too mechanically contrived. Here, one feels, are books written to meet a need and to cater for a market, while Janet McNeill's come from the urge to give form to ideas and impressions which must out. This may be to do less than justice to a story like *Pirate's Island* (1968) which explores the mysteries of a commonplace urban scene through the eyes of a poet—or a liar. Sheila, a wisp of a girl who lives in the Shambles and has Rod Ridgeway, a born delinquent with enormous strength and no sense, for brother, escapes from an uncomfortable home into the imaginary world which she has built out of the undigested fragments of her reading. When she and her fat friend Gordon try to make these dreams come true, the real world becomes a dangerous place. The book applies a successful formula and is compellingly readable, but one feels, even while in the grasp of an effective story-teller, that this is artifice rather than art.

There is a similar reaction to a different theme in *The Hallersage Sound* (1966). Here the scene is a pair of Pennine towns, one prosperous, the other in decline. Hallersage has nearly everything, but Holly Bridge has the Tykes, an up-and-coming Group. These amiable young men become the excuse for gang-warfare between the towns, into which Norman and his girl-friend Ril get reluctantly drawn. The scene, the theme, the language are all topical. This is the strength and the weakness of the book. It speaks urgently to the readers to whom it is directly addressed, but themes and idioms change, and—as Townsend, who started life as a journalist, knows—nothing is staler than yesterday's news.

These books all bear the marks of their origin. This author has a journalist's panache, the sharp brisk style, the surface shrewdness, the gift for smelling out the human story behind a social problem. He has also the journalist's shallowness, the fondness for clichés of situation and character as well as phrase. No other writer of the day shows more professional competence, but he makes the reader hanker after a touch of amateurism, a hairline crack in the varnish.

Neither Anne Barrett nor Eric Allen rivals Townsend in

professional skill, but each has something rather more precious, a vein of innocence. Noel Streatfeild, with characteristic shrewdness, called *Songberd's Grove* (1957) 'a fairy tale of a London street', and there is indeed a folk-tale quality in Anne Barrett's agreeable book. The Singer family, appropriately enough, come to live in Songberd's Grove. This is a shabby terrace near the Regent's Canal. Neglect and the spite of the small children who live there cannot quite disguise the former splendours of the houses, but they look like 'a collection of grimy old black-clothed women all huddled together; their toothless mouths the uncurtained windows; the saggy, uneven roofs their battered hats.' Martin Singer, in Number 7, is a boy of no more than average intelligence and physique, but he has a feeling for form and order. Living, as he had done, in Aunt Emmeline's house, he had been offended not so much by her snobbishness but by the lack of style—he could not abide the sloppy lettering which proclaimed their house as 'Emandalf'. He is the boy to dig the essential Songberd's Grove out of its casing of filth, that is, if Lennie will let him. Lennie is the gang-leader. Building up his image from a synthesis of his film heroes, Lennie favours lounging pyjamas and a monogrammed dressing-gown. ('Cor, he really had been studying the films!') Lennie employs his gang to minister to his own comforts and to suppress individuality among the tenants of Songberd's Grove. Anyone foolish enough to give his front door a coat of paint has the work undone by next daybreak, and minor accidents occur to those who oppose Lennie's will.

Lennie makes an interesting study. His father was a prize-fighter, now deceased, but his mother, determined that her beautiful son shall not take after the Basher, has brought him up in the belief that Dad had been a florist. The spoilt boy reacts predictably. A wreath-maker's son living in Songberd's Grove seems fair game to his school-fellows, but the Basher's son bashes them. He then sets about destroying anything which by its beauty may remind him of his supposed father.

Here the book ceases to be a fairy tale, in which, of its very nature, there is no room for psychology. It is not a straight fight between Martin and Lennie, between good and evil. The subtleties of the situation enrich the development and resolution of an exciting and satisfactory story, which ends with the restoration of Songberd's Grove and Lennie on his way to heavyweight honours.

*Songberd's Grove* is about the preservation of the quality of life. *The Latchkey Children* (1963) is about the preservation of personal integrity. There is not much gracious living for Billandben and Froggy. These are the latchkey children. Their parents are out at work and the kids look after themselves, coming and going with their latchkeys in the tall yellowbrick flats. There is implicit criticism of a social system which produces this situation, but Eric Allen does not labour his point. Nor does he make much of Etty's mother, who has a car but no Saturday dinner, just 'mouldy old sandwiches, and bits of yellow egg falling all over the place and that'. Saturday dinner matters. During the week the kids feed themselves, Froggy on the remains of Sunday's joint, Billandben—who lives in a real house—on cold chicken from the fridge.

Life is a serious business for the latchkey children, and the gaunt cliffs of flats do not lend themselves to play. Their pleasure is centred on, and symbolized by, the tree. It is a real tree, battered and worn bare by the feet and seats of many children who scramble and swing on it. It is the best thing in the children's playground. But the Council decides to take it down and replace it with 'one simulated locomotive in a sand/cement aggregate;' that is, a concrete engine. It is not altogether a bad idea, but it is a symbol of adult arrogance; no one had asked the children what they thought. The latchkey children fight for their right to the same kind of freedom in their play that they have perforce in their home life. They call a public meeting, and Goggles makes a fine speech, unfortunately in the pouring rain. ' "That's what always happens," said Goggles. "Just when everything's going fine it starts to rain." ' They involve the news-media, visit Parliament and the L.C.C., precipitate a strike of council workmen. They have a wonderful time, in which the tree *qua* tree is almost forgotten. After the great public meeting Duke Ellington Binns, the West Indian, goes over to the tree. 'On the knuckly part where the twig put out a leaf in spring a fragment of bark was still left. The boy picked if off methodically, digging at it with his fingernails.'

Although the social issues are real, *The Latchkey Children* maintains a light tone. It is an entertaining story with social undertones, not a social tract. Eric Allen draws a set of attractive portraits, well on the right side of caricature (and Charles Keeping gave them highly satisfactory forms in his remarkable illustrations). The adults are for the most part treated humorously, but with some realism. One has met Mr Frisby, the Vicar of St Justin's, with his 'great white teeth as if he were wearing a collar backwards in his mouth as well as round his neck.' Mr Frisby consoles Goggles for the loss of his tree by inviting him to join the Youth Club, where there is 'a wide variety of activities—sing-it-yourself sessions, general knowledge quizzes, ping-pong . . .' The reader is on Goggles's side: 'even a grown-up hadn't any right to be as stupid as all that.' Then there is the Honourable and Gallant Member who, having failed to listen to Goggles's appeal for help, dismisses him with ' "Just remember—if ever I can be of service to any of my future constituents, here is where you can always find me. I am yours to command." '

The latchkey children are on their own. Even the well-disposed adults never really listen. The balance of society is disturbed, as it is in almost all the books which try sincerely to present the problems of urban adolescence. The best of them— Paul Zindel's stories of the wilderness in which American youth wanders, for example—are examples of special pleading. Almost alone among creative writers H. F. Brinsmead is concerned to adjust the balance. Although Mrs Brinsmead lets the reader know where her sympathies lie, she is normally a detached narrator. In *Beat of a City* (1966) she abandons the role of observer. Her angry interpolations spoil the symmetry of the book, which by strict standards is her least satisfactory work. Mrs Brinsmead, however, has something to say about the beat generation, and she is worth hearing.

Sydney Ernest Green, philosopher of the jazz clubs, gave the generation its motto: 'We are the only generation to be born superior to our parents.' Syd is 'backing expansion in all branches of construction', that is, he is an apprentice bricklayer dedicated to doing as little as possible for as much as possible. Syd comes from the underprivileged half, although he

*From* The Latchkey Children (*see page 225*)

hasn't missed much. When he was small his mother worked as a waitress 'so that her blue-eyed son might have the finest possible perambulator, the biggest teddy-bear, and the reddest tricycle. Of course, she had left him for twelve hours a day at the best possible crèche.' His friend Sabie comes from the other half; he has no money of his own, apart from what he gets by pawning his mother's hats, but he has the benefits of much philosophical advice from his intellectual mother. These two young men are going somewhere fast, if nowhere in particular. Into their urban path drops Raylene, alias Muscles from Mussel Flat, who comes to town to meet the wild people and to find Blade O'Reilly who rides a Bonneville motor cycle— stolen—and looks like a prince of darkness.

Raylene also drops into the path of Mary. Mary is the touchstone of this story, a girl who walks in both worlds. She sings at Gospel meetings for her Uncle Stefan the minister, but she is not out of place, despite her clean face, at the Blue Beat dance club. Mary would be too good to be true, but for her habit of collecting stray dogs, cats and delinquents.

It is Mary, with help from her uncle, policemen, probation officers and boredom, who lights candles in the eyes of these lost children. It is a long job and there is no final and complete success. What has been proved is that there is something after all behind the emptiness in the eyes of Syd, Sabie and Raylene. Not Blade. Blade O'Reilly, who rides down old women with his stolen bike, is beyond Mrs Brinsmead's compassion. The best she can do is to deflate Blade. In fact Raylene does it with a flick-knife, and he shrinks 'like an apple after a long winter'.

*Beat of the City* is no more tidy than back-street Melbourne. It is a messy hotch-potch of anger, violence, prejudice, love, confusion; in fact a picture of life. It breaks most of the traditional and formal rules of the novel, but it rises above them. The subject-matter has decreed that this should be the last book mentioned in my survey. In some ways it does not make a satisfactory conclusion. One might have preferred a more elegant and cultivated work of art. The flaws in *Beat of the City* are formal, however; in its passionate concern for human beings, its criticism of society, the serious and humorous truth of its characterization, its strong angry style, this is clearly an important novel of our time. In it the traditions of the children's novel, their roots reaching back strongly to their origins in E. Nesbit at the dawn of the century, are preserved and renewed.

# Children's Books for Adults

ADULTS USUALLY READ children's books for professional reasons. Teachers, parents, librarians, all read them in order to assess their suitability for and to estimate their effect upon young readers. Incidentally, no doubt, they derive personal delight from the experience, but this is not the principal objective.

Although I have had many rewarding contacts with children in the shared enjoyment of books, my own concern with children's books has mainly been personal. I read them because I enjoy them as literature. Believing that there are many readers who would find pleasure in the best of the books designed for children, but who have no occasion for finding a way through the tangled paths of children's literature, I have ventured to add a list of twenty books which seem to me to possess to a high degree the qualities which mature readers look for in a novel. The selection is obviously a personal one and is not intended to represent some Olympian view of 'best books'. Nor is it intended to help adults to look curiously, or condescendingly, at what is being written for the kids. These books can stand up for themselves and can be read with the same quality of critical attention that 'adult' books demand.

Ruth M. Arthur *A Candle in her Room*, Victor Gollancz, *see* p. 201

Henri Bosco *The Boy and the River*, Oxford University Press, *see* p. 88

L. M. Boston *A Stranger at Green Knowe*, Faber & Faber, *see* p. 139

H. F. Brinsmead *Pastures of the Blue Crane*, Oxford University Press, *see* p. 159

John Christopher   *The Guardians*, Hamish Hamilton, *see* p. 51

Helen Cresswell   *The Night-watchmen*, Faber & Faber, *see* p. 112

Brian Fairfax-Lucy and Philippa Pearce   *The Children of the House*, Longman Young Books, *see* p. 174

Antonia Forest   *The Ready-made Family*, Faber & Faber, *see* p. 171

Leon Garfield   *Smith*, Longman Young Books, *see* p. 34

Alan Garner   *The Owl Service*, Collins, *see* p. 126

Russell Hoban   *The Mouse and his Child*, Faber & Faber, *see* p. 118

Tove Jansson   *Moominland Midwinter*, Benn, *see* p. 138

Herbert Kaufmann   *Red   Moon   and   High   Summer*, Methuen, *see* p. 97

William Mayne   *A Swarm in May*, Oxford University Press, *see* p. 167

Philippa Pearce   *Tom's Midnight Garden*, Oxford University Press, *see* p. 198

K. M. Peyton   *Flambards*, Oxford University Press, *see* p. 177

Stephanie Plowman   *Three Lives for the Czar*, Bodley Head, *see* p. 83

Ian Serraillier   *The Silver Sword*, Jonathan Cape, *see* p. 29

John Rowe Townsend   *The Intruder*, Oxford University Press, *see* p. 206

Henry Treece   *The Dream-Time*, Brockhampton Press, *see* p. 67

# *Index*

*Printed in Great Britain
by W & J Mackay Limited, Chatham*